HOMEGROUND

Homeground

KATHRYN TRUEBLOOD & LINDA STOVALL, EDITORS

AMERICAN LITERATURES SERIES

A CO-PUBLISHING PROJECT OF
BEFORE COLUMBUS FOUNDATION
AND
BLUE HERON PUBLISHING, INC.

Homeground
American Literatures Series

Kathryn Trueblood & Linda Stovall , Editors

ISBN 0-936085-36-3

The American Literatures Series is a co-publishing project of Before Columbus Foundation and Blue Heron Publishing, Inc.

Publication of this book has been supported by a grant from the Lannan Foundation and a grant from the Portland, Oregon, Metropolitan Arts & Culture Council.

Blue Heron Publishing, Inc.
24450 NW Hansen Road
Hillsboro, Oregon 97124
503.621.3911

Interior design: Dennis Stovall
Cover art: Linda Sawaya. Copyright © 1996 by Linda Sawaya
Cover composition: Dennis Stovall and Linda Sawaya

First edition, May 1996

LIBRARY OF CONGRESS CATALOGING IN PUBLICATION DATA

Homeground / Kathryn Trueblood & Linda Stovall, editors.
      p.   cm. — (American literatures series)
      Contents: My Oakland, there is a there there / Ishmael Reed — Home is where the music is / Victor Hernández Cruz — Where one starts from / Nash Candelaria — Going home / Colleen McElroy — Home is every place / Pico Iyer — Borders / Thomas King — Hiroshi from Hiroshima / Lawson Fusao Inada — Leaving Yuba City / Chitra Banerjee Divakaruni — Homesickness / Joseph Geha — Immigrant mother / Shirley Geok-lin Lim.
      ISBN 0-936085-36-3 (alk. paper)
      1. Home—Fiction.   2. American prose literature—Minority authors. 3. American prose litearture—20th century.   4. Ethnic groups—United States— Fiction.   5. Immigrants—United States—Biography.   6. Immigrants—United States—Fiction.   7. Ethnic groups—United States.   8. Place (Philosophy)— Fiction. 9. Place (Philosophy).   10. Home.
      I. Trueblood, Kathryn, 1960–   II. Stovall, Linda, 1940– III. Series: American literatures series (Berkeley, Calif.).
PS648.H55H66 1996
818' .540808355—dc20   96-13690
                                                              CIP

Printed in the United States of America on pH-balanced paper.

Permissions and Credits

The editors of this collection would like to thank
the board of directors of the
Before Columbus Foundation —

alta, Rudolfo Anaya, Marie Anderson, Johnnella Butler,
Bob Callahan, Lawrence DiStasi, Victor Hernández Cruz,
Andrew Hope, Yuri Kageyama, David Meltzer, Simon Ortiz,
Ishmael Reed, Gundars Strads, Kathryn Trueblood,
Gerald Vizenor, Shawn Wong,

the staff who assisted with *Homeground* at
Blue Heron Publishing —

Elizabeth Jackson, Erin Leonard, Ingrid Opsahl,
Meisha Rosenberg, Jessica Shulsinger, Susan Skarzynski,
Dennis Stovall, William Woodall,

and the granting organizations whose support made
publication of this book possible — the Lannan Foundation
and the Portland, Oregon, Metropolitan Arts & Culture Council.

CONTENTS

Introduction

This collection of fiction and nonfiction launches a new anthology series through the combined forces of two organizations whose aim has long been to redefine mainstream literature in America. Founded in 1976 by a group of writers, editors, educators, and small press publishers, the Before Columbus Foundation has promoted for 20 years an inclusive literary vision through its American Book Awards, panels, seminars, and publications. Blue Heron Publishing, a 10 year-old press with books for educators and writers, young adult fiction, and literary collections, has sought from its inception to promote diversity in its books and periodicals.

We picked "home" as the subject for the initial book because it is a common denominator; no matter how little we know about each other's tribe, we can agree on the instinct for home, in all its brave and bizarre forms. Deciding on a series title did not prove to be as easy. We intentionally avoided use of the word "multicultural," which is rather ironic considering that the Before Columbus Foundation was the first to coin the term. In Ishmael Reed's words, multiculturalism describes "a cultural gumbo," a situation in which cultures and subcultures exist with their own integrity intact alongside other cultures with whom they jostle and share mutual influences. Although these last two decades have seen the on-going revision of the literary canon, the term multicultural has lately been appropriated and used to distinguish between what is mainstream and what is outside or other. It's not uncommon in school libraries to find that multicultural itself has become a separate category lumping together feminists and writers of color. This view of multiculturalism encourages traditional distortions of history, overlooks Euro-American cultural identities, and generally ignores the fact that we are a syncretic, hybrid society. To us, the term multicultural is not a description of a category of American writing but a definition of all American writing. So we chose to call our *multicultural* series, "American Literatures." Plural.

The beauty of good stories is their resistance to facile categorization and crass generalization. Not only do stories keep company across time and borders, they render the particularity of the human experience. If we define culture as ways of living transmitted from one generation to another, then nothing comes closer to personal culture than home, and homeground is a vision that asks for farsightedness.

At its most expansive, that vision resides in plurality. Ishmael Reed writes gracefully, sometimes satirically, as he takes a memory tour among the ethnic groups that make up the California neighborhoods he's considered home, and examines them for degrees of racism, classism, and friendliness. For Victor Hernández Cruz, home is located in the music and poetry that floats between Puerto Rico and New York City, a joyful accompaniment to his Indian-Spanish-African family story. For Chicano author Nash Candelaria, childhood encompassed the New Mexico of his family heritage and the Anglo-Catholic neighborhoods of Los Angeles, both of which he identifies with and has been at times rejected by.

Other writers in this collection explore the many forked roots that reach into and out of homeground, routes that often encircle the globe. For them, home can be as much memory as place, and therefore not lost but carried within, just as to bring an anchor home means to draw it towards its vessel. For Pico Iyer, who even as a child traveled among foreign lands, airports and strange hotels seem like home, but as a world citizen, he regrets having no allegiance to or passion for a particular country. Then too, home is the place where one is native like a plant to the land, without the constrictions of boundaries. Thomas King renders the story of a Native American mother traveling from a reservation in Canada to Las Vegas who becomes trapped between two national boundaries because she refuses to recognize any country but Blackfoot. Colleen McElroy, daughter of a military man, like Iyer, knew homes around the world, and as an adult with a loving St. Louis family to return to, is still peripatetic. Her poetic memoir reflects on reactions to a Black woman both in and outside the United States.

Do we know home by leaving it or losing it? Lawson Inada describes a Japanese teenager working in his grandfather's fish market with a recent immigrant from Hiroshima whose home has been rendered a wasteland. Perhaps we find home by having to construct it of new materials. Chitra Divakaruni tells the story of a 20 year-old Indian woman who leaves her parents' home in the middle of the night to escape rigid traditions that include an impending arranged marriage. Joseph Geha's immigrant from Beirut bears his war injuries with dignity while trying to absorb American culture through television and learn a new language with all the resulting confusion and humor. For Shirley Lim, aspirations for her native-born child supersede her own ambivalence towards the United States as an immigrant mother from Malaysia. We say a truth drives home or hits home when it has found a mark in the heart unerringly. Laura Kalpakian reaches beyond her grandmother's cheery assimilation-tinted stories to envision her Armenian ancestors as they fled from Turkish terrorism in the 1920s. She pieces together the remnants of Turkish rugs, jewels sewn in corsets, passports and other family documents to create a fictional history, and in the process identifies herself more fully.

Home is a word of paradox and antipode. The very sense of belonging the word home carries — to be at home in a place or oneself — implies the degree of loss if one cannot find or feel it. Lawrence DiStasi survives the economic ups and downs of his Italian father and ends up housed with an aunt and uncle where he finds most in common with his displaced grandmother. Russell Leong explores the self-destructive impulses of a man neither at home in his religion nor his sexuality who wanders Asia and ultimately faces the transience of the human embrace. Generally used to denote the place of one's domestic affections, the word home is also applied to institutions, often places of refuge or retreat from family. Sandra Scofield, as a child, finds respite from the feud between her mother and grandmother when she is boarded at a convent school and thrives within its walls.

Within the same family or ethnic group, the customs and conventions of home or its icons can diverge widely. Naomi Shihab Nye compares her well-loved older home, which everywhere shows signs of its own biography, to her brother's new upscale home, devoid of history, and contemplates their different responses to a shared Palestinian heritage. Robin Hemley reveals how a Jewish family creates a

11

sustaining mythology about itself despite divisions between relatives from eastern and western Europe.

The desire to belong or protect is fierce. Military strategy has us home in on a target. Frank Chin's contribution focuses on the streets as home when Asian gang members in San Diego lay violent claim to turf. In extensive interviews with kids, parents, police, and community activists, Chin sees family structure turned on its head when children become more powerful than their parents.

Finally, we say that something has been brought home to us when we've found an epiphany. There are many such within these pages. Welcome home.

— The Editors

THOMAS KING

BORDERS

When I was twelve, maybe thirteen, my mother announced that we were going to go to Salt Lake City to visit my sister who had left the reserve, moved across the line, and found a job. Laetitia had not left home with my mother's blessing, but over time my mother had come to be proud of the fact that Laetitia had done all of this on her own.

"She did real good," my mother would say.

Then there were the fine points of Laetitia's going. She had not, as my mother liked to tell Mrs. Manyfingers, gone floating after some man like a balloon on a string. She hadn't snuck out of the house, either, and gone to Vancouver or Edmonton or Toronto to chase rainbows down alleys. And she hadn't been pregnant.

"She did real good."

I was seven or eight when Laetitia left home. She was seventeen. Our father was from Rocky Boy on the American side.

"Dad's American," Laetitia told my mother, "so I can go and come as I please."

"Send us a postcard."

Laetitia packed her things, and we headed for the border. Just outside of Milk River, Laetitia told us to watch for the water tower.

"Over the next rise. It's the first thing you see."

"We got a water tower on the reserve," my mother said. "There's a big one in Lethbridge, too."

"You'll be able to see the tops of the flagpoles, too. That's where the border is."

When we got to Coutts, my mother stopped at the convenience store and bought her and Laetitia a cup of coffee. I got an Orange Crush.

"This is real lousy coffee."

"You're just angry because I want to see the world."

"It's the water. From here on down, they got lousy water."

"I can catch the bus from Sweetgrass. You don't have to lift a finger."

"You're going to have to buy your water in bottles if you want good coffee."

There was an old wooden building about a block away, with a tall sign in the yard that said "Museum." Most of the roof had been blown away. Mom told me to go and see when the place was open. There were boards over the windows and doors. You could tell that the place was closed, and I told Mom so, but she said to go and check anyway. Mom and Laetitia stayed by the car. Neither one of them moved. I sat down on the steps of the museum and watched them, and I don't know that they ever said anything to each other. Finally, Laetitia got her bag out of the trunk and gave Mom a hug.

I wandered back to the car. The wind had come up, and it blew Laetitia's hair across her face. Mom reached out and pulled the strands out of Laetitia's eyes, and Laetitia let her.

"You can still see the mountain from here," my mother told Laetitia in Blackfoot.

"Lots of mountains in Salt Lake," Laetitia told her in English.

"The place is closed," I said. "Just like I told you."

Laetitia tucked her hair into her jacket and dragged her bag down the road to the brick building with the American flag flapping on a pole. When she got to where the guards were waiting, she turned, put the bag down, and waved to us. We waved back. Then my mother turned the car around, and we came home.

We got postcards from Laetitia regular, and, if she wasn't spreading jelly on the truth, she was happy. She found a good job and rented an apartment with a pool.

"And she can't even swim," my mother told Mrs. Manyfingers.

Most of the postcards said we should come down and see the city, but whenever I mentioned this, my mother would stiffen up.

So I was surprised when she bought two new tires for the car and put on her blue dress with the green and yellow flowers. I had to dress up, too, for my mother did not want us crossing the border looking like Americans. We made sandwiches and put them in a big box with pop and potato chips and some apples and bananas and a big jar of water.

"But we can stop at one of those restaurants, too, right?"

The border was actually two towns, though neither one was big enough to amount to anything. Coutts was on the Canadian side and consisted of the convenience store and gas station, the museum that was closed and boarded up, and a motel. Sweetgrass was on the American side, but all you could see was an overpass that arched across the highway and disappeared into the prairies. Just hearing the names of these towns, you would expect that Sweetgrass, which is a nice name and sounds like it is related to other places such as Medicine Hat and Moose Jaw and Kicking Horse Pass, would be on the Canadian side, and that Coutts, which sounds abrupt and rude, would be on the American side. But this was not the case.

Between the two borders was a duty-free shop where you could buy cigarettes and liquor and flags. Stuff like that.

We left the reserve in the morning and drove until we got to Coutts.

"Last time we stopped here," my mother said, "you had an Orange Crush. You remember that?"

"Sure," I said. "That was when Laetitia took off."

"You want another Orange Crush?"

"That means we're not going to stop at a restaurant, right?"

My mother got coffee at the convenience store, and we stood around and watched the prairies move in the sunlight. Then we climbed back in the car. My mother straightened the dress across her thighs, leaned against the wheel, and drove all the way to the border in first gear, slowly, as if she were trying to see through a bad storm or riding high on black ice.

The border guard was an old guy. As he walked to the car, he swayed from side to side, his feet set wide apart, the holster on his hip pitching up and down. He leaned into the window, looked into the back seat, and looked at my mother and me.

"Morning, ma'am."

"Good morning."

"Where you heading?"

"Salt Lake City."

"Purpose of your visit?"

"Visit my daughter."

"Citizenship?"

"Blackfoot," my mother told him.

"Ma'am?"

"Blackfoot," my mother repeated.

"Canadian?"

"Blackfoot."

It would have been easier if my mother had just said "Canadian" and been done with it, but I could see she wasn't going to do that. The guard wasn't angry or anything. He smiled and looked towards the building. Then he turned back and nodded.

"Morning, ma'am."

"Good morning."

"Any firearms or tobacco?"

"No."

"Citizenship?"

"Blackfoot."

He told us to sit in the car and wait, and we did. In about five minutes, another guard came out with the first man. They were talking as they came, both men swaying back and forth like two cowboys headed for a bar or a gunfight.

"Morning, ma'am."

"Good morning."

"Cecil tells me you and the boy are Blackfoot."

"That's right."

"Now, I know that we got Blackfeet on the American side and the Canadians got Blackfeet on their side. Just so we can keep our records straight, what side do you come from?"

I knew exactly what my mother was going to say, and I could have told them if they had asked me.

"Canadian side or American side?" asked the guard.

"Blackfoot side," she said.

It didn't take them long to lose their sense of humor, I can tell you that. The one guard stopped smiling altogether and told us to park our car at the side of the building and come in.

We sat on a wood bench for about an hour before anyone came over to talk to us. This time it was a woman. She had a gun, too.

"Hi," she said. "I'm Inspector Pratt. I understand there is a little misunderstanding."

"I'm going to visit my daughter in Salt Lake City," my mother told her. "We don't have any guns or beer."

"It's a legal technicality, that's all."

"My daughter's Blackfoot, too."

The woman opened a briefcase and took out a couple of forms and began to write on one of them. "Everyone who crosses our border has to declare their citizenship. Even Americans. It helps us keep track of the visitors we get from the various countries."

She went on like that for maybe fifteen minutes, and a lot of the stuff she told us was interesting.

"I can understand how you feel about having to tell us your citizenship, and here's what I'll do. You tell me, and I won't put it down on the form. No one will know but you and me."

Her gun was silver. There were several chips in the wood handle and the name "Stella" was scratched into the metal butt.

We were in the border office for about four hours, and we talked to almost everyone there. One of the men bought me a Coke. My mother brought a couple of sandwiches in from the car. I offered part of mine to Stella, but she said she wasn't hungry.

I told Stella that we were Blackfoot and Canadian, but she said that that didn't count because I was a minor. In the end, she told us that if my mother didn't declare her citizenship, we would have to go back to where we came from. My mother stood up and thanked Stella for her time. Then we got back in the car and drove to the Canadian border, which was only about a hundred yards away.

I was disappointed. I hadn't seen Laetitia for a long time, and I had never been to Salt Lake City. When she was still at home, Laetitia would go on and on about Salt Lake City. She had never been there, but her boyfriend Lester Tallbull had spent a year in Salt Lake at a technical school.

"It's a great place," Lester would say. "Nothing but blondes in the whole state."

Whenever he said that, Laetitia would slug him on his shoulder hard enough to make him flinch. He had some brochures on Salt Lake and some maps, and every so often the two of them would spread them out on the table.

"That's the temple. It's right downtown. You got to have a pass to get in."

"Charlotte says anyone can go in and look around."

"When was Charlotte in Salt Lake? Just when the hell was Charlotte in Salt Lake?"

"Last year."

"This is Liberty Park. It's got a zoo. There's good skiing in the mountains."

"Got all the skiing we can use," my mother would say. "People come from all over the world to ski at Banff. Cardston's got a temple, if you like those kinds of things."

"Oh, this one is real big," Lester would say. "They got armed guards and everything."

"Not what Charlotte says."

"What does she know?"

Lester and Laetitia broke up, but I guess the idea of Salt Lake stuck in her mind.

The Canadian border guard was a young woman, and she seemed happy to see us. "Hi," she said. "You folks sure have a great day for a trip. Where are you coming from?"

"Standoff."

"Is that in Montana?"

"No."

"Where are you going?"

"Standoff."

The woman's name was Carol and I don't guess she was any older than Laetitia. "Wow, you both Canadians?"

"Blackfoot."

"Really? I have a friend I went to school with who is Blackfoot. Do you know Mike Harley?"

"No."

"He went to school in Lethbridge, but he's really from Browning."

It was a nice conversation and there were no cars behind us, so there was no rush.

"You're not bringing any liquor back, are you?"

"No."

"Any cigarettes or plants or stuff like that?"

"No."

"Citizenship?"

"Blackfoot."

"I know," said the woman, "and I'd be proud of being Blackfoot if I were Blackfoot. But you have to be American or Canadian."

When Laetitia and Lester broke up, Lester took his brochures and maps with him, so Laetitia wrote to someone in Salt Lake City, and, about a month later, she got a big envelope of stuff. We sat at the table and opened up all the brochures, and Laetitia read each one out loud.

"Salt Lake City is the gateway to some of the world's most magnificent skiing.

"Salt Lake City is the home of one of the newest professional basketball franchises, the Utah Jazz.

"The Great Salt Lake is one of the natural wonders of the world."

It was kind of exciting seeing all those color brochures on the table and listening to Laetitia read all about how Salt Lake City was one of the best places in the entire world.

"That Salt Lake City place sounds too good to be true," my mother told her.

"It has everything."

"We got everything right here."

"It's boring here."

"People in Salt Lake City are probably sending away for brochures of Calgary and Lethbridge and Pincher Creek right now."

In the end, my mother would say that maybe Laetitia should go to Salt Lake City, and Laetitia would say that maybe she would.

We parked the car to the side of the building and Carol led us into a small room on the second floor. I found a comfortable spot on the couch and flipped through some back issues of *Saturday Night* and *Alberta Report*.

When I woke up, my mother was just coming out of another office. She didn't say a word to me. I followed her down the stairs and out to the car. I thought we were going home, but she turned the car around and drove back towards the American border, which made me think we were going to visit Laetitia in Salt Lake City after all. Instead she pulled into the parking lot of the duty-free store and stopped.

"We going to see Laetitia?"

"No."

"We going home?"

Pride is a good thing to have, you know. Laetitia had a lot of pride, and so did my mother. I figured that someday, I'd have it, too.

"So where are we going?"

Most of that day, we wandered around the duty-free store, which wasn't very large. The manager had a name tag with a tiny American flag on one side and a tiny Canadian flag on the other. His name was Mel. Towards evening, he began suggesting that we should be on our way. I told him we had nowhere to go, that neither the Americans nor the Canadians would let us in. He laughed at that and told us that we should buy something or leave.

The car was not very comfortable, but we did have all that food and it was April, so even if it did snow as it sometimes does on the prairies, we wouldn't freeze. The next morning my mother drove to the American border.

It was a different guard this time, but the questions were the same. We didn't spend as much time in the office as we had the day before. By noon, we were back at the Canadian border. By two we were back in the duty-free shop parking lot.

The second night in the car was not as much fun as the first, but my mother seemed in good spirits, and, all in all, it was as much an adventure as an inconvenience. There wasn't much food left and that was a problem, but we had lots of water as there was a faucet at the side of the duty-free shop.

One Sunday, Laetitia and I were watching television. Mom was over at Mrs. Manyfingers's. Right in the middle of the program, Laetitia turned off the set and said she was going to Salt Lake City, that life around here was too boring. I had wanted to see the rest of the program and really didn't care if Laetitia went to Salt Lake City or not. When Mom got home, I told her what Laetitia had said.

What surprised me was how angry Laetitia got when she found out that I had told Mom.

"You got a big mouth."

"That's what you said."

"What I said is none of your business."

"I didn't say anything."

"Well, I'm going for sure, now."

That weekend, Laetitia packed her bags, and we drove her to the border.

Mel turned out to be friendly. When he closed up for the night and found us still parked in the lot, he came over and asked us if our car was broken down or something. My mother thanked him for his concern and told him that we were fine, that things would get straightened out in the morning.

"You're kidding," said Mel. "You'd think they could handle the simple things."

"We got some apples and a banana," I said, "but we're all out of ham sandwiches."

"You know, you read about these things, but you just don't believe it. You just don't believe it."

"Hamburgers would be even better because they got more stuff for energy."

My mother slept in the back seat. I slept in the front because I was smaller and could lie under the steering wheel. Late that night, I heard my mother open the car door. I found her sitting on her blanket leaning against the bumper of the car.

"You see all those stars," she said. "When I was a little girl, my grandmother used to take me and my sisters out on the prairies and tell us stories about all the stars."

"Do you think Mel is going to bring us any hamburgers?"

"Every one of those stars has a story. You see that bunch of stars over there that look like a fish?"

"He didn't say no."

"Coyote went fishing, one day. That's how it all started." We sat out under the stars that night, and my mother told me all sorts of stories. She was serious about it, too. She'd tell them slow, repeating parts as she went, as if she expected me to remember each one.

Early the next morning, the television vans began to arrive, and guys in suits and women in dresses came trotting over to us, dragging microphones and cameras and lights behind them. One of the vans had a table set up with orange juice and sandwiches and fruit. It was for the crew, but when I told them we hadn't eaten for a while, a really skinny blonde woman told us we could eat as much as we wanted.

They mostly talked to my mother. Every so often one of the re-

21

porters would come over and ask me questions about how it felt to be an Indian without a country. I told them we had a nice house on the reserve and that my cousins had a couple of horses we rode when we went fishing. Some of the television people went over to the American border, and then they went to the Canadian border.

Around noon, a good-looking guy in a dark blue suit and an orange tie with little ducks on it drove up in a fancy car. He talked to my mother for a while, and, after they were done talking, my mother called me over, and we got into our car. Just as my mother started the engine, Mel came over and gave us a bag of peanut brittle and told us that justice was a damn hard thing to get, but that we shouldn't give up.

I would have preferred lemon drops, but it was nice of Mel anyway.

"Where are we going now?"

"Going to visit Laetitia."

The guard who came out to our car was all smiles. The television lights were so bright they hurt my eyes, and, if you tried to look through the windshield in certain directions, you couldn't see a thing.

"Morning, Ma'am."

"Good morning."

"Where you heading?"

"Salt Lake City."

"Purpose of your visit?"

"Visit my daughter."

"Any tobacco, liquor, or firearms?"

"Don't smoke."

"Any plants or fruit?"

"Not any more."

"Citizenship?"

"Blackfoot."

The guard rocked back on his heels and jammed his thumbs into his gun belt. "Thank you," he said, his fingers patting the butt of the revolver. "Have a pleasant trip."

My mother rolled the car forward, and the television people had to scramble out of the way. They ran alongside the car as we pulled away from the border, and, when they couldn't run any farther, they stood in the middle of the highway and waved and waved and waved.

We got to Salt Lake City the next day. Laetitia was happy to see us, and, that first night, she took us out to a restaurant that made really good soups. The list of pies took up a whole page. I had cherry. Mom had chocolate. Laetitia said that she saw us on television the night before and, during the meal, she had us tell her the story over and over again.

Laetitia took us everywhere. We went to a fancy ski resort. We went to the temple. We got to go shopping in a couple of large malls, but they weren't as large as the one in Edmonton, and Mom said so.

After a week or so, I got bored and wasn't all sad when my mother said we should be heading back home. Laetitia wanted us to stay longer, but Mom said no, that she had things to do back home and that, next time, Laetitia should come up and visit. Laetitia said she was thinking about moving back, and Mom told her to do as she pleased, and Laetitia said that she would.

On the way home, we stopped at the duty-free shop, and my mother gave Mel a green hat that said "Salt Lake" across the front. Mel was a funny guy. He took the hat and blew his nose and told my mother that she was an inspiration to us all. He gave us some more peanut brittle and came out into the parking lot and waved at us all the way to the Canadian border.

It was almost evening when we left Coutts. I watched the border through the rear window until all you could see were the tops of the flagpoles and the blue water tower, and then they rolled over a hill and disappeared.

CollEEN McElroy

GOING HOME:
A POETIC MEMOIR

My travels began in St. Louis Missouri, not going to it, but coming from it. There I learned how to see myself as both separate from and a part of several lives. This has happened repeatedly over the years: going away seems to bring me back to whom I have become. Wherever I go, I take pieces with me. That is how my story begins and continues: with pieces, bits of things remembered, details of home moving on a fuzzy landscape. Smells, sounds, textures clearer even than names and dates. My mind recording changes. My life growing out of events that occurred away from home. The world giving me a sense of home. So that is how I will tell it, a story where I move away from and back to whom I have been and what I have become. This is my chronometry of travels — the bits and pieces, my goings and comings.

Each trip reorders my map until like some ancient sailor, the known world is dead center. The rest spirals out. Spokes and arcs, light and water, an aside where it all belongs.

To get out of town, you had to pass the fountain in front of Union Station. The Wedding of Rivers. The pull of the mighty Mississippi. Then on to Crave Coeur (kids said *Grieve Car* in Missouri French). After that it was a clear shot. Of course you avoided the old men on benches and the old women in their kitchens and the snaggle-tooth children and the rococo statues at the fountain shooting rusty water that keeps going nowhere.

I'm still out here on that road. Occasionally getting caught in cul-de-sacs, a thousand and one shops. Avoiding the final exit.

Chile, why do you go to all them places? I never heard of such. Nobody in our family ever did all that going. Why you always got to be going?

Because they're there — those places. Everything we know is in constant motion. Earth, air, water. This room, this piece of paper, these words. All traveling along some map, through systems in motion. Rising, falling, willingly or forced we are brought together at some point. We move apart, move closer, move away. It is natural to move. As natural as breathing or dying or loving or freedom. All that movement didn't stop with the Emancipation.

What are you? he said. Serious, I answered: *Negro. No,* he said. *Not what are you called, but what do you claim? America?* I answered. And he said: *I am German. Verstehen? This place is the place of my people. What place holds your people to this earth?* It was the first time I was asked that question. And never asked at home.

> One two three O'Leary
> Four five six McCleary
> Allen Adams Grunewald Carey
> Ten O'Leary Dandy

What you remember: jump rope songs, ol man Farrow's store, the all-white playground at the end of the street, races down Ash Hill, the eight-block walk to school — no bus. Getting out.

They have torn down every house you've ever lived in. The house on Kennerly gone. Aunt Jennie's house on St. Ferdinand gone. The flat over Mrs. Scales' bar gone. The house on McMillan gone. And all the others mushed in a new riddle of one way streets leading to vacant lots. Not one damn map familiar and comfortable.

Tonight, another ubiquitous immigrant salutes the good ol days. I remember, says the fat man, when this land was free — we come here with nothing more than what my daddy could put on a half load wagon. Weren't nothing here but some scraggly trees, a few Indians, and lots of rattlesnakes. Carved everything we own outta this dirt. Funny, I think, no black cowboys. No Bill Picketts or Isom Darts or Nat Loves? No black folks heading West for Oklahoma and the territories, stopping off in St. Louis for one last home-cooked meal?

Pick a color: black, white, black and white, white and black.

Eighth grade. We graduated 8th grade in those days. No one expected us to do better. Cote Brilliante School. The system was George Washington Carver. Our bootstraps hooked to a libretto. All year we practiced. "The Caravan," an operetta. With Bedouins, Arabs, and slaves. I could sing every role, but Mr. Billups found me no matter where I hid. Off-key, he'd shout. Off-key.

What twisted mind let thirty-two black kids sing about caravans and slaves on a hot day in June 1947 in the middle of St. Louis?

A woman whose lip peels back to gum and nasal ridge brags of her descent from English stock. She loves all that is old world, except its dysentery, scarlet fever, plague, and syphilis. When the round of questions on heritage ends on your plate, she asks: Where do you live, dear?

You nod, your safest bet. Everyone is polite. They speak in confidential tones of conquests. Give each other gentled names. Nothing is as it seems. Adventure means plunder. They are pirates turned captains of industry.

Just in case you'll never get it right, he clarifies: We were giving it away, from Indian Hills clear to Cherokee. The names slip off his tongue: Potawatomee, Unondoga, Shawnee....Good little towns, he says, my brother was the sheriff round about the time the Crees migrated here. Don't 'member too many of the colored — 'cept that one town had 'em all. Jebediah...

The thieves are counting their jewels. They give each coin a name of exclusion. Their women are bent under the weight.

And you wonder how migrations fared under the guns of cavalry and manacles and back breaking marches with no time to stop for babies or sore feet.

> Cherries cherries in my basket
> Heel toe stamp and over
> Gold and silver in my basket
> Front and over heel toe

You still remember eighth grade, don't you? In those days your folks graduated eighth grade. Nobody thought they could do more. "The Caravan" and whole class was a choir. Most could sing. Not you. The boys sang all the slave parts: *We are old with labor/bended low/and our steps are weary/weary and slow.* The girls sang answers: *Heed not the slaves melancholy song/Heed not their moaning along.* Everyone laughed when you sang: The *guards are forming a-head.*

Your problem has always been mouth. Most folks expect you to prove the truth, yet they accept the other stuff. Well, here's the truth: you were on your way to a planet of three moons and somehow got side-tracked here. Once you landed, there was no turning back. But in your world, the dead are white and walk backwards. The rest just are. Same problem as here.

Now the statistics: In the black 12–16% — depending on the calculator. In the service 25% In the pen 55% On the pity of welfare 65% On the move 35% Abroad 03% Two of them male.

Girl, what you doing out there by yourself. Best be careful among those foreigners.

What are you? he said. Serious, I answered: *Negro. Not where but who? American?* He says: *I am German. Verstehen? This place is the place of my people. What place holds your people to this earth?* Silence. It is the first time I have been asked that question. And never at home. Silence. *How can you understand someone else's history if you don't know your own? Do not come back until you can answer the question.* I don't.

Watusi. Xhosa. Eritrean. Seminole. Chinese. Saxon. Which names matter? Herr Doktor Professor what I remember is eighth grade. Cote Brilliante School. An operetta I couldn't sing.

James' boy wants to marry a Eurasian girl, Mama says. Don't know what's happening to this family. First you go off and stay for Lord knows how long with all them foreigners, then your brother gets himself a wife from one of them places in the Pacific and brought her here to St. Louis. Colored people got enough trouble without all that mess. And James he's fit to be tied now. Course, the girl looks like your cousin Mae.

What else is there left to say? Your aging cousins show you their fur coats. They have traded them for men. Mink as mean as their eyes. Your aunt, their mother, greets you as always with hostile indifference. She thinks you've passed over. Not dead but just as well in a sea of pink faces.

What travelers invent for themselves is a journey of unimaginable lengths.

I am standing in the middle of a dusty square. The sun is boiling and tropical. A woman comes up to me. She wears something Punjabi. Speaks Haitian. Eats European, fork in left hand always. She is thirsty. I hand her a map. She sticks it full of pins and falls asleep. When she dreams, she smiles. When the bus arrives, she demands a ticket. Home.

In the right light, my mother looks a bit like her mother, but she really favors her father, my grandfather, Papa. Papa who worked for Anheuser. Papa who gave me my long legs and slender fingers. Papa who died before I began all this traveling stuff. Now I do it with his memory in my head. Odd since it was my mother's mother, Mama, who always greeted us when we came home.

My mother and I have similar feet, long and narrow. Made for walking my grandmother would say. Grandma had feet with ankles that ended right on the ground, and a roll of flesh around the heels like a small inner tube. She had feet that grew corns like an annual crop. Her feet could dig into the earth, walk a mile, and dance as if they had wings. I knew those feet didn't like shoes, but when we came home from one of my father's tours of duty, my grandmother's feet virtually flew down the stairs of that house on Kennerly and didn't even touch the ground. She wouldn't know which of us to hug first. She sort of scooped us all against her, and we fell into one of those clumsy hugs that involved too many people squished together at strange angles, bits of them left out in the open like extra body parts. She'd grab me around my ears and neck leaving my left shoulder wedged between her chest and my mother's armpit. My left side picked up the heat from those women. My right side stuck out unattached and cold in the nippy St. Louis air. Ready to go again.

Come September and Mama sent me home for school: In St. Louis where I'd get a good education in a colored school, the family said. And my cousins Irma Jean and Cora Jean squealing like birds whose nest had been mangled: *Colleena Mobeena Stick Stack Steena.* And everyone moving in sort of a circle of laughing and ooh-ing and ahh-ing and *Lord Jesus, so long a time....*

The first problem of adjustment upon returning any place is that everything seems smaller than you remember. I remembered the house on Kennerly as bigger than any place we'd lived in the Army. I remembered rows of coffee-colored flats with white-washed stoops. Or my Aunt Jennie's house set in a block of houses with long summer porches. Jennie, who always took you back when you came home. What I saw when I returned was a line of squat houses made of fake brick with postage-stamp front porches painted faded yellow and blue, and all that curlicue wrought iron. Houses where one neighbor knew exactly what the other neighbor was doing. Houses stacked together wall-to-wall — like those houses of cards Daddy built to show me how strong a deck could be.

> Heel toe kiss O'Malley
> Pull him way back in the alley
> Soap and water gums and belly
> End to end O'Malley

What are the telltale signs of the inveterate traveler? She loves the act of traveling, the motion, the confusion of tickets and luggage, strangeness waiting like a present about to be opened.

What is home if the road that draws you away from it is more familiar, more comforting? Home is what you find when you get there. Home is any place on this planet. And no silver arch over the "Mighty Miss" to pin you there. They got some of us everywhere: Grandma said. In Ecuador, in 1977 on the seventh day of the seventh month, I stood at the equator: latitude 0'00. In Istanbul, I stood with one foot in Asia and the other in Europe.

The only sunrise I ever want to see is over the wing tip of a 747 at 35,000 feet. Otherwise, don't wake me before noon.

Overseas, I am always the sight to see. Some turn, smile, say: *Buon giorno* or *Buenos dias* or *Comment allez-vous* or *G'day t'ya*. Some just grin: *coffee? tea?* Their treat. In the market on Fiji, the vendors were pretty and black and when they learned my name they called me: *Col-lee-een, and I* started tripping cause I heard my mama calling me home when I had to run swimming among fireflies and all those bad boys trying to get me in trouble.

Out in the world, I think of Josephine Baker, the singer, *La Bakaire*. Me and Josephine, a long way from St. Louie.

On the Isle of Majorca, near the home of Junipero Serra who wrestled the Indians of the Californias into Christianity, three boys and an old man stand outside my car for an hour and a half while I rest my swollen feet. In the end, they consent to one photo — none of them smiling. In Belgrade, everyone stared, jeered, flapped behind me like geese. My trick: find the dullest store-front display (old keys, sockets and wrenches, shoelaces and heelcaps) When a crowd gathered (and it would) straining to see what it was I saw — this strange black woman in Western clothing — slip away and leave them there. It always worked.

You always remember men who smiled shyly, their eyes soft as a caress: Stëin and Chaupè…Stephanovic and Nikki…Lau and Georgio and Anton…They taught you languages you'll never forget. Some nights you still dream them.

Perhaps everything you love should be put on wheels.

Outside, the sun is making its daily come-back. And the sea is dancing its one damn dance again. But yours is a water sign, and that's what this is all about. This moving. You are making love. The sheets are hot, the air is hot, your skin is hot, your lover. Lips, arms, skin. Where are you traveling now? You've always liked lovers with strong thighs. After all, someone has to carry all those damn bags. And you always overpack.

When the plane bound for New Jersey left the Azores, the last landmark we saw was the castle, Torre-de-Belem. Our pilot tipped the wings so we'd catch that final glimpse of land. It was a noticeable lurch, the kind taken by pilots who still dreamed of the old days and wars when they skimmed the clouds to avoid ground fire. Beneath us, the sunset turned leaves gold and red, then we winged out over the endless ocean — going home.

My greatest hassles with customs agents have always been Stateside. How did you pay for this ticket? they ask. Where were you born? Why did you go to these places? Do you know anyone there? Is there anyone at home who can vouch for you?

Is there anyone home?

> Heel toe cross and over
> Heel toe back and over
> Put O'Leary in the clover
> Cross and over heel toe

When we stepped into the terminal in New Jersey, I discovered culture shock in reverse. I'd landed in a sea of black faces. Away from home for a few months, and I find myself swimming in a sea of black faces. Hundreds of black folks everywhere and of every shade. Not just some scattered here and there in the cities of Europe or Asia. Black folks swirled around me, words echoing with the sounds of Texas, Georgia, Missouri, New York — and all in color. Out of the country, I was the stranger, stared at because I was the curiosity, the exotic, the myth they'd told stories about. Out of the country, white Americans thought they knew me better than I knew myself. But Stateside was another matter. Straight color like so much White and so much Black, I couldn't breathe without pushing against it. All answers depended on color. Three hundred years of racism, a history of slavery, and headlines about Supreme Court decisions became eyeball to eyeball looks. Folks looked knives, looked buzz-saws and grenades. "They look like damn-it-I'll-bite-you," Mama said. Somewhere overseas, I'd lost the knack of that look. Somewhere, I'd dropped my mask and stood up, "Black and the hell with you, I'm here." Now I was home and color was straight out and head on. Color was the prison where, like any concentration camp, both the guards and the inmates were bound by the rage.

He says, *It says here you've traveled quite a bit. Yes, I say. Visa stamps on almost every page. An old passport, I tell him. He picks up the entry stamp. Turns the pages again. Triangles, squares, blue ink, green ink* — half the world turned into symbols. He brings the stamp down slowly. *Don't you ever stay home?* he asks. *I am home,* I say.

She was Japanese, short and muscular. I didn't give a damn. I stood my ground, skinny black legs and all. Three other inbound planes had landed, and that was the last luggage cart in customs and it was mine. She squatted, stared, yanked the cart, said something that sounded like sand hitting the side of a bowl. I held fast. Yanked back. Turned street. It's always surprising how "fuck you" translates instantly in all languages.

Somewhere in the late afternoon of that first day home, when my body clock was collapsing under the change in time zones I listened to the rhythms of the house.

Home alone with the children gone now and the rest of the family in the Midwest. If I'm quiet I can still hear the familiar sounds of home. Perhaps I hear my Aunt Jennie saying: Chile, you are so brave. Go out there and see this world. Wish I could go with you. Or my Grandmother pulling out old photographs to match the ones I'm showing her of places she'll never see. That's your Uncle Roman, she says, just so I won't lose track of the family. And that's you, she says. A silhouette done at the carnival when you was just about five years old. But you so big now. I member when you was no bigger than this. Then she pops her fingers and hardly a sound comes out and we both laugh because Grandma could never make her fingers pop. And my father will cook a meal of a thousand starches highlighted with greens and beans and beets. And my mother will shake her head and say: I just don't understand. Full grown and always on the go. And I'll look at the tapestry hanging over my grandmother's sofa. The one with the desert scene, a hand at the tent flap, one eye peeking out.

One two three O'Leary
Give the basket to McCleary
Pinch her if she hollers dearie
That's O'Leary Dandy

The plane was filled with orphans, babies belted in airline cradles all the way from Korea. Chicago was the last leg of their trip. Two nuns accompanied them, but no one else could touch them, not even hold them when they cried. Against regulations. Finally, an hour outside of Chicago they fell asleep. Then we went into a holding pattern over O'Hare. It was too quiet. All the babies woke up. The plane nosed through the heavy cloud cover and rocketed past the lights of the city with forty orphans wailing.

Thirty-two of us singing "The Caravan." Four will be dead before they're twenty. Eight more before they're thirty. One will be an opera singer, the toast of Europe naturally. Two will head corporations, one of them bankrupt on someone else's savings and loan scandal. One will dance on Broadway. One form his own singing group. He'll be famous. One day, on tour, I'll stop by his hotel. The concierge will not admit me to his room.

There's a name somewhere on the tip of your tongue. Like an island in a sea of words. Nadi. Majorca. Krk. Ischia. Langkawi. Why does it always taste so good to say names in foreign languages? Like loving someone you can hardly bear to touch? Smells like flowers — sweet plumeria, raw rafflesia. The texture of washed silk. A crisp ticket for a new port. The body adjusts, sighs. Beautiful you think, beautiful. You move.

Even now, you can recite entire verses of "The Caravan."

Home. I turned to the window. The air lanes were dotted with planes, some like the American carrier I had traveled on — others with foreign designations. I've traveled them as well. The airfield held a strange kind of symmetry, planes lined up wing tip to wing tip, underbellies dragging or pointed noses painted like beaks. When the airport limo turned onto the highway, I watched cars zip past. Too many colors, too many different faces, too many billboards for "buy this," and roadside stores selling a little bit of that. A fast talking disc jockey handed out bad news on the hour every hour. And we ease past the strangeness of airports, heading where? Home ain't but a place, I tell myself.

Why you got to go to all those places? Mama asks. Because they are there, I say. All that going and coming, she says. Always going home, I think.

Pico Iyer

Home Is Every Place

By the time I was nine, I was already used to going to school by trans-Atlantic plane, to sleeping in airports, to shuttling back and forth, three times a year, between my parents' (Indian) home in California and my boarding school in England. Throughout the time I was growing up, I was never within 6,000 miles of the nearest relative — and came, therefore, to learn how to define relations in non-familial ways. From the time I was a teenager, I took it for granted that I could take my budget vacations (as I did) in Bolivia and Tibet, China and Morocco. It never seemed strange to me that a girlfriend might be half a world (or 10 hours flying time) away, that my closest friends might be on the other side of a continent or sea.

It was only recently that I realized that all these habits of mind and life would scarcely have been imaginable in my parents' youth; the very facts and facilities that shape my world are all distinctly new developments, and mark me as a modern type.

It was only recently, in fact, that I realized that I am an example, perhaps, of an entirely new breed of people, a transcontinental tribe of wanderers that is multiplying as fast as international phone lines and Frequent Flyer programs. We are the Transit Loungers, forever heading to the Departure Gate, forever orbiting the world. We buy our interests duty-free, we eat our food on plastic plates, we watch the world through borrowed headphones. We pass through countries as through revolving doors, resident aliens of the world, impermanent residents of nowhere. Nothing is strange to us, and nowhere is foreign. We are visitors even in our own homes.

This is not, I think, a function of affluence so much as of simple circumstance. I am not, that is, a jet-setter pursuing vacations from Marbella to Phuket; I am simply a fairly typical product of a movable sensibility, living and working in a world that is itself increasingly small and increasingly mongrel. I am a multinational soul on a multicultural globe where more and more countries are as polyglot and restless as airports. Taking planes seems as natural to me as picking up the phone, or going to school; I fold up my self and carry it around with me as if it were an overnight case.

The modern world seems increasingly made for people like me. I can plop myself down anywhere and find myself in the same relation of familiarity and strangeness: Lusaka, after all, is scarcely more strange to me than the foreigners' England in which I was born; the America where I am registered as an "alien"; and the almost unvisited India that people tell me is my home. I can fly from London to San Francisco to Osaka and feel myself no more a foreigner in one place than another; all of them are just locations — pavilions in some intercontinental Expo — and I can work or live or love in any one of them. All have Holiday Inns, direct-dial phones, CNN, and DHL. All have sushi and Thai restaurants, Kentucky Fried Chicken and Coke. My office is as close as the nearest fax machine or modem. Roppongi is West Hollywood is Leblon.

This kind of life offers an unprecedented sense of freedom and mobility: tied down to nowhere, we can pick and choose among locations. Ours is the first generation that can go off to visit Tibet for a week, or meet Tibetans down the street; ours is the first generation to be able to go to Nigeria for a holiday to find our roots — or to find they are not there. At the lowest level, this new internationalism also means that I can get on a plane in Los Angeles, get off a few hours later in Jakarta, check into a Hilton, order a cheeseburger in English, and pay for it all with an American Express card. At the next level, it means that I can meet, in the Hilton coffee shop, an Indonesian businessman who is as conversant as I am with Michael

Kinsley and Magic Johnson and Madonna. At a deeper level, it means that I need never feel estranged. If all the world is alien to us, all the world is home.

I have learned, in fact, to love foreignness. In any place I visit, I have the privileges of an outsider: I am an object of interest, and even fascination; I am a person set apart, able to enjoy the benefits of the place without paying the taxes. And the places themselves seem glamorous to me, romantic, as seen through foreign eyes: distance on both sides lends enchantment. Policemen let me off speeding tickets, girls want to hear the stories of my life, pedestrians will gladly point me to the nearest Golden Arches. Perpetual foreigners in the transit lounge, we enjoy a kind of diplomatic immunity; and, living off room service in our hotel rooms, we are never obliged to grow up, or even, really, to be ourselves.

Thus, many of us learn to exult in the blessings of belonging to what feels like a whole new race. It is a race, as Salman Rushdie says, of "people who root themselves in ideas rather than places, in memories as much as in material things; people who have been obliged to define themselves — because they are so defined by others — by their otherness; people in whose deepest selves strange fusions occur, unprecedented unions between what they were and where they find themselves." And when people argue that our very notion of wonder is eroded, that alienness itself is as seriously endangered as the wilderness, that more and more of the world is turning into a single synthetic monoculture, I am not worried: a Japanese version of a French fashion is something new, I say, not quite Japanese and not truly French. Comme des Garcons hybrids are the art form of the time.

And yet, sometimes, I stop myself and think. What kind of heart is being produced by these new changes? And must I always be a None of the Above? When the stewardess comes down the aisle with disembarkation forms, what do I fill in? My passport says one thing, my face another; my accent contradicts my eyes. Place of Residence, Final Destination, even Marital Status are not much easier to fill in; usually I just tick "Other."

And beneath all the boxes, where do we place ourselves? How does one fix a moving object on a map? I am not an exile, really, nor an immigrant; not deracinated, I think, any more than I am rooted. I have not fled the oppression of war, nor found ostracism in the places where I do alight; I can scarcely feel severed from a home I have barely known. Yet is "citizen of the world" enough to comfort me? And does taking my home as every place make it easier to sleep at night?

Alienation, we are taught from kindergarten, is the condition of the time. This is the century of exiles and refugees, of boat people and statelessness; the time when traditions have been abolished, and men become closer to machines. This is the century of estrangement: more than a third of all Afghans live outside Afghanistan; the second city of the Khmers is a refugee camp; the second tongue of Beverly Hills is Farsi. The very notion of nation-states is outdated; many of us are as crosshatched within as Beirut.

To understand the modern state, we are often told, we must read V.S. Naipaul, and see how people estranged from their cultures mimic people estranged from their roots. Naipaul is the definitive modern traveler in part because he is the definitive symbol of modern rootlessness; the singular qualification for his wanderings is not his stamina, nor his bravado, nor his love of exploration — it is, quite simply, his congenital displacement. Here is a man who was a foreigner at birth, a citizen of an exiled community set down on a colonized island. Here is a man for whom every arrival is enigmatic, a man without a home — except for an India to which he stubbornly returns, only to be reminded of his distance from it. The strength of Naipaul is the poignancy of Naipaul: the poignancy of a wanderer who tries to go home, but is not taken in, and is accepted by another home only so long as he admits that he's a lodger there.

There is, however, another way of apprehending foreignness, and that is the way of Nabokov. In him we see an avid cultivation of the novel: he collects foreign worlds with a connoisseur's delight, he sees foreign words as toys to play with, and exile as the state of kings. This touring aristocrat can even relish the pleasures of Low culture precisely because they are the things that his own high culture lacks: the motel and the summer camp, the roadside attraction and the hot fudge sundae. I recognize in Nabokov a European's love for America rooted in America's very youthfulness and heedlessness; I recognize in him the sense that the newcomer's viewpoint may be the one most conducive to bright ardor. Unfamiliarity, in any form, breeds content.

Nabokov shows us that if nowhere is home, everywhere is. That instead of taking alienation as our natural state, we can feel partially adjusted everywhere. That the outsider at the feast does not have to sit in the corner alone, taking notes; he can plunge into the pleasures of his new home with abandon.

We airport-hoppers can, in fact, go through the world as through a house of wonders, picking up something at every stop, and taking the whole globe as our playpen, or our supermarket (and even if we don't go to the world, the world will increasingly come to us: just down the street, almost wherever we are, are nori and salsa, tiramisu and *naan*). We don't have a home, we have a hundred homes. And we can mix and match as the situation demands. "Nobody's history is my history," Kazuo Ishiguro, a great spokesman for the privileged homeless, once said to me, and then went on, "Whenever it was convenient for me to become very Japanese, I could become very Japanese, and then, when I wanted to drop it, I would just become this ordinary Englishman." Instantly, I felt a shock of recognition: I have a wardrobe of selves from which to choose. And I savor the luxury of being able to be an Indian in Cuba (where people are starving for yoga and Tagore), or an American in Thailand, to be an Englishman in New York.

And so we go on circling the world, six miles above the ground, displaced from time, above the clouds, with all our needs attended to. We listen to announcements given in three languages. We confirm our reservations at every stop. We disembark at airports that are self-sufficient communities, with hotels, gymnasia, and places of worship. At customs we have nothing to declare but ourselves.

But what is the price we pay for all of this? I sometimes think that this mobile way of life is as novel as high-rises, or the video monitors that are rewiring our consciousness. And even as we fret about the changes our progress wreaks in the air and on the airwaves, in forests and on streets, we hardly worry about the changes it is working in ourselves, the new kind of soul that is being born out of a new kind of life. Yet this could be the most dangerous development of all, and not only because it is the least examined.

For us in the Transit Lounge, disorientation is as alien as affiliation. We become professional observers, able to see the merits and deficiencies of anywhere, to balance our parents' viewpoints with their enemies' position. Yes, we say, of course it's terrible, but look at the situation from Saddam's point of view. I understand how you feel, but the Chinese had their own cultural reasons for Tiananmen Square. Fervor comes to seem to us the most foreign place of all.

Seasoned experts at dispassion, we are less good at involvement, or suspensions of disbelief; at, in fact, the abolition of distance. We are masters of the aerial perspective, but touching down becomes more difficult. Unable to get stirred by the raising of a flag, we are sometimes unable to see how anyone could be stirred. I sometimes think that this is how Rushdie, the great analyst of this condition, somehow became its victim. He had juggled homes for so long, so adroitly, that he forgot how the world looks to someone who is rooted, in country or belief. He had chosen to live so far from affiliation that he could no longer see why people choose affiliation in the first place. Besides, being part of no society means one is accountable to no one, and need respect no laws outside one's own. If single-nation people can be fanatical as terrorists, we can end up ineffectual as peacekeepers.

We become, in fact, strangers to belief itself, unable to comprehend many of the rages and dogmas that animate (and unite) people. Conflict itself seems inexplicable to us sometimes, simply because partisanship is; we have the agnostic's inability to retrace the steps of faith. I could not begin to fathom why some Moslems would think of murder after hearing about *The Satanic Verses*; yet sometimes I force myself to recall that it is we, in our floating skepticism, who are the exceptions, that in China or Iran, in Korea or Peru, it is not so strange to give up one's life for a cause.

We end up, then, a little like nonaligned nations, confirming our reservations at every step. We tell ourselves, self-servingly, that nationalism breeds monsters, and choose to ignore the fact that internationalism breeds them too. Ours is the culpability not of the assassin, but of the bystander who takes a snapshot of the murder. Or, when the revolution catches fire, hops on the next plane out.

In any case, the issues in the Transit Lounge are passing; a few hours from now, they'll be a thousand miles away. Besides, this is a

40

foreign country, we have no interests here. The only thing we have to fear are hijackers — passionate people with beliefs.

Sometimes, though, just sometimes, I am brought up short by symptoms of my condition. They are not major things, but they are peculiar ones, and ones that would not have been so common 50 years ago. I have never bought a house of any kind, and my ideal domestic environment, I sometimes tell my friends, is a hotel-room. I have never voted, or ever wanted to vote, and I eat in restaurants three times a day. I have never supported a nation (in the Olympic Games, say), or represented "my country" in anything. Even my name is weirdly international, because my "real name" is one that makes sense only in the home where I have never lived.

I choose to live in America in part, I think, because it feels more alien the longer I stay there. I love being in Japan because it reminds me, at every turn, of my foreignness. When I want to see if any place is home, I must subject the candidates to a battery of tests. Home is the place of which one has memories but no expectations.

If I have any deeper home, it is, I suppose, in English. My language is the house I carry round with me as a snail his shell; and in my lesser moments I try to forget that mine is not the language spoken in America, or even, really, by any member of my family.

Yet even here, I find, I cannot place my accent, or reproduce it as I can the tones of others. And I am so used to modifying my English inflections according to whom I am talking to — an American, an Englishman, a villager in Nepal, a receptionist in Paris — that I scarcely know what kind of voice I have.

I wonder, sometimes, if this new kind of non-affiliation may not be alien to something fundamental in the human state. The refugee at least harbors passionate feelings about the world he has left — and generally seeks to return there; the exile at least is propelled by some kind of strong emotion away from the old country and towards the new — indifference is not an exile emotion. But what does the Transit Lounger feel? What are the issues that we would die for? What are the passions that we would live for?

Airports are among the only sites in public life where emotions are hugely sanctioned, in block capitals. We see people weep, shout, kiss in airports; we see them at the furthest edges of excitement and exhaustion. Airports are privileged spaces where we can see the primal states writ large — fear, recognition, hope. But there are some of us, perhaps, sitting at the Departure Gate, boarding passes in hand, watching the destinations ticking over, who feel neither the pain of separation nor the exultation of wonder; who alight with the same emotions with which we embarked; who go down to the baggage carousel and watch our lives circling, circling, circling, waiting to be claimed.

Ishmael Reed

My Oakland, There Is a There There

My stepfather is an evolutionist. He worked for many years at the Chevrolet division of General Motors in Buffalo, a working-class auto and steel town in upstate New York, and was able to rise from relative poverty to the middle class. He believes that each succeeding generation of Afro-Americans will have it better than its predecessor. In 1979 I moved into the kind of neighborhood that he and my mother spent about one third of their lives trying to escape. According to the evolutionist integrationist ethic this was surely a step backward, since "success" was seen as being able to live in a neighborhood in which you were the only black and joined your neighbors in trying to keep out "them."

My neighborhood, bordered by Genoa, Market Street, and Forty-Eighth and Fifty-Fifth streets in North Oakland, is what the media refer to as a "predominantly black neighborhood." It's the kind of neighborhood I grew up in before leaving for New York City in 1962.

My last New York residence was an apartment in a brownstone, next door to the building in which poet W.H. Auden lived. There were trees in the backyard, and I thought it was a swell neighborhood until I read in Robert Craft's biography of Stravinsky that when Stravinsky sent his chauffeur to pick up his friend Auden, the chauffeur would ask, "Are you sure Mr. Auden lives in this neighborhood?" By 1968 my wife and I were able to live six months of the year in New York and the other six in California. This came to an end when one of the people I sublet the apartment to abandoned it. He had fled to England to pursue a romance. He didn't pay the rent, and so we were evicted long-distance.

My first residence in California was an apartment on Santa Ynez Street, near Echo Park Lake in Los Angeles, where I lived for about six months in 1967. I was working on my second novel, and Carla Blank, my wife, a dancer, was teaching physical education at one of Eddie Rickenbacker's camps, located on an old movie set in the San Bernardino Mountains. Carla's employers were always offering me a cabin where they promised I could write without interruption. I never took them up on the offer, but for years I've wondered about what kind of reception I would have received had they discovered that I was black.

During my breaks from writing I would walk through the shopping areas near Santa Ynez, strolling by vending machines holding newspapers whose headlines screamed about riots in Detroit. On some weekends we'd visit novelist Robert Gover (*The One Hundred Dollar Misunderstanding*) and his friends in Malibu. I remember one of Gover's friends, a scriptwriter for the *Donna Reed Show*, looking me in the eye and telling me that if he were black he'd be "on a Detroit rooftop, sniping at cops," as he reclined, glass of scotch in hand, in a comfortable chair whose position gave him a good view of the rolling Pacific.

My Santa Ynez neighbors were whites from Alabama and Mississippi, and we got along fine. Most of them were elderly, left behind by white flight to the suburbs, and on weekends the street would be lined with cars belonging to relatives who were visiting. While living here I observed a uniquely Californian phenomenon. Retired men would leave their houses in the morning, enter their cars, and remain there for a good part of the day, snoozing, reading newspapers, or listening to the radio.

I didn't experience a single racial incident during my stay in this Los Angeles neighborhood of ex-Southerners. Once, however, I had a strange encounter with the police. I was walking through a black working-class neighborhood on my way to the downtown Los Angeles library. Some cops drove up and rushed me. A crowd gathered. The cops snatched my briefcase and removed its contents: books and notebooks having to do with my research of voodoo. The crowd laughed when the cops said they thought I was carrying a purse.

In 1968 my wife and I moved to Berkeley, where we lived in one Bauhaus box after another until about 1971, when I received a three-book contract from Doubleday. Then we moved into the Berkeley Hills, where we lived in the downstairs apartment of a very grand-looking house on Bret Harte Way. There was a Zen garden with streams, waterfalls, and bridges outside, along with many varieties of flowers and plants. I didn't drive, and Carla was away at Mills College each day, earning a master's degree in dance. I stayed holed up in that apartment for two years, during which time I completed my third novel, *Mumbo Jumbo*.

During this period I became exposed to some of the racism I hadn't detected on Santa Ynez or in the Berkeley flats. As a black male working at home, I was regarded with suspicion. Neighbors would come over and warn me about a heroin salesman they said was burglarizing the neighborhood, all the while looking over my shoulder in an attempt to pry into what I was up to. Once, while I was eating breakfast, a policeman entered through the garden door, gun drawn. "What on earth is the problem, officer?" I asked. He said they'd got word that a homicide had been committed in my apartment, which I recognized as an old police tactic used to gain entry into somebody's house. Walking through the Berkeley Hills on Sundays, I was greeted by unfriendly stares and growling, snarling dogs. I remember one pest who always poked her head out of her window whenever I'd walk down Bret Harte Way. She was always hassling me about parking my car in front of her house. She resembled Miss Piggy. Though my landlord was a congenial intellectual, I came to think of this section of Berkeley as "Whitetown."

Around 1974, we found ourselves again in the Berkeley flats. We spent a couple of peaceful years on Edith Street, and then moved to Jayne Street, where we encountered another next-door family of nosy, middle-class progressives. I understand that much time at North Berkeley white neighborhood association meetings is taken up with discussion of and fascination with blacks who move through the neighborhoods, with special concern given those who tarry, or who wear dreadlocks. Since before the Civil War, vagrancy laws have been used as political weapons against blacks. Appropriately, there has been talk of making Havana — where I understand a woman can get turned in by her neighbors for having too many boyfriends over — Berkeley's sister city.

In 1976 our landlady announced that she was going to reoccupy the Jayne Street house. I facetiously told a friend that I wanted to move to the most right-wing neighborhood he could think of. He mentioned El Cerrito. There, he said, your next-door neighbor might even be a cop. We moved to El Cerrito. Instead of the patronizing nosiness blacks complain about in Berkeley, I found the opposite on Terrace Drive in El Cerrito. The people were cold, impersonal, remote. But the neighborhood was quiet, serene even — the view was Olympian, and our rented house was secluded by eucalyptus trees. The annoyances were minor. Occasionally a car would careen down Terrace Drive full of white teenagers, and one or two would shout, "Hey, nigger!" Sometimes as I walked down The Arlington toward Kensington Market, the curious would stare at me from their cars, and women I encountered would give me nervous, frightened looks. Once, as I was walking to the market to buy magazines, a white child was sitting directly in my path. We were the only two people on the street. Two or three cars actually stopped, and their drivers observed the scene through their rearview mirrors until they were assured I wasn't going to abduct the child.

At night the Kensington Market area was lit with a yellow light, especially eerie during a fog. I always thought that this section of Kensington would be a swell place to make a horror movie — the residents would make great extras — but whatever discomfort I felt about traveling through this area at 2 A.M. was mixed with the relief that I had just navigated safely through Albany, where the police seemed always to be lurking in the shadows, prepared to ensnare blacks, hippies, and others they didn't deem suitable for such a neighborhood.

In 1979 our landlord, a decent enough fellow in comparison to some of the others we had had (who made you understand why the Communists shoot the landlords first when they take over a country), announced he was going to sell the house on Terrace Drive. This was the third rented house to be sold out from under us. The asking price was way beyond our means, and so we started to search for another home, only to find that the ones within our price range were

46

located in North Oakland, in a "predominantly black neighborhood." We finally found a huge Queen Anne Victorian, which seemed to be about a month away from the wrecker's ball if the termites and the precarious foundation didn't do it in first, but I decided that I had to have it. The oldest house on the block, it was built in 1906, the year the big earthquake hit Northern California but left Oakland unscathed because, according to Bret Harte, "there are some things even the earth can't swallow." If I was apprehensive about moving into this neighborhood — on television all-black neighborhoods resemble the commotion of the station house on *Hill Street Blues* — I was later to learn that our neighbors were just as apprehensive about us. Were we hippies? Did I have a job? Were we going to pay as much attention to maintaining our property as they did to theirs? Neglected, the dilapidated monstrosity I'd got myself into would blight the entire block.

While I was going to college I worked as an orderly in a psychiatric hospital, and I remember a case in which a man was signed into the institution after complaints from his neighbors that he mowed the lawn at four in the morning. My neighbors aren't that finicky, but they keep very busy pruning, gardening, and mowing their lawns. Novelist Toni Cade Bambara wrote of the spirit women in Atlanta who plant by moonlight and use conjure to reap gorgeous vegetables and flowers. A woman on this block grows roses the size of cantaloupes.

On New Year's Eve, famed landscape architect John Roberts accompanied me on my nightly walk, which takes me from Fifty-Third Street to Aileen, Shattuck, and back to Fifty-Third Street. He was able to identify plants and trees that had been imported from Asia, Africa, the Middle East, and Australia. On Aileen Street he discovered a banana tree! And Arthur Monroe, a painter and art historian, traces the "Tabby" garden design — in which seashells and plates are mixed with lime, sand, and water to form decorative borders, found in this Oakland neighborhood and others — to the influence of Islamic slaves brought to the Gulf Coast.

I won over my neighbors, I think, after I triumphed over a dozen generations of pigeons that had been roosting in the crevices of this house for many years. It was a long and angry war, and my five year-old constantly complained to her mother about Daddy's bad words about the birds. I used everything I could get my hands on, including chicken wire and mothballs, and I would have tried the clay owls if the only manufacturer hadn't gone out of business. I also learned never to underestimate the intelligence of pigeons. Just when you think you've got them whipped, you'll notice that they've regrouped on some strategic rooftop to prepare for another invasion. When the house was free of pigeons and their droppings, which had spread to the adjoining properties, the lady next door said, "Thank you."

Every New Year's Day since then our neighbors have invited us to join them and their fellow Louisianans for the traditional Afro-American good-luck meal called Hoppin' John. This year the menu included black-eyed peas, ham, corn bread, potato salad, chitterlings, greens, fried chicken, yams, head cheese, macaroni, rolls, sweet potato pie, and fruitcake. I got up that morning weighing 214 pounds and came home from the party weighing 220.

We've lived on Fifty-Third Street for three years now. Carla's dance and theater school, which she operates with her partner, Jody Roberts — Roberts and Blank Dance/Drama — is already five years old. I am working on my seventh novel and a television production of my play *Mother Hubbard*. The house has yet to be restored to its 1906 glory, but we're working on it.

I've grown accustomed to the common sights here — teenagers moving through the neighborhood carrying radios blasting music by Grandmaster Flash and Prince, men hovering over cars with tools and rags in hand, decked-out female church delegations visiting the sick. Unemployment up, one sees more men drinking from sacks as they walk through Market Street or gather in Helen McGregor Plaza on Shattuck and Fifty-Second Street, near a bench where mothers sit with their children waiting for buses. It may be because the bus stop is across the street from Children's Hospital (exhibiting a brand-new antihuman, postmodern wing), but there seem to be a lot of sick black children these days. The criminal courts and emergency rooms of Oakland hospitals, both medical and psychiatric, are also filled with blacks.

White men go from door to door trying to unload spoiled meat. Incredibly sleazy white contractors and hustlers try to entangle people into shady deals that sometimes lead to the loss of a home. Everybody knows of someone, usually a widow, who has been deceived into paying thousands of dollars more than the standard cost

48

for, say, adding a room to a house. It sure ain't El Cerrito. In El Cerrito the representatives from the utilities were very courteous. If they realize they're speaking to someone in a black neighborhood, however, they become curt and sarcastic. I was trying to arrange for the gas company to come out to fix a stove when the woman from Pacific Gas and Electric gave me some snide lip. I told her, "Lady, if you think what you're going through is an inconvenience, you can imagine my inconvenience paying the bills every month." Even she had to laugh.

The clerks in the stores are also curt, regarding blacks the way the media regard them, as criminal suspects. Over in El Cerrito the cops were professional, respectful — in Oakland they swagger about like candidates for a rodeo. In El Cerrito and the Berkeley Hills you could take your time paying some bills, but in this black neighborhood if you miss paying a bill by one day, "reminders" printed in glaring and violent typefaces are sent to you, or you're threatened with discontinuance of this or that service. Los Angeles police victim Eulia Love, who was shot in the aftermath of an argument over an overdue gas bill, would still be alive if she had lived in El Cerrito or the Berkeley Hills.

I went to a bank a few weeks ago that advertised easy loans on television, only to be told that I would have to wait six months after opening an account to be eligible for a loan. I went home and called the same bank, this time putting on my Clark Kent voice, and was informed that I could come in and get the loan the same day. Other credit unions and banks, too, have different lending practices for black and white neighborhoods, but when I try to tell white intellectuals that blacks are prevented from developing industries because the banks find it easier to lend money to Communist countries than to American citizens, they call me paranoid. Sometimes when I know I'm going to be inconvenienced by merchants or creditors because of my Fifty-Third Street address, I give the address of my Berkeley studio instead. Others are not so fortunate.

Despite the inconveniences and antagonism from the outside world one has to endure for having a Fifty-Third Street address, life in this neighborhood is more pleasant than grim. Casually dressed, well-groomed elderly men gather at the intersections to look after the small children as they walk to and from school, or just to keep an eye on the neighborhood. My next-door neighbor keeps me in stitches with his informed commentary on any number of political comedies emanating from Washington and Sacramento. Once we were discussing pesticides, and the man who was repairing his porch told us that he had a great garden and didn't have to pay all that much attention to it. As for pesticides, he said, the bugs have to eat, too.

There are people on this block who still know the subsistence skills many Americans have forgotten. They can hunt and fish (and if you don't fish, there is a man who covers the neighborhood selling fresh fish and yelling "Fishman," recalling a period of ancient American commerce when you didn't have to pay the middleman). They are also loyal Americans — they vote, they pay taxes — but you don't find the extreme patriots here that you find in white neighborhoods. Although Christmas, Thanksgiving, New Year's, and Easter are celebrated with all get-out, I've never seen a flag flying on Memorial Day, or on any holiday that calls for the showing of the flag. Blacks express their loyalty in concrete ways. For example, you rarely see a foreign car in this neighborhood. And this Fifty-Third Street neighborhood, as well as black neighborhoods like it from coast to coast, will supply the male children who will bear the brunt of future jungle wars, just as they did in Vietnam.

We do our shopping on a strip called Temescal, which stretches from Forty-Sixth to Fifty-First streets. Temescal, according to Oakland librarian William Sturm, is an Aztec word for "hothouse," or "bathhouse." The word was borrowed from the Mexicans by the Spanish to describe similar hothouses, early saunas, built by the California Indians in what is now North Oakland. Some say the hothouses were used to sweat out demons; others claim the Indians used them for medicinal purposes. Most agree that after a period of time in the steam, the Indians would rush en masse into the streams that flowed through the area. One still runs underneath my backyard — I have to mow the grass there almost every other day.

Within these five blocks are the famous Italian restaurant Bertola's, "Since 1932"; Siam restaurant; La Belle Creole, a French-Caribbean restaurant; Asmara, an Ethiopian restaurant; and Ben's Hof Brau, where white and black senior citizens, dressed in the elegance of a former time, congregate to talk or to have an inexpensive though quality breakfast provided by Ben's hardworking and courteous staff.

The Hof Brau shares its space with Vern's market, where you can shop to the music of DeBarge. To the front of Vern's is the Temescal Delicatessen, where a young Korean man makes the best po'boy sandwiches north of Louisiana, and near the side entrance is Ed Fraga's Automotive. The owner is always advising his customers to avoid stress, and he says good-bye with a "God bless you." The rest of the strip is taken up by the Temescal Pharmacy, which has a resident health adviser and a small library of health literature; the Aikido Institute; an African bookstore; and the internationally known Genova Deli, to which people from the surrounding cities travel to shop. The strip also includes the Clausen House thrift shop, which sells used clothes and furniture.* Here you can buy novels by J. D. Salinger and John O'Hara for ten cents each.

Space that was recently occupied by the Buon Gusto Bakery is now for rent. Before the bakery left, an Italian lady who worked there introduced me to a crunchy, cookielike treat called "bones," which she said went well with Italian wine. The Buon Gusto had been a landmark since the 1940s, when, according to a guest at the New Year's Day Hoppin' John supper, North Oakland was populated by Italians and Portuguese. Those days a five-room house could be rented for forty-five dollars a month, she said.

The neighborhood is still in transition. The East Bay Negro Historical Society, which was located around the corner on Grove Street, included in its collection letters written by nineteenth-century macho man Jack London to his black nurse. They were signed, "Your little white pickaninny." It's been replaced by the New Israelite Delight restaurant, part of the Israelite Church, which also operates a day-care center. The restaurant offers homemade Louisiana gumbo and a breakfast that includes grits.

Unlike the other California neighborhoods I've lived in, I know most of the people on this block by name. They are friendly and cooperative, always offering to watch your house while you're away. The day after one of the few whites who lives on the block — a brilliant muckraking journalist and former student of mine — was robbed, neighbors gathered in front of his house to offer assistance.

In El Cerrito my neighbor was indeed a cop. He used pomade on his curly hair, sported a mustache, and there was a grayish tint in his brown eyes. He was a handsome man, with a smile like a movie star's. His was the only house on the block I entered during my three-year stay in that neighborhood, and that was one afternoon when we shared some brandy. I wanted to get to know him better. I didn't know he was dead until I saw people in black gathered on his doorstep.

I can't imagine that happening on Fifty-Third Street. In a time when dour thinkers view alienation and insensitivity toward the plight of others as characteristics of the modern condition, I think I'm lucky to live in a neighborhood where people look out for one another.

A human neighborhood.

---

* Of all the establishments listed here, only the Siam restaurant, the Aikido Institute, and the Genova deli remain.

Victor Hernández Cruz

Home Is Where the Music Is*

I was born in a barrio with the name of a Taino fruit: El Guanabano. Located in the central or urban area of the town of Aguas Buenas, Puerto Rico, some 35 minutes from San Juan. The streets of El Guanabano were not yet paved. When it rained everything became a mess, the downpour created a small river flowing down to the town plaza, the red dirt making the stream appear to be guava juice. Kids would jump outside to play in the torrential tropical showers.

The humidity, the mountain entanglement of lucid bush, spontaneity of trees, and the improvisation of the foliage invented creatures berserk through mating calls of nocturnal *coquis* — a kind of toad chirping in choral concerto. The native inhabitants of the island were certain that trees were the home of spirits, so they sang poetry to them, asked them in what direction were they walking. To walk the

mountains was to encounter the trees as individuals. You could hide from the rain under a Palo de Guayacan; to see from a distant mountain curve a Palo de Roble is to recognize its almost whiteness separating it from the bold green. The fruit of Aguas Buenas is the mamey, a native fruit tree; it has been ripened into ice cream and melted into malt. A tall Palo de Maga points into the clouds while inviting its liquid down. A scattered Palo de Almacigo brushes up arboresque into a Palo de Maria, assisting in the process of fertilization. A Palo de Hiquera hangs round-gourds, oval and festive mobiles, worked into bowls by Arawak-speaking hands or into *cacique*-size maracas to mark the meters of a poem within the *arieto*. Encountering a Palo de Ceiba is like first communion, sacred to the Tainos; some are hundreds of years old, a huge trunk and roots can take over a region. Lizards fleeting like electrical charges or suspended motionless for hours awaiting the trajectory of a predestined singular fly. Iguanas, mini crocodiles by the rivers. At night under the mosquito nets the world was a kaleidoscope of sounds, insects, dogs, the dance of trees like layers in the wind. The *cucubanos* (fire flies) sparkling in the dark, we kids would run after them and palm them right out of the air, put them in clear glass jars, and watch them light up in unison as if we were holding a star in our hands.

All the houses were made of wood; if there was any cement, it was down by the structures that surrounded the plaza where the middle class supposedly dwelled. The windows were small doors that swung open. Many of the houses were elevated off the earth creating a space underneath, a place where chickens and roosters roamed wild in their persistent flirtation that ended up being the eggs on your plate.

Skinny brown legs accompanied packs of mothers heading towards the river to wash clothes. The women used to bang the clothes against the river rocks, hitting the dirt out with pieces of boards as they sang and gossiped, talking, laughing, exchanging information, saying things no man could imagine. We children disappeared into the flora, playing by the eternal contemplation of the cows. Jumping into the river, all of us boys and girls butt naked, with a giggling and mirth that was recorded by the trees.

The fertile land around us was full of coffee and tobacco, which were the two prominent agricultural crops. We had our own coffee label, "El Jibarito." Coffee was always conducive to conversation, its aroma was the melody of the morning. The *campesino* custom of the three o'clock cup still maintains its fanatics, like court in session with jury and all. Unlike the custom of *la siesta*, the afternoon repose, which is fading in these regions. A rest during the day is bad for production; you can't fall asleep on the machine. If they found you horizontal in bed at one-thirty in the afternoon in the northern longitudes, urbanites might christen you lazy, or worse, useless to the economy.

The center of town was full of tobacco workshops known as "*chin-chales*" in the island vernacular. My grandfather, Julio El Bohemio, was a well known *tabaquero*. He was a picturesque character who created a legend for himself as a singer; men were always looking for him to render serenades to the sleeping women of their fancy. In the dark of night the silence was broken by guitar strings and harmonic voices in bolero; those songs' lyrics have stayed with me through all metamorphoses of regions and climates. My grandfather used to sing "...I want the love of a dark skin women, those bronze ladies of my native earth..." to the ears in the heart of the night. They sang Cuban, Mexican, Argentinian, Chilean songs written by composers who were popular poets.

The *chin-chals* were active places, for the *tabaqueros* in the Caribbean were notorious for their socialist and anarchistic politics, philosophers of the masses, dramatic declaimers of poetry, and, as in the case of my grandfather, singers of the love-romance songs sometimes known as *tragedia*. Many *tabaqueros* were rebels and *independentistas* (those who wanted freedom from Spanish, and then North American, possession of the island). Within the context of Caribbean agricultural workers, *tabacconists* had a much more leisurely work process, freeing their minds for contemplation and aesthetic flight. Coffee pickers, by comparison, had to battle bees all day long, and cane cutters had to chop vigorously under the Caribbean sun. A significant number of *tabaqueros* went on to become great labor leaders, writers, and historians.

It was within the *chin-chals* of Aguas Buenas that my imagination first heard poetry declaimed, thrown outloud in coordination with head and hands weaving. I was only a child amidst the tobacco leaves, taken there by my grandfather or my uncle Carlos who used to go and recite poetic standards like "El Brindis Del Bohemio." My uncle continued this tradition of declaiming into the frozen zones of New York's lower East Side tenements.

Tobacco production employed a good proportion of the town. There were farmers who cultivated the plants in the mountain ranchos, taking meticulous care of them, watching out for tobacco worms and other harmful insects. There was a period allowed for the tobacco leaves to age and dry so that they could acquire their deep aromatic *cafe con leche* color; the timing had to be perfect, for while they wanted a drying of the leaves, they did not want to lose all the moisture. Some men dedicated themselves to hauling stacks of bundled tobacco down to the *despalilladoras*. *Despalillar* — to remove the center stem from the tobacco leaf — was a task that was accomplished by women; old and young worked side by side, telling stories, reviewing every shadow of public and private life. Nothing escaped their scrutiny, the narratives making the passage of time painless. Once the leaves were done, they were bundled again and sent to all the local *chin-chales* where the men rolled them into various styles of cigars. The finished cigars were picked up and taken to these massive *fábricas* for packaging; some of the workers specialized in putting on the ring or little gold wrapper that identified the company and the cigar type. All day they put those little wedding bands on the tips of cigars, keeping an eye out for those that appeared to be damaged. It was also within these cigar terminals where they were arranged into their handsome boxes. The whole process took some six months after which the town went into a slumber.

It is recounted by those who lived this epoch that the *tabaqueros* were paid well. They had their golden age. They dressed well: white linen *guayaberas*, two-tone shoes with white on the top, pra-pra sombreros. The area around the plaza was full of places to dance and hear the best orchestras of the day. *Cafetin* rumor has it that once Ramito, Puerto Rico's best-known *trovador*, spinner of mountain music, came to hang out with the *tabaqueros* of El Guanabano. They went into such a jubilance and frolic of singing and scratching *quiro*, stomping and dancing that through beat and vibration they caused an abandoned and ageing wooden house next door to collapse. My grandfather filled the air on Fridays with a white suit and a white Panama sombrero. I remember him walking off towards town gleaming clean like white chalk under the pretext of going to the *colmado* to buy a pound of *café*, and vanishing through the hole of a *cuatro* guitar for two days.

My grandmother Tina must've known him well; when he sculptured that bohemian mischievous grin on his Jibaro face, his features were such that he could have been a *campesino* from the Rio Plata region of Argentina where the tangos that he sang so well were born. Tina Velasquez Ortiz had Africa inside of her, a dark, tall, heavy-set woman whose family hailed from the mountain,

Jaqueyes, which is seen from the center of town like a towering wall. Situated as we are not far from the coast, we have a substantial amount of African blood, which in one way or another runs through the community. We are truly *criollos* and a visual festival. The term *criollo* has meant many different things through different historical periods and regions of Latin America; in some areas it designates a Spaniard born in the New World. To us in Puerto Rico, it has come to mean the mixing of the cultural elements of the Indian, the Spanish, the African — a tripolarity that we recognize in music, dance, physical looks, and cuisine.

My grandmother fell ill with cancer at 46. In the interior of a small wooden house, I could see her laying in a hammock swinging and singing the pain away, a singing that scaled into a humming that went through the house like a humid vapor. The air had an odor of rubbing alcohol mixed with medicinal plants, a kerosene lantern flickering in her room making shadows dance on a wooden cross. She had eight children, one right after the other plus one that died at birth. My mother's tribe would have been nine, but eight was enough. She was slowly being eaten by time, dissolving like chocolate in the sun.

Through a rewind of archived pictures, a Caribbean *mulata* fries *alcapurrias* in the combustion of barrio life, green bananas, *yautia* — part African, part Indian. How did she walk when she was nineteen at the instant my grandfather, Julio El Bohemio, saw her in the Maria-go-round of plaza coquetry? Did his voice swell in the balada producing spacious gardens of flowers? She drops a handkerchief, they take a stroll into the night, the scent of a mamey tree, within a glance my mother was born.

My mother was the oldest of the eight children and she spent her teenage years helping rear her brothers and sisters. She had her father's gift of singing, and into the despair of the necessities of materialism and the limitations imposed on the female by a strong rural machismo, she sang her transcendental boleros. She married young and stayed in the local area where the extended family was in forceful practice.

In the rural communities women used to give birth within their own homes with the assistance of a midwife, *comadrona*. Into the scenario of my mother's advanced stages of labor, Dona Lola, the *comadrona* who brought me into the world, came in smoking a cigar and flinging herbs towards the sinistral and dextral of the ambiance, as if fishing spirits with hooks so that they can come forward to assist, to align the celestial with the biological process at hand. I was born on a Sunday between five and six in the morning. My mother remembers that Dona Lola made it to seven o'clock mass at the local Catholic church, Los Tres Santos Reyes.

The wooden house where I was born was painted a passion-fruit yellow, adding to the rainbow formed by all the houses on the street. You throw brush with what you got, a blue home next to an orange kiosk, natural wood made gray by age. Gauguin could have come here before going to Tahiti. The color spectrum exhausting itself as the Guanabano housing drops down the sloped street. Time slowly transformed the street into other hues, other textures.

Through a series of chance circumstances, my old house has now been converted into a *cafetin* — a small community bar and grocery store, a place where men gather to drink, cultivate the art of conversation, tell jokes. Through a further set of coincidences, the *cafetin* came under the ownership of a cousin of my mother's, Julio Hernández Hernández, who was what I would designate as a popular poet of our town. Not a poet of text or literature but a versifier, his poems written in the traditional Spanish forms of *coplas* and *decimas*. His compositions approximate the limericks of boleros, the same sentimental, emotional sphere in a language of preconceived formula. Like all popular poets, he had the ability to declaim his verses from memory; going into his *cafetin* always meant the possibility of a spontaneous outburst of recitation.

The tobacco workshop where my grandfather rolled was directly across the street from where we lived. He worked next to his lifelong friend, Alegria, spicing the rolling of cigars by singing in duo. In the mornings the *tabaqueros* would put a little money together and hire a reader to come in and read the newspaper, *El Imparcial*; other times the *tabaqueros* would hire a reader to come read them a chapter of a book a day. It seems that all the *tabacconists* in Aguas Buenas were Socialist. It was the party of my grandfather, Julio EL Bohemio, and that's how my grandmother voted too; my mother tells me that when she became eligible to vote, she also voted for the socialist party. They were all that way through some kind of popular spirit and not as intellectuals inspired by some economic ideals which penetrated them through readership. Melodies and people's anarchy rose from the salt of the earth, from a sector where the only things affordable sometimes were pride and emotion. Songs entered the leaves to be heard on some future plane within the eventual aroma of smoke.

In the late '40s and the early '50s, people were speaking of a place called Nujol; it caused a lot of agitation in all sectors of the town. Relatives already up in the northern ledge were sending letters inflating and inflaming imaginations and hopes. There was trouble in paradise. How did that happen in a place so fertile? The greater portion of the rural population was still feeling the effects of many years of Spanish exploitation by remote control, shipping medieval economic plans in coffins to the Americas. The conquest still bubbling in the veins. Even objects felt the despair. The pineapple was turning sour in the mountains of sweet music. Where the coffee grew, where the cane was tall, where aboriginal cigar was grown and rolled — they say that they saw the devil run, being chased by necessity from the inferno, his very home.

The Puerto Rican tribal-social network helped ease the scarcity of food. Many families heard the call of the yonder, the whispers of the north. People in knots started to untangle and maneuver. Children were left with relatives while the adults were flying Eastern Airline propeller planes to the Bronx. Once up there, stumble around the English looking for employment, set up a home, and send for their children.

New York City has been a center for Caribbean immigrants since the late eighteen hundreds. Exiled Cuban and Puerto Rican revolutionaries established la Sociedad Republicana de Cuba y Puerto Rico in the 1860s to assist in the cause of those on the islands fighting against Spanish colonialism.

Most of the new arrivals from the Antilles moved into the lower West Side, an area with an established Spanish community; there were Spanish and Argentinian restaurants, book stores, and a Spanish Cultural Center that continues to exist today. Perhaps many of these Spaniards were Andalus merchant seamen who came on work visits through the Brooklyn Navy Yard docks, near the areas of Red Hook and Williamsberg, which was also where the first Puerto Rican families settled into sometime after the 1900s. Later, after the 1920s, the Puerto Rican community started to *sofrito* spice the East Harlem area around 100th street. *Tabaqueros* constituted a strong force in this first wave of migration.

In El Guanabano, the commotion of cement trucks mixed with the whirlwind of families who were organizing themselves to jump off the edge of the world. It was not the upper classes that had to leave; the bourgeois never leave where they are milking. In proportion to the population of the island, it was one of the most dimensional cases of human exodus. People were tying boxes like *pasteles* with banana leaves and heading for the iron bird. My mother wanted to know why people kept borrowing that antique heavy iron we had that had to be fed charcoal, when they were going to fold the clothes after ironing and place them in the suitcases to wrinkle again. Puerto Ricans were obsessed with ironing apparel in those days, and they used a homemade starch to get a crease on a pair of pants that could have cut you; women used to complain that they even had to iron their husbands' underwear. This anti-wrinkle mania is something that could be studied. El Guanabano was in a ruckus with public cars taking people to the airport in the mornings and afternoons: tears, hugs, farewells. My grandfather walked through the chaos with a fine grip on his guitar.

My own family jumped on one of those massive waves of island evacuation. The decision was beyond anything I could comprehend. I was busy trying to split "*alaorrobas*" seeds in half in a boys' game known as "*gallitos*." It was our time to go forward into the regions beyond the mountains, from the comforts and hardships of Aguas Buenas to industry and entertainment, to the jungle of concrete and lights in the hyperborean windows of Manhattan.

I have always been haunted by the strong impression that the first gulps of cold winter air registered in my childhood nostrils. We migrated from the tropics in the middle of winter. What did we know coming from one extreme to another, like putting the sun in the freezer. In New York it was snowing; those who love contrast could satisfy themselves here. We went to the traditional immigrant neighborhood of New York — the lower East Side where the tenement buildings towered like magic over us. Had someone poured cement on the mountains, I wondered, recalling all those cement trucks back home. A cold metallic incense permeated the ether, the olfact of steel, iron, cement, and glass.

English was just a scattering of noise coming out of people's mouths — who could arrange that strange new furniture, where would one sit? Walking slowly, I picked up neighborhood jargon, stoop yap, hallway vocabulary; out on the streets children exchanged information. Puerto Rican kids had apparently arrived before we did, for I encountered many that were already speaking English, hanging it like fragmented and distorted Cubist paintings. The lower East Side was full of accents. English waved, leaned, flew, got squashed, shredded, sautéed, made into puree. Italian, Polish, Jewish thoughts danced their own angles into Shakespeare.

On the street where we lived, there was still a Jewish synagogue lingering from the past life of the neighborhood that was erasing right before our eyes. The local stores were full of things I'd never seen. Jars of sauerkraut, pickles, knishes, winter hats with ear flaps that made people look like sputniks, a new empire of gadgetry like that which opened up the eyes of Pinzon, the Spanish explorer. Bubbling it was, flashing, dashing, darting, a new vertical comprehension — cars, buses, subways.

The encounter between rural and urban landscape, a debate released through migration, a discussion of spacial tempos, city versus tropical paths are steeped in my consciousness and echo through my poetic creation. This for me is the center of metaphor, sharp contrast that keeps one in northern metros aware of profound elsewhere. El Guanabano — view of the mountains; the lower East Side — view of the Empire State Building. A pendulum swinging between the heat and the cold. The Spanish and English coming together, giving a multiple choice of sounds to select from for objects, experience, emotion, sensation. For me, writing in straight English or Spanish is always a process of translation — it is a duality that opens up a third dimension beyond the actual semantics. What comes first in Spanish could come last in English. This same polarization can create problems; it is to the advantage of a writer to be bilingual, but for the general speaker it would be best to be anchored in a native tongue before venturing off into another language. The great Spanish poet Migual Unamuno said something to the effect that, "Language is the blood of the spirit." Consequently it is through words that we fulfill our personality. Without a strong linguistic spine, you could fold into a mush of blah-blah. Because language represents a world, we can see the contradictions that besiege the users of the Spanish language in the United States; the world it is from is not in their presence. Words have lives of their own, it is what we fit into, were they not here before us. Experience is the word that passes through the things that we do. Language is a cultural attitude accumulated over the centuries; when I write in Puerto Rican Spanish — the first sounds that my body heard and felt when I played in El Guanabano was the ambit of fruits in harmony with boiling manioc — I am writing in a language which has Taino, Arabic-Gypsy-Berber Desert Wind, African words. In addition, many new vocals were created by the collision of all that energy and diction in the Caribbean.

The Spanish radio programs kept us warm. Flowing from an Emerson radio was Puerto Rican, Cuban, Santo Domingo, Argentinian, Chilean, Mexican music. Being Latin American mestizo is a condition supplied by the criss-crossing of multi-nations. The cultures go one into another as through the common root language, an extended nationalism that includes the entire continent. We danced to the guarachas of Cuba, beat our feet to the rancheras of Mexico, became sad and nostalgic to the boleros of Trio San Juan.

My father, who had gone to New York and was already settled and working when we arrived, found our railroad flat on the lower East Side. It was on the third floor facing the backyard, a steel fire escape hung immediately outside one of the windows. It offered a view uptown towards 14th street, a Con Edison electrical plant with pipes systematically dispensing smoke into the sky. Looking to the right, your eyes focused upon the long stretch of brick mountains that made up the edifices of the Avenue D housing projects. We could hear the fog horns of ships on the East River in the mornings as we drank Cafe Bustelo, getting ready to go out and wrestle with the streets.

In our household there was a constant dialogue, debate, discussion, argument, chaos, fights between my mother and father as to when we would get back to Aguas Buenas. Originally the plan was that they would be in New York to work for a period, gather some money, and eventually work our way back home. Every year we would make plans to leave that never got beyond the motions of my mother starting to pack the luggage. Puerto Ricans perfected the art of packaging. They used to encase clothes, personal knickknacks, and even tree bark like sardines into cans. Rumor has it that back in the '50s, when transportation was bad, Puerto Ricans knew how to get to the airports on public trains.

In the public schools the teachers prohibited the use of Spanish among the island children who were recent arrivals. They would come and say, "Shisssh-hush, speak in English, it's what's going to get you ahead" or they'd say, "You're in America now." Looking out the window, we knew we were on the East Side, an aspect of America. A group of us once got in trouble because we used to have to sing the National Anthem at the beginning of each day. Every time it came to the part "Oh say can you see," most of the students in the class — we were all still learning English — heard "Oh Jose can you see." So we always sang it this way while we all mumbled something to the two Joses in the room. The teacher — I think her name was Mrs. Straus — was old and had a crooked finger. When she said "Hey you" and pointed, the person sitting next to who she meant would always stand up. When she hooked an ear into how we were singing, she separated a group of us — maybe because we had the highest pitch — and made us stay after class. She told us we had to bring our parents in, which was the most embarrassing thing. So we did, but what was that for? Our parents spoke no English and there was no one around to translate. So there was Mrs. Straus talking with our island mothers; our mothers just kept saying, "Yeah-yeah-yeah." One of them knew how to say the word Right, going, "Rye-rye." They figured another way to get out of it was by shaking their heads up and down because this would give the impression that they were absorbing information.

As the bricks aged we entered the age of flowers — walking molasses, cha-cha boots, bolero blouses. Mothers found places to make white dresses for their daughters. The youth had inherited the Caribbean spirit of fiesta and carnival and used any excuse to have a party. Over in the Avenue D projects, we'd borrow an apartment, and walked the neighborhood to the fringes inviting every girl we saw. With our portable record players, we formed a bembe anywhere — in the school yard, up on the roof. There we were, sons and daughters of the Antilles throwing pachanga steps, dancing slow to the doo-wop of "The Paragons Meet The Jesters."

The years washed the red mountain dirt from our shoes, but the abyss created by the migration remained like a root-canal cavity in the wisdom molars, hungry for excavation and filling. Puerto Rican musicians and writers made the journey up north for reasons of economy and because of the traditional restlessness of artists. It was an opportunity for the writers to get a bird's eye view of island politics and culture and their extension in the diaspora.

The music and the songs would go back to the island to become part of the cultural panoramas of a Caribbean nation. Culture produced in the streets of New York would take the airplanes with the people who are in continuous reverse migration — there is something like an on-going back and forward shaft keeping those in the North resupplied with tropical resistance.

Cuban and Puerto Rican musicians met in the clubs and large ballrooms of Manhattan, discussing with each other new levels of rhythms and poly-rhythms. On 110th street there was the now defunct Park Palace Ballroom where the music was on fire way before it traveled downtown to the famous Palladium. I was too young in the early '50s to make it to these dramas of island life in the states. It was like *fiestas patronales* indoors. I watched my Uncle Juan and my Aunt Chela get glazed up with those shoes that used to look like glass to go to these Mambo groves. With their friends they would form balls to take the subway together to 53rd where the Palladium was. They would all get back late, couples kissing all over the hallways, leaning against brass mailboxes, then taking off their shoes to walk up the marble stairs. In the mornings when I was sent out to get bread for the coffee, I could sense the lingering scent of gardenia perfume throughout the hallway.

The music of the guitar and the music of the drum came together in the ears and hearts of a generation that was bilingual and bred in the States. Everything was jumping with Symphony Sid in the City; he had a late night radio program playing the New York based Cuban and Puerto Rican music (it wasn't called Salsa then, that can came later). A dance called la pachanga, which featured some vicious foot stomping, was knocking buildings down. My generation developed a boogaloo with Latin rhythms and English lyrics; dancers started jumping all around the floor. Building roofs were stretched with conga drum hide and something was playing them.

On a clear, warm summer night of my youth I was trying to search for some sleep, staring from a third floor window at the moon, which seemed to be falling into one of the pipes of the Con Edison plant; there was too much energy elevating up. Out on the street a group was drumming an African beat through which they were weaving a deep Gypsy *canto hondo* that sang of Spain, Goya and Velazquez paintings melting onto Bantu shrines, someone shaking native maracas into the brick Bohíos. As I looked down towards the sound, they appeared like a gathering of agricultural tribes in a fertility fest — Hindu Gypsies, Andaluces, Asturians, Arabs, Congolese, nomadic Berber shepherds. It was such a kaleidoscope that I decided to paint the fire escape gold. By morning it was dry and the drums had turned to strings. The troubadours were praising a lady, studying her walk they measured the meter of the verse. The morning light brought images out of haze.

I remembered then, sitting in the sunshine out on the fire escape, the songs of my grandfather, Julio El Bohemio, the proclaimer of poems around the old *chin-chal* of tobacco in the town of my childhood. The mountain, Jagueyes, blocked out the projects. Sitting upon the golden mineral, I got the urge to write, to tell a story as if from a balcony, use the juices of a guanabana for ink. I knew I would some day go back with words, searching for the past in the future. I knew my body was right, right where it was. With Hugh Masekela, I second the emotion when he put out the album, "Home Is Where The Music Is."

---

* Title of a Hugh Masekela album.

Nash Candelaria

Memoirs of a Bourgeois Chicano Writer

"Home," T.S. Eliot said in one of his poems, "is where one starts from." Growing up, I really had two homes: a home/house, which is what many think of when they use the word home, and a home*land*, which roots me in the culture and history that helped define my work as a Chicano writer.

Although I was born in Los Angeles, I consider the state of New Mexico my homeland. Here existed the first known record of a Candelaria in what is now the United States of North America. She was a widow, a refugee of the 1680 Pueblo Revolt when the Pueblo Indians drove the Spanish settlers out of New Mexico into exile in the area of El Paso, Texas, and Juarez, Mexico. Thirteen years later the Spanish settlers returned, and in 1706 the Widow Candelaria and her two sons were numbered among the founding families of the city of Albuquerque. My father was born on a farm in Los Candelarias, a rural area just north of what was then the city limits.

I first left New Mexico in the womb of an 18 year-old bride accompanied by her 22 year-old bridegroom on their combined honeymoon and move away from home. They were no doubt exhilarated, confused, frightened, and relieved at being able to bring forth this conceived-before-marriage new life away from the prying eyes and tsk-tsking of family, friends, and neighbors. Five months later this love-child shouted his first *grito* to the world in Los Angeles, a Californian by default rather than intent.

Forty-plus years later, when I was participating in one of those New Age seminars that the Golden State was known for in the 1970s, the seminar leader turned to a large map of the United States mounted on the wall. "Show me home," she said.

There was no doubt in my mind. Immediately, with no need to think, I pointed to the state of New Mexico. The heart knows. I think there is something in our genes that remembers home. It's as if a thin umbilical connects me back through the generations to those early pioneers. Connects me with pride in their courage and faith, their toughness, their endurance, in spite of whatever cruelty and ignorance was the norm in those early days. Connects me to the spirit that brought these strangers over ocean and desert to this alien country to help create this land of many cultures.

I am a true child of New Mexico's cultures: the Spanish whose surname I bear; the Native American which many in my family will not admit to and whose looks and complexion I share; and a dollop of Anglo like a latter day grace note to remind me that I am part of the mainstream, no matter what anyone else may surmise from my physical appearance.

But don't be misled. I was no stranger to my homeland although born and raised in Los Angeles. From that first *grito* to the forty-plus-years-later finger on the map, there were many returns — temporary for the most part. In the early years, these backs and forths were more than the summer visits they would later become, for my father had passed a U.S. Civil Service examination, one of the first Hispanos to do so. He had chosen to become a Railway Mail Clerk, working the mail on trains, instead of a Border Patrol officer — candidates for both jobs took the same examination back then. So that instead of life along the border of Mexico and the United States, there was that migrant movement to wherever shiny, parallel rails merged in the beckoning distance. El Paso when I was still a babe in arms. Albuquerque where we lived for short periods of time. Then later, and permanently, Los Angeles.

During this migrant time, we lived in rented places that were house rather than home. There was a little house on Roma Avenue in Albuquerque from which I went to an elementary school that no longer exists. Where the boys in the first grade chased a new student who did not speak their language. That student: me. The language I no longer spoke: Spanish. My vigilante pursuers: little brown faces like myself, intolerant of this...this...traitor. This villain. This stuck-up no-better-than-themselves who dared to be different. The race to my house through an empty lot. Preferring to run through the low branched, stinging tamarisks that lacerated my face rather than submit to the fists of my pursuers. To arrive breathless and in tears. Learning one of life's early lessons in intolerance: that no group, even one that itself suffers from prejudice, is immune from such attitudes.

Later there was the little stucco house on Fruit Avenue — since demolished to make way for urban renewal — where I attended the third grade at St. Mary's Parochial School. I had a hopeless crush on our teacher, Sister Mary Margaret, a beautiful, disciplinary nun. Her face shone out of that starched, white headdress covered by a wimple that was black like the austere, shapeless uniform that hid the rest of her from worldly eyes except for her pale hands and the polished black shoes that peeked from the hem of that full, black skirt.

During that same time, my headstrong younger sister had been enrolled in the all-girls St. Vincent's Academy where, my father threatened, the nuns would put some discipline into her. I'm not sure how well the nuns succeeded. What I do remember is that one day my sister's teacher asked the first-grade children, "What nationality are you?" What a question with which to confront the brown-faced girls whose parents probably spoke Spanish and who were no doubt confused about how to answer. There was no confusion in my sister's reply. "American!" she said with six year-old authority.

When, near the end of that school year my father was transferred permanently to Los Angeles, I solemnly promised Sister Mary Margaret that I would write, fully expecting a reply in perfect Parker penmanship that would acknowledge that I was special to her. I never received that letter. That was the last of living in New Mexico. From then on we lived in Los Angeles where I had been born.

But our New Mexico roots went deep. In later years, when researching the family genealogy to share with my sons, I discovered something amazing and unexpected. I saw the proliferation of surnames as the years went back, an incredible web of connections. In just a few generations there were many names: Candelaria, Rivera, Nuanes, Dalton, Armijo, Gutierrez, Sanchez, Gonsales, Sisneros, Martines, Duran, Perea. All of them of direct line ancestors. From the present back to those first Spanish settlers of New Mexico represents about 13 generations. Standing here now, if I add up all my progenitors, each of whom had two parents, the total would come to over 8,000 people. I could rent a hall — a big one — and hold a convention.

Can you imagine a family reunion of 13 generations of your ancestors? If you have trouble getting along with some of your relatives now, think about 8,000 of them. Their clothes would differ — as would their levels of education and literacy, and the social assumptions on which they base their lives. The way language changes you might not even be able to communicate with them easily. The black sheep might be there with rope burns around his neck where he was suspended from a nearby tree. The family gossip would be pointing out exactly which tree he hung from. And somewhere in that crowd might be your twin, that other you who lived in another time, raising serious doubts about your uniqueness, not to speak of your disbelief in reincarnation.

All this gave me pause about tracing my ancestral roots. First of all, it is sheer accident that I'm known by the surname Candelaria. In a matrilineal society I would have been known as Rivera. The arbitrary custom of being tagged forever by that one name completely blinded me to all the other names that are an equal part of my history. In a sense, it made me realize that I am a brother to many — not just in spirit and attitude, but in blood. I must be related to half the people in New Mexico! For all the real meaning in the surname Candelaria, I might as well have a bar code stamped on my forehead or a binary number like 101101 identifying me in this computer age. A name is a convenient, arbitrary handle. Certainly a useful means of identification as well as a means by which we can trace the connections that spiderweb back through history to tribe, clan, and family. But it is not my true identity.

Yet, while New Mexico receded into the background with our permanent move to Los Angeles, my homeland of New Mexico remained forever, as much a part of me as black hair and brown eyes and dark complexion.

My parents rented houses to begin with. They did not move to those Chicano enclaves of East Los Angeles and Boyle Heights, although we had family friends and cousins who did. We were, my parents insisted, Americans with every right to live wherever we pleased.

There were many houses before we settled into what I remember as my home/house: 1247 West 59th Street. It was a Los Angeles neighborhood of frame and stucco houses built in the 1920s. A mix of working class, middle class neighbors. A solid, New Deal, vote for Franklin Delano Roosevelt neighborhood. The country wasn't out of the Depression yet — it would take World War II to do that. But people seemed to be getting along.

Next door on one side lived the childless couple who owned two dry cleaning shops. On the other side lived Major MacDonald and his wife. He had retired from the Army after being in charge of the mess at West Point, the highlight of his career. I never heard him talk about World War I, which had been just 20 years prior. A big, genial, thoroughly nice Irish American from New York with an equally friendly, almost childlike wife. When Major MacDonald died a few years later, Mrs. MacDonald would be found wandering the streets in confusion and tears — a lost soul.

Across the street lived Joanna Chlarson, a flaming redhead my sister's age, whose father was a house painter. Next door to her lived Mrs. Heisenbuttle, a crippled, white-haired widow. Since she did not move around readily, Mrs. H. delighted in sitting bright-eyed on her front porch watching the comings and goings of the neighborhood, especially the young people with all their energy and activity.

I can still remember the excitement when my parents bought that house in 1939. My father was then 34 years-old, my mother 30 — both younger than my sons are now. It was a different world they lived in, having come to their majority during the Great Depression when something like 20 percent of American men were out of work. My father was the first of his family to leave the farm and New Mexico, while my mother had said good-bye to the urban barrio of Los Barelas, the poorest section of Albuquerque that was the way-station for many displaced farm families who had lost or sold their land and were now trying to make their way in the city.

This was the first house they had owned, and they felt very lucky to buy it — the fulfillment of an American dream. The down payment, though, had come hard — it was blood money. For my father had been at work on board a Southern Pacific Railway train that had crashed head-on with another train in the Imperial Valley of California. A brakeman had thrown a switch the wrong way. There was a long list of dead and a longer list of injured, including my father.

Because money was tighter than usual while father was in the hospital, we moved to a small apartment from the comfortable house that we rented. He had suffered a back injury, something that plagued him off and on for the rest of his life. And it was the insurance settlement from the accident that became the down payment on my parents' first house. The place that, looking back on my growing up years, I think of as home.

We were the only brown faces in the neighborhood. Among the very few in school and church. Brown faces were something you only saw in the mirror. Or when we visited cousins or family friends in the Projects in the barrios of East Los Angeles or Boyle Heights. Or back where it all began. Back in New Mexico. It was the place where we lived the longest when I was growing up. The place, that along with my homeland of New Mexico, formed me.

Three blocks east, on Vermont Avenue, was John Muir Junior High School that my sister and I attended. Along several blocks of Vermont Avenue was everything a growing youngster needed.

There was the local movie theater, purveyor of dreams during Saturday matinees. In the evening parents could see on the screen the swells in their fancy New York apartments wearing fabulous clothes, ready to go out and dine at the Ritz. On Bank Night, between features, the manager would come on stage and draw numbers while the audience prayed to fill a row on their Keno cards so they could win actual cash money. "Come on number 17! Junior needs a new pair of shoes!"

Down the block and across 58th Place was the Thrifty Drug Store. Next door was Kress's variety store where I bought my first tennis racket for fifty cents and indulged in Big Little books when I had the money. Ten cents would buy you a fat little volume of the abridged *Tom Sawyer* or *Treasure Island* or, better yet, *Tarzan Of The Apes* or *Buck Rogers*.

On the corner of Vermont and Slauson Avenues was the local branch of the Bank of America where my father deposited his paycheck. It was just across the street from the local Sears, Roebuck & Company store where my sister worked part-time as a sales clerk as soon as she was old enough. And cater-corner from Sears was the local food market where, during those tight-money times, you could buy a dozen small oranges for — if I remember correctly — one cent. Oranges that my mother would put in my brown paper, school-lunch bag. When I ate them, they dripped and squirted their sticky, sweet juice on my hands and face, causing embarrassment in front of my school friends who had less messy matters to contend with in their lunch sacks.

Then north and south, a few blocks either way, were two other anchors of my childhood: south on 64th Street was the public library that with the movies and radio in those pretelevision days fed my thirsting imagination; while north on 57th Street was Nativity Church, the Catholic residence of God who stared hard into my wretched little soul, knowing exactly what kind of a sinner I was.

What more could a growing boy need? Never mind that we were the only brown faces in the neighborhood. Among the very few in our schools. The world was a wonderful place. People were friendly. It was a home in which I learned about other people, about other worlds.

In addition to my neighborhood friends, there were school and church friends. Even now it amazes me how children reach out into the world, unafraid and trusting. It can be intimidating to meet strangers, but there is a certain radar that tells you when you've met a new friend. I went unselfconsciously into the world with never a thought of rejection and so encountered none.

In the neighborhood you got to be friends — well, because you were there. When you're not near the people you like, you like the people you're near. When it comes to playing hide-and-seek or kick-the-can, the more the merrier. My closest neighborhood pals were Mickey and Ralph Laszlo, whose stepfather owned a vending machine business. On rainy days we would sit in their garage playing Monopoly and sneaking some of the vending machine peanuts stored there.

I was drawn to church friends by proximity too, although for the most part I saw them only on Sundays. It didn't matter how your last name was spelled or pronounced, although my Catholic friends tended heavily toward Irish with names like Blesser, Ennis, Fitzpatrick, Mannion, O'Brien. We had something in common greater than compatible names: faith and the watchful eyes of priest and nuns to see that we behaved.

Public school was different. Proximity could be a factor. Especially if you sat next to a cute girl. The only common faith was the belief that the bell would ring promptly at three o'clock so you could escape this purgatory.

The two main threads from which school friendships were woven, at least for boys, were sports and grades. If you were good at sports, everybody wanted you to be on their team, whether in physical education class or after school. If you got good grades, you earned a certain respect and notoriety, as long as you weren't a teacher's pet, a brown nose, or a grind. Not to speak of the occasional desperate whisper during an exam, "Psst. Candelaria — What's the answer to number four?"

Like neighborhood and church, public school opened new worlds. There was my friend, Dave Wright, a redhead whose grandparents came from England and who reveled in novels by H. Rider Haggard like *She* or books about Lawrence of Arabia. There was my friend, Len Ash, whose Jewish father came over on a boat from England as a young man. What a revelation! I thought only WASPs came from England. There were Protestant friends of all shapes, sizes, and ancestries. There were my Sephardic Jewish friends who spoke Spanish better than I did, only they called it Ladino.

During the most remembered football season of that period I played halfback for two sandlot teams. One day I would be on the team from St. Columcille's with my Catholic friends. The next day I would be with my friends in the AZA league, an organization for Jewish boys. Because I was a ringer, there was a crisis before the first AZA game. Calling a quick huddle, my friend Bob Bloch decided that I should adopt a pseudonym: Moishe Candleberg! The referee never understood why we were laughing so hard that we almost fumbled the kickoff.

So it was that from home, the place I started from, the wider world opened up. Friends, neighbors, school, church, books, movies. Then in summers there was the annual pilgrimage to my New Mexico homeland. After about three days, my parents, especially my father, had the screaming meemies from the over attention and wrangling from relatives — especially my father's family — who insisted we visit them first, stay with them first, eat with them first. Damned if we did; damned if we didn't. Like the baby claimed by two women in the presence of King Solomon, we were pulled in different directions until the least crazy-making move was to drive back to Los Angeles, a decision that did not require royal wisdom. But in those few days, for all the turmoil, I wallowed in an embarrassment of family attention — especially from my country cousins. My sister and I were their city cousins, something special.

It was as if I lived in two worlds. There was Los Angeles and mainstream middle America where we were different and in the minority, making our way in the white, Anglo world. And there was New Mexico where family and friends were like us. The conflict growing up was: Can we belong to both worlds? Or must we, like others we knew, belong to only one and if so, which one? Or finally, like a few rare, tortured, and alienated souls, would we belong to neither?

Loss of innocence dawns gradually as you are growing up. We lived in that neighborhood in blissful unawareness for 15 years. Early in 1954, a few months after I had returned from service in the U.S. Air Force, my parents sold their frame house on West 59th Street.

During that time there was one of those great upheavals that permanently alters a city's landscape. The Harbor Freeway was being built, stretching from the shore at San Pedro Bay through central Los Angeles to the Civic Center and then north to Pasadena. One of the houses we had rented when I was a boy turned into a massive concrete pillar helping hold up six lanes of fast, crowded, smog-belching freeway traffic. It was as if the Wicked Witch of Detroit had transformed it with a touch of her wand.

The families displaced by this advancing juggernaut had to find elsewhere to live. My parents were the first in our immediate neighborhood to sell to a Black family. Oh, the outrage and hysteria of some of our neighbors. The childless couple next door who owned two dry cleaning shops were especially incensed.

"You just wait!" the man threatened my father. "I'm going to find out where your new house is and move the biggest, dirtiest, ugliest, trashiest family I can find right next to you."

Then a neighbor woman and fellow Catholic accosted my mother with her own injection of venom. "We should have known," the woman said. "When you moved into the neighborhood, we circulated a petition to keep out Mexicans. But we didn't get enough signatures."

My mother was stunned to learn this fifteen years after the fact. She didn't stay stunned long. She was a strong person, gentle and giving, but she didn't suffer idiots lightly. Anger took over — plus her strong belief that we could live anywhere we wanted and sell our house to whomever we wanted and the hell with you, madam!

Years later, suffering an acute attack of nostalgia, I drove through that aging neighborhood. I made my way along Vermont Avenue, up 59th Street past the junior high school and our old house to Normandie Avenue, and south toward Florence Avenue.

Most of the old stores were gone, replaced by others. Some of these had failed, leaving abandoned store fronts with broken windows and paint-can-sprayed graffiti. Across the windows of still functioning businesses were heavy, black bars of iron grillwork. Off to the side of many entryways were folding accordion metal grates, not quite as thick as the window grills. These would be drawn across store fronts at night and secured with heavy padlocks. And the movie theater was gone! Where did neighborhood children go to indulge their dreams?

Then even later, in 1992, that part of Los Angeles was the scene of riots after the verdict of the first Rodney King trial.

All things, of course, age and decline, but perhaps they can be renewed. I prefer to remember this home/house as it was during my childhood. The good things remain forever, and I carry that memory deep within me the way I carry my heritage from my New Mexico homeland.

LAWSON
FUSAO INADA

HIROSHI
FROM HIROSHIMA

I. SMALL THINGS

He was "Hiroshi from Hiroshima." That's all I knew about him.
Along with the fact that he arrived early and stayed late. And, for
such a big, strong man, we were all surprised by how little he ate —

some small things
wrapped in a small paper bag.
A bag he folded carefully,
and brought back the next day.

This was the summer of 1954.
I was working in my grandfather's
famous fish store
and busy doing three things:

1. Making payments on my new,
   metallic blue '49 Ford —
   which, for 1954
   and eight-hundred bucks,
   was worth working for;

2. Working out at night,
   running along country roads
   with friends, in anticipation
   of our senior football season;

3. Trying to figure out a way
   to approach a certain person.

And, oh, there were some cool clothes
down the street at the Peacock Department Store.

II. Parallel Lives

Hiroshi, I believe, had some connections
with my grandfather. Some network
was at work, some relations
in the way that all people from the old country
appeared to be part of one family.

And maybe they were.
For instance, it wasn't until long after
my grandfather had passed,
that I found out, in passing,
that he had had another family in Japan,
that his first wife had died over there,
and somewhere over there
were his grandchildren my age,
and we were leading parallel lives.

III. Skill

So, early one morning, Hiroshi arrived.
Or, rather, he was already there
when I arrived with my uncles to open the door.
They nodded at him (I had never seen him before),
and he went immediately to work.

Now, the strange (or interesting) thing is,
except for office or telephone work
(which I didn't know how to do, either;
but I could drive, picking up and delivering
all over greater Fresno, including
outback country towns),

well, Hiroshi could do everything.
From the minute he put on his apron,
he could do it all.
And with such efficiency, grace, and skill,
that by the next day he was already

the favorite of our regular customers.

These old people would come in —
people of many colors, languages,
places of origin —

and wait for him to wait on them.

IV. Waiting For Hiroshi

Actually, it was "uncanny," as they say —
because here was this new guy,
just off some boat, in a new country,
and instead of being like a "fish out of water,"

he was functioning proficiently
by some kind of "telepathy."
Looking back, I'd say there was some kind of
"immigrant empathy" involved, some kind of
"mutuality" at work, some kind of
"unstated message" communicated

which comes down to *trust*,
which comes down to *understanding*
what you've all gone through
back home, down home, and here,

as you stand, waiting for Hiroshi.

V. Samurai

So, yes, these elders would come in,
point, signal, nod, whatever,
and whatever it was they wanted,
they got: fresh, sparkling,
            personalized to perfection.

Say they wanted a pound-chunk
off that big piece of seabass;
Hiroshi would size it up, slice
like a samurai, zap — one pound!

Say they wanted that whole chicken,

those squid, that abalone,
fixed just so — plus,
wrapped in ice for the trip back home;
they got it, precisely.

Say you needed something
for soup or stew;
or, some friends were coming
over for barbecue
and you needed that rascal
skinned and filleted, just so;
there it was, exactly.

And the next time, happy,
you'd come and tell Hiroshi,
in your smile and language,
just how great it was...

VI. "Unpreferred"

Maybe I didn't exactly feel rejected,
but I had to get used to being "unpreferred" —

by these elders, including relatives,
who always waited for Hiroshi.

And I didn't feel threatened, either —
because there were always

other things to do, others to wait on,
and, as both my uncles took vacations,

and my grandfather came in less and less,
I was even given duties in the office;

thus, I made deliveries, answered the phone,
and urged Hiroshi that it was time to close.

VII. Better

One thing I learned that summer:
I was "pretty good," I was "okay,"
but I could learn to get better.

VIII. "WAR"

Not that I was going to take over the store.
My way lay across the tracks, at college.

And the way things were going in West Fresno,
with old businesses not meeting new "codes,"

and whole buildings being torn down
in the "war" called "Urban Renewal,"

something we didn't want to face
stared at us like a gap-toothed smile:

our home, this ethnic, colored district,
had seen its day, was giving way

to empty space; thus, the fish market
is a parking lot where nobody parks.

IX. WATCH

So, that summer,
I learned
my place —

one of the
young ones,
one of the
new ones,

a good kid
at heart,
but without
the wherewithal
and wisdom
of decades
of survival.

You earn
respect.
You pay for
trust.
You experience
experience.

In the meantime,
here was a kid
you had to watch —

a kid who could
crush your tofu
while wrapping
with one hand
and waving at a
passing girl
with the other.

You had to watch
him while he weighed;
you had to supervise
at his shoulder
as he cut; otherwise,
you'd get home
and be surprised;

you had to watch
him on prices;
you had to watch
him on change.

Watch that kid!
Watch what's
going on
all around!

Next week, that kid
and everything else
will be gone!

X. "Hiroshima"

Still, perhaps some things never change.
Because another interesting, strange thing is,
no one had to show Hiroshi "the ropes" —

because from that very first day,
he not only knew how we did things

(including making blocks of ice
in a buried tank of saltwater),

or where things were, but he also knew
where we kept every little thing stored.

So this store, which my grandfather claimed
he designed and started from "nothing"
in 1912, as the first such store in the region,
just may have been part of "something" —

an ancient, time-honored, archetypal pattern
of workable history and proven tradition;

thus, Hiroshi, had he answered the phone,
might have said: "Hello, Hiroshima Fish Store!"

XI. "Mezu-rah-shi"

As it was, with my limited Japanese,
we only exchanged very few words.

And usually it was "mezu-rah-shi!" —
or, his way of saying "How special!"

And I'd nod, acknowledging his quaint way
of acknowledging the very ordinary.

For instance, the very ordinary, daily,
early morning trip to the train depot

was usually cause for a "mezu-rah-shi"
or two; sometimes, just crossing the tracks

would do (well, looking back, I suppose
those tracks *were* "special," since they seg-

gregated people into "colored" and "white"),

and certainly while waiting for ordinary
freight or (dining) passenger trains to pass...

Then, at the depot, there'd be those
"mezu-rah-shi" crates to lift and load —

big as dripping coffins, slippery, hazardous
and heavy for our steel hooks to handle...

We'd grunt, shove, lift, shove some more,
and after I'd sign for the stuff, feeling

proprietary, the station clerk would offer us
ordinary coffee in ordinary paper cups...

XII. Acknowledging the Qualities

But that wasn't the half of it,
since back at the store
there was all that
relifting, unpacking, repacking to do,
which, in my fashion,
consisted of a lot of slamming,
bashing, prying, crunching,

while Hiroshi carefully but swiftly
undid his crates like packages,
stacking each intact board, each nail,
in neat little piles —

all the while
acknowledging the qualities
of human-sized halibut from Alaska,
salmon thick as thighs
from the Oregon coast,
big-eyed bottom-dwellers of the Baja,
and masses of slippery, prickly,
sometimes wriggling
shrimp or squid or perch
or mackerel or even octopi
from as far away
as the waters of Hawaii
and the Gulf of Mexico...

And, everything, every single day,
while being repacked in fresh, clean ice,
merited a "mezu-rah-shi!"

XIII. Grain

Then there were the crates of jars
and canned goods from all over the world —

each item feeling "special"
on its way to the shelves.

And as for the sacks of rice, of course!
Tons of rice, stacks of rice

from Arkansas, Texas, California —
grain by "mezu-rah-shi" grain!

XIV. The Little Details

Sometimes, he'd work alongside
my semi-retired grandfather
for hours, putting pieces of salmon
to cure in miso casks, and the way

they carried on, talking, talking
about such common, ordinary things,

I got the impression that it didn't
take much to get grown men focused
on the little details of life…

And Hiroshi was not only a grown man,
but he may have had a wife…

XV. "First String"

I, too, was a man,
and when the truck
full of rice arrived,
I was more than ready
for those 100-pound sacks,

and it took deftness,
quickness, strength,
skill, and balance,
to hoist and shoulder
each sack, careful

not to slip as you
made your wary way
from the street, through
the busy store, past
the walk-in refrigerator,
the walk-in freezer, to
the storage room in back.

One trip, and you
started to sweat;
two trips, and you
breathed real breath.

Hiroshi, however, seeing
all that, all that rice,
got into a "mezu-rah-shi"
trance, stuck a sack
under each thick arm
like taking toddlers
off to bed, and two-
by-two, had the truck
unloaded in no time,
before the surprised
driver finished a Coke.

Another thing I learned
that summer: I may
have been "first string"
in football, but, boy,
this *man* was a *rope*!

XVI. "Moht-tai-nai"

Then there was that other word:
        "Moht-tai-nai" —

        "What a shame"
                and
        "What a waste"
                combined.

Hiroshi first uttered this
over an open crate of clams —
live clams, but some whose
shells had broken in transit.

We had to throw those away.
"Moht-tai-nai," "Moht-tai-nai"

    all day.

XVII. Founding Concepts

When I think about it,
those two words —
"mezu-rah-shi" and
"moht-tai-nai" — were
the founding concepts
of the very business:

my grandfather's genius
was knowing his *special*
customers and *special* fish;

thus, everything was fresh,
and very little was wasted.

Plus, grandfather and fish
were honest — take his word
and their flesh for it:
"Fresh" means *fresh!*

The only time my grandfather
made a mistake in ordering
was when he called the same
old fishery in San Diego
on a busy December day:

"We don't sell fish to Japs!"

XVIII. Combined

Oh, well — he had heard worse
since 1907, when he arrived.
He was ready, and still fresh.

Thus, the concentration camps
were just "mezu-rah-shi" and
"moht-tai-nai" combined.

XIX. In Whatever Language

I think about that all the time.
Not a day goes by when someone
doesn't reflect upon those words —
"mezu-rah-shi" and "moht-tai-nai" —
in whatever language, as the two
words that best depict the history,
landscape, and people of America.

XX. Blessings and Connections

At the end of that summer,
before Hiroshi left (wherever
he went, I'm sure it was with
my grandfather's blessings and connections),
and before I got my set of new, tubeless,
whitewall tires, along with new, "fullmoon" hubcaps,
we had to make our seasonal (what I called)
"run to the dump."

Now, the advantages of living on the West Side
were several:

1. Boy, it sure was "multicultural —
   or, we were at least as colorful
   as those splendid species of fish;

2. Gee, we sure had "e-z" access
   to the new Highway 99 freeway —
   which cut a huge swath through
   the middle of our side of town,
   displacing families, churches,
   businesses, whole neighborhoods
   in the process, concretely cut-
   ting our community in half and
   stranding my grandfather's home
   on the bank of a traffic-river;

3. Gosh, we sure had fun playing
   "Monopoly" in the new, upscale,
   "color-coded-housing projects —

   because, by golly, old porches
   and thick shade trees couldn't
   upgrade and improve themselves;

   and, like the making of camps,
   somebody else always made good
   money in community development;

4. Wow, despite our fabled, exotic
   "China Alley" and our authentic,
   ethnic, historic business district
   in the fabled heart of California,
   you didn't have to hassle tourists
   experiencing the real experience;

5. And, right-o — we had the city dump!

So I took the truck around to the back of the store,
in the alley, where we stored the trash
(and where, in the old days, in the American
"back-of-business" tradition, my mother was born);

now, instead of a tiny house and yard,
only an ancient, fragrant orange tree remained —
the rest was space for delivery trucks to back into,
and over in the corner was the trash.

Rather, it used to be a pile of trash —
smashed planks and crumpled cardboard —
but Hiroshi had managed to dismantle
and reassemble everything into symmetrical
stacks according to size, so that it resembled
a lumberyard and recycling center combined;

thus, the "trash" took on a kind of "value" —
which is why, several times, I surprised
some fleeing winos making off with our trash!

(And, come to think of it, my grandfather
built a dandy doghouse and little storage shed
with those fish-crate boards, so I suppose
those winos built a structure for sleeping.)

Whatever, it was still trash bound for the dump,
and Hiroshi loaded up the truck in nothing' flat,
while I was chatting with an old high school friend
and new streetwalker, at the end of the alley.

We were ready for our "run to the dump"!
And, along the way, I remembered how exciting
it had been, for a kid out of the camps,
to go with his dad in our pickup Model A
(our "affordable Ford"), hauling our extravagant
surplus of, hard to believe, branches and leaves,
and along the way the kid might get a Pepsi!

Or, later on, without telling anyone, I walked
out there with Gilbert Martinez, "exploring,"
and we came back riding on a bike he found!

And, later on, we'd ride out there on bicycles,
and we always found something — and once,
on the same day, Gilbert found a puppy and a gun!

So, yes, a "run to the dump" was something!
It was like an adventurous journey to the mountains,
because those massive, smoldering mounds
were like volcanoes, the tallest things around,
and it was dangerous out there, and to get there
you went through several geographical changes.

First, you went through your shady neighborhoods;
then, you passed the wasteland of projects;
then, when you got to the outskirts of town,
you were "down South" in the cottonfields

where, way out there by the monstrous slaughterhouse,
beyond the massive, choking, smoking tallow works,
way out there beyond the Snake Road Hut, surrounded
by cottonfields, was the road-house known as "Jericho."

Jericho, it was rumored, had a sentinel on the roof
who could spot plainclothes cops coming for miles.
Jericho, we very well knew, had some sentinel dogs
that, if they weren't chained, would have you
and your bicycle (and maybe your car), for supper.
Jericho was like a hospital — downright "surgical"!

So I was tooling along, hummin', reminiscin',
making sure the load was steady,
not paying much mind to Hiroshi,
who was a quiet guy anyway,

and when we arrived at the dump,
I'm the one who said "mezu-rah-shi,"

figuring the size and scope of the place
would impress him —

but, nope, he didn't say a thing.

And then, when I back up to unload —
backing up to one of the many mounds,
finding a smooth way through the rubble,
watching out for glass,
watching out for metal,
watching out for wood with nails —

this is when, for the first and only time,
Hiroshi decides to get lazy!

That is, I'm up on the truck, with gloves,
grunting and shoving and tossing
things off like crazy,

while Hiroshi, with bare fingers, carefully
picks and chooses
pieces of wood,
pieces of cardboard,
and goes over there, slowly, seriously,
to lay them in neat and separate piles!

And then, as I'm working up a decent sweat,
he proceeds to stop altogether!
And just stands there!

And here's this big, strong guy,
this grown man,
just standing there with his hands at his side,
looking around at the smoldering piles,
shaking his head
and gazing about
with this glazed look in his eyes,
muttering:

> "Moht-tai-nai!
> Moht-tai-nai!
> Moht-tai-nai!
> Moht-tai-nai!"

Chitra Banerjee Divakaruni

Leaving Yuba City

She has been packing all night. It's taking a long time because she knows she must be very quiet, mustn't wake up the family. Father and mother in the big bedroom downstairs. He sharp and angular in his crisp ironed night-pajamas, lying on the bed-lamp side because he reads the Punjabi newspaper before he sleeps. Her body like a corrugation, a dark apologetic crease on her side of the big white bed, face turned away from the light, or is it from her husband, *salwaar-kameez* smelling faintly of sweat and dinner spices. Brother and his new wife next door, so close that all week bits of noise have been flying through the thin wall at her like sparks. Murmurs, laughter, bed-creaks, small cut-off cries, and once a sound like a slap, followed by a sharp in-drawn breath like the startled start of a sob that never found its completion. And directly underneath her bedroom, grandfather, propped up on betel-juice stained pillows to help him breathe, slipping in and out of dreams, nightmares where he calls out in his asthmatic voice hoarse threats in a dialect she does not understand.

She moves on tiptoe like she imagines, from pictures seen in magazine advertisements, a ballerina would move. Actually she is more like a stork, with that same awkward grace as she balances stiff-legged on the balls of her feet. She curls her toes in, then pushes them out, her for-the-first-time painted toes that splay fuchsia pink with just a hint of glitter through the crowded half-dark of her bedroom. She moves back and forth between suitcase and dresser, maneuvers her way around the heavy teak furniture that father chose for her. Armchair. Dressing table. Narrow single bed. They loom up in the sad seep of light from her closet like black icebergs. Outside, wind moves through the pepper trees, whispering her name through the humid night. *Sushma, Sushma, Sushma.* She has been holding her breath, not realizing it, until her chest begins to feel like there are hands inside, hot hands with fuchsia-pink nails, scraping the lining of her lungs, pummeling to be let out. Now she releases it in a rush, shaking her head with a small, embarrassed laugh.

She had seen the nail polish two weeks back. She'd been wandering through the meager cosmetics section of the India House drugstore, killing time as she waited for grandfather's asthma prescription to be filled. She hadn't been looking for anything. What was the use when mother and especially father believed that nice girls shouldn't wear makeup? But the bottle leaped out at her, so bright and unbelonging in that store with its dusty plastic flowers in fake crystal vases on the counter. *Take me, take me,* it called, a bottle from a book she had read in grade school, what was it, a girl falling through a hole in her garden into magic. But this voice was her own, the voice that cried into her pillow at night. *Take me, take me.* There in the store she had looked up at the faded Christmas streamers wrapped like garlands around the pictures of the gods hanging above the cash register. Ganesha with his inscrutable elephant head, Krishna with his calm flute, his eyes like opaque water. *My life.* Her fingers had closed around the fuchsia bottle. That's when she knew she was leaving.

So when at brother's wedding all the relatives said, now it's Sushma's turn, and Aunt Lakshmi told her mother she knew just the right boy back in Ludhiana, college graduate, good family, how about sending them Sushma's photo, that one in the pink *salwaar-kameez* with her hair neatly double-braided, it was not hard to sit quietly. Sit with a smile on her face, tracing the gold-embroidery on the border of her sari, letting the voices flow around her, *Sushma Sushma*

Sushma, like the wind in the pepper trees. Because she had already withdrawn her savings, two years salary from working at the Bharat Spices grocery, money her mother thought she was keeping for her wedding jewelry. The twenty-dollar bills lay folded under her mattress, waiting like wings. Below the bed was the old suitcase she had taken down from the attic one afternoon when no one was home, taken down and dusted and tom off the old Pan Am tag from a forgotten long-ago trip to India. Even her secondhand VW Bug was filled with gas and ready.

Now she pauses with her arms full of satiny *churidars, kurtas* with tiny mirrors stitched into them, transparent gauzy *dupattas* in sunset colors. What is she going to do with them in her new life in some rooming house in some downtown she hasn't even decided on, where she warms a can of soup over a hot plate? But she packs them anyway because she can't think of what else to do. Besides, she has only two pairs of jeans, a few sweaters, and one dress from when she was in high school that she's not sure she can still fit into. Three nightgowns, long-sleeved, modest-necked. From old habit she folds them in neat, flat, gift-box rectangles. Comb, toothbrush, paste, vitamin pills. She puts in the bottle of hair oil and lifts it out again. *Nice girls never cut their hair. They let it grow long, soft as silk, braided tightly down their backs.* That's what father and mother had looked for when they arranged brother's marriage. She stands in shadow in front of the mirror with its thick, bulging frame. She pouts her lips like the models on TV, narrows her eyes, imagines something wild and wicked and impossible, a frizzy permed mass radiating from her face, short hair brushing the bare nape of her neck light as a lover's kiss. She throws in the bottle of nail polish.

It's time for the letter now, the one she has been writing in her mind all week. *I'm leaving,* it says. *I hate you hate the old ways you're always pushing onto me. Don't look for me. I'm never coming back.* Or, *I'm sorry, I had to go. I was suffocating here. Please understand.* Or perhaps, *Don't worry about me. I'll be fine. I just want to live on my own for a while. Will contact you when I'm ready.* She pauses, pen poised over paper. No. None of it is right. The words, the language. How can she write in English to her parents who have never spoken to her in anything but Punjabi, who will have to have someone translate the lines and curves, the bewildering black slashes she has left behind?

She walks down the steps in the dark, counting them. *Nineteen, twenty.* The years of her life. She steps lightly on them, as though they have not been cut into her heart, as though she can so easily leave them behind. She puts her hand on the front door, steeling herself for the inevitable creak, for someone to wake and shout, *kaun hai?* For the pepper trees to betray her, *Sushma Sushma, Sushma.* The suitcase bumps against her knee, bulky, bruising. She bites off a cry and waits. But there is only the sound of the neighbor dog barking.

And she knows, suddenly, with the doorknob live and cold under her palm, that it's going to happen, that the car will start like a dream, the engine turning over smooth, smooth, the wind rushing through her open hair, the empty night streets taking her wherever she wants to go. No one to catch her and drag her back to her room and keep her under lock and key like they did with Prema last year until they married her off. No one to slap her around or scream curses at her, *shameless bad luck girl,* or accuse her of having smeared mud on the family name. And sometime tomorrow, or next week, or next month, when she's far far away where no one can ever find her, Las Vegas, Los Angeles, she'll pick up a phone and call them. Maybe the words will come to her then, halting but clear, in the language of her parents, the language that she carries with her for it is hers, too, no matter where she goes. Maybe she'll be able to say what they've never said to each other all their lives because you don't say those things even when they're true. Maybe she'll say, *I love you.*

Notes:

Yuba City: town in Northern California where many Indian immigrants from Punjab have settled.

Churidar-kurta, salwar-kameez: Indian pants with long tunic, traditional wear for Punjabi girls.

Dupatta: scarf to be worn with *churidar-kurtas* and *salwar-kameejee.*

Kaun hai: who's there?

Joseph Geha

Homesickness

He doesn't look at all like what the American cousins expect. They are second- and third-generation, and maybe they have watched too many TV documentaries. They envision some gaunt greenhorn in an Ellis Island overcoat, but this is 1975, and what they find is a little fellow, dressed as if he's just stepped out of a Disco club — platform shoes, Flamenco snug-trousers, a glossy shirt, electric blue with enormous collar points. His hair is neatly trimmed but the sideburns are shaved completely away. The cousins trade glances. Stylish in Beirut, maybe, but this is America, Toledo, Ohio. Then, when he flinches at the sudden buzz of the baggage carrousel, they can only shake their heads. *Musq'een*, they think, *poor chap*. What will they do with this one?

This one speaks a labored, school room English; better, anyway, than their Arabic. When he listens, it is with his head cocked toward them, as if favoring one ear.

"Mister Jameel?" he repeats their names as if they are questions, "Mister Habeeb?" Adding *Mister* to the first name is an Old Country show of respect.

His name is Samir.

"I'm Henry," says Cousin Habeeb. "Call me Hank."

"And drop the *Mister*," says Cousin Jameel, extending a hand. "I'm Jimmy."

"In America," says Cousin Habeeb, "you can be Sam."

"Like Uncle Sam," adds Cousin Jameel. "Very American."

"*Pardon?*" Samir asks with a French inflection. He does not understand.

No matter. Cousin Habeeb can start him in the stock room of his Monroe Street carry-out and, as his English improves, train him up to the cash register.

"Pardon?"

Musq'een, the cousins think, maybe the *poor chap* is a little deaf.

Cousin Habeeb arranges for Samir to have a tiny flat above the carryout. Sundays, the cousins have him over for Old Country meals — grape leaves, eggplant stew, raw kibbee with vinegary onions.

Samir's first Sunday in America is sunny and hot and they take him to the Toledo Zoo. He loves the elephants. The smell of their dung, he says, reminds one of steamy vegetables — no? Their laughter surprises him.

As they are leaving the zoo, Cousin Jimmy points to the exit gates to show how the monogram TZ has been fashioned into their wrought iron design. The cousins laugh. Get it? TZ is funny because, as even Cousin Jimmy knows, *teezee* is Arabic for *my ass.* See? And Americans don't know this. Get it now? Toledo Zoo. TZ?

Next Sunday is rainy so the cousins take Sam to the Toledo Museum of Art. The Modern Gallery reminds everyone of being in church, whispers echoing *ssss-ssss* in the high arched ceiling. Then a man's voice knifes through the shuffle of feet and hushed murmurs to pronounce, "Good grief, will you look at *that?*"

The cousins stop short and turn. As does everyone else in the crowded gallery. *That,* everyone sees, is a painting by an artist named R. Motherwell, three thick black strokes against a white background, and the man who spoke is still shaking his head in dismay. "I could do *that* myself." Then he adds, "With my eyes shut!"

He is speaking to his wife, a grayish woman who is shrinking next to him. By the way he looks about for some response, he seems to expect everyone in the gallery to applaud his daring and honesty.

But there is no response, so he shifts his weight from one foot to the other then tugs his belt up a bit, like a street tough. His eye falls on Sam. And no wonder — Samir is staring directly at him in bewilderment.

"Right, Sport?" he asks Samir.

Sam cocks his head toward his left ear as if he hasn't quite heard, then in the same motion extends the gesture, touching hand to forehead in a kind of salute. Beaming, the man turns back to his wife.

"C'mon, Sport," Cousin Hank whispers as he motions Sam through the arch toward the museum coffee shop.

"Sbort?" Sam asks when they are seated.

"*Sp*-ort," Cousin Jimmy says, "*Spuh- spuh-*," stressing the *P* sound which does not exist in Arabic. The museum coffee shop is arranged to look like a European cafe — tiny, glass-topped tables beneath Cinzano umbrellas — and Jimmy glances about to see if people are watching. He lowers his voice, "A sport is like baseball or football, see?"

"And in America," Cousin Hank says, "a guy who plays is called a sport too."

Sam seems to turn in on himself while he translates. "Soccer?" he asks.

"Yeah, that's the idea. Soccer is a sport." Jimmy gives him a moment, then asks, "Do you follow the game?"

"Me?" Sam says in English. He lifts his chin and clicks his tongue — *tch!* — Old Country for *No*.

"Do you follow any sports at all?"

"Really, no," he says, as if turning down a request.

"It's a shame," Cousin Jimmy shrugs, glances over at Cousin Hank. "Sports are big in America."

"Very big," adds Cousin Hank. "In America most guys follow a sport. And there are seasons: baseball, football, basketball, all year round. Right now, for instance, it's baseball season."

Cousin Jimmy kinks an eyebrow. "In America all the schools have baseball teams. Even the *churches*, some of them. Even businesses!"

"They say that baseball is..." Cousin Hank hesitates. An announcer on television says this all the time, and Hank wants to be sure he has it right. "Baseball is the all American pastime."

"And all you do is keep tabs on the Mud Hens, follow the Tigers up in Detroit — "

"The *great* American pastime."

"Catch a Reds game now and then — "

"How?" Sam says, perplexed. He is breathing through his mouth.

"Radio," Cousin Jimmy says.

"And TV," Cousin Hank adds. "

"And before you know it —

"And before you know it," Cousin Hank echoes, "you *are* a sport! All American!"

In the flat above the carry-out, Samir awakens to an intermittent hissing in his right ear; yawning makes it go away. In a while, he finds himself staring lazily at the wall beside his cot, at ancient wallpaper patterns of identical flower bursts. They must have once been red, but are now faded to pale almost colorless flesh tones. Then, abruptly and with startling clarity Samir sees that these flower bursts look exactly like clusters of puffy-cheeked little faces. Children. Staring, he sees that all the children are holding little pink hands to the sides of their open mouths, and all the mouths are screaming.

Samir turns quickly away, blinking. These are only the pictures of flowers, he assures himself, flowers and nothing more. That night, getting into bed, he averts his gaze and quickly turns out the light. But in the first light of morning, he gives in. Using a length of twine, he takes a rough measurement of the wall next to his bed. Then, reluctantly, he goes downstairs with his key to the carry-out. He hopes no permission is needed for what he is about to do because he would not be able to explain it, neither in English nor in Arabic. There is tool drawer in the back room. The store's giant spools of wrapping paper are kept back there too.

Later, when the job is finished, the entire wall alongside his bed is covered. Gathered at the top and tacked in bunches, the wrinkly brown sheets look something like curtains.

The carry-out downstairs closes at six, and afterward there are no *ahwa* coffee houses here in the near-downtown, no neighbors to make noise, no voices, no footsteps even. Escaping the silence, Samir takes walks beyond the neighborhood.

Most of the houses in America look closed at night, with shades drawn and those large pull-down doors facing the street. At first Samir thought the doors opened to attached family shops that were

99

closed just now, probably for some American holy day. He was amazed that everyone in America had shops. When the cousins heard this ("You mean garages?") they laughed until the tears rolled down their cheeks.

"Everybody in America has cars," Cousin Jameel said. "But first things first. You save up for a television first."

Sam begins saving for a television, putting away a good portion of his salary each week. He expects laughs from it, and singing, a relief from the silence of nights in the flat. But there is another reason to buy a television. Back in Beirut his sponsors, members of a peace network, had told him that his English would improve rapidly if he listened to the radio and to *le television*. In America, they said, everyone calls *le television* the *teefee*. Had he heard of the *teefee*?

No, not by that name, perhaps. Even so, did they think that Sam was some mountaineer from one of the remote villages? He felt obliged to mask his indignation, however; these peace workers were not his cousins, yet they had lied to officials on his behalf, afterward had helped him bury his uniform with the shiny buttons; from the charity of their own pockets they paid for the sending of telegrams to America, to his American cousins Habeeb and Jameel.

"This is a famous story called 'Apple Pie and Coffee,'" Cousin Jimmy says. They are at the counter of the Yankee cafe and he is speaking English and yet he begins with *"Il-hasloh,"* the Arabic *And thus. "Il-hasloh,* Man comes here from Beirut, doesn't speak a word of English. Not one word."

"A greenhorn," Cousin Hank offers, so eager is he to laugh.

"He's a greenhorn, this man. So his American cousins find him a place to stay."

"Like we found for you."

"And next they get this man a job."

"Factory work, something where you don't need English. Like on the line at Willy's Jeep, nut to bolt, nut to bolt."

"*You* wanna tell him the story?" Cousin Jimmy is from Zahleh. The men of Zahleh all have the Zahlawi temper — fierce, but gone in a blink. "*Il-hasloh,* every day at noon all this *musq'een* can do is sit there at the lunch counter and watch the other workers eat. Why?"

"No English." Cousin Hank is too quick to answer. Nervous, he twists one way then the other on his counter stool.

"*Il-hasloh*, every day this greenhorn, he comes home from work and he is starving. 'Why?' his cousins ask him, and he tells them.

"His eldest cousin is a clever man." Cousin Jimmy pauses to see if Cousin Hank has anything to say to this. Cousin Hank says nothing. "Tomorrow at the lunch counter," the greenhorn's eldest cousin says, "just repeat these words to the waitress: *Apple pie and coffee.*

"*Abble bie and coffee, abble bie and coffee*," the man says it over and over so he won't forget, *abble bie and coffee, abble bie and coffee.*

"Next day he sits at the lunch counter and he tries it. *Abble bie and coffee*. And the waitress says "Yes sir," and she brings it to him. Next day, same thing. Apple pie and coffee. Every day, same thing. He is a happy man, lucky to have the advice of such a clever cousin."

Cousin Jimmy pauses a long time, and once more Cousin Hank looks as if he wants to laugh.

"*Il hasloh?*" Cousin Jimmy asks, the way Arab story tellers traditionally turn the question on their listeners. *And thus?*

"*Il-hasloh*," Samir responds properly.

"*Il-hasloh*," Jameel says, after a few weeks, this greenhorn, he's had enough apple pie and coffee! He tells his cousin and the cousin gives him this advice, "Tomorrow say these words to the waitress: Hamburger sandwich and coffee."

"Next day — " Cousin Hank prods.

"Next day," Jimmy pauses as if to stress that *he* on the other hand is a patient man, "the greenhorn sits at the counter and says to the waitress, *Hamburger sandwich and coffee*. And the waitress says, *You want onions and catsup on that?* A couple minutes pass while the greenhorn thinks, another couple minutes, and then he says...," and here, finally, Cousin Jimmy turns to Cousin Hank who, blurting out "*Abble bie and coffee!*" nearly falls off his stool laughing.

Cousin Jimmy laughs, too, and when they have both settled down, they look at Samir and then at one another.

"I don't know," Cousin Jimmy says. "Maybe we ought to send this one back."

But Sam's face turns so pale at this that Hank slides him his water glass, and like an echo, Cousin Jimmy must repeat again and again that he was only joking, only joking, only joking.

In America the sidewalks remain empty even as the climate heats through July and into August. Only in the shopping plazas on weekend afternoons does he see people in any numbers walking outside. The American faces fascinate Samir — clerks, shoppers, noon hour workers taking their lunches on benches in the sun, all of them are good-looking people. Not like the Bourj Plaza in Beirut. Here he sees no leprosy at all, not even the leonine look that indicates its onset; nor is there a single face, not a single one, with the scars of smallpox.

At night, downtown, the only faces are of those going in or coming out of the bars along parts of Monroe and Madison, and the *sharameet* who stand outside the bars and stare at him shamelessly until he learns to cross the street. In the Old Country there were *sharameet*, too, but here none of them appeal to Samir, neither the black ones nor the white. Here they are called hookers. The word alone frightens him.

Walking at night, Sam is approached by a young *ahbid*, a black man, wearing an expensive looking sports jacket. Corralling Sam toward a lamp post, the black man reveals a display of jeweled watches kept hidden beneath his jacket sleeve. He is selling them.

Sam lifts his chin sharply and clicks his tongue — *tch!* But the peddler doesn't understand no; he keeps pleading and calling Samir his man.

"My man," the *ahbid* says, his voice thinning to a whine, "this one has seven*teen* jewels. And this one here, this one here's *Swiss* made! C'mon, my man."

Sam tries to step around but the *ahbid* thrusts out a hand, fingers outstretched, and the fingers are laden with rings, both men's and women's.

"Got solid silver sterling, got solid gold sterling, too."

Sam does not want a ring or a watch, but he does not want trouble, either. He feels the threat of physical danger, a familiar tensing that he hasn't felt since coming to America. His head clears. He stands still, cocks his good ear, readying himself for anything.

The *ahbid* notices that something has changed. "Take it easy now. Hey, now, look what I got here for my man." He holds out a small brown plastic box the size of a cigarette package, clicks a dial along its side. A tinny voice comes from an ear piece at the end of a pink wire. It is a miniature radio. The voice is announcing a baseball game.

"How much?" Sam asks.

When people ask, he tells them the ear piece is to help with the English. Which is true. And it fills up his head, which is also true, but this he does not tell anyone. Because how can he explain it? What do they know of when everything is quiet, and you are listening, listening. Back home there were those who went crazy from listening too hard. These would step out into the street and fire the shot-pots just to watch everybody else listening jump. Some fell to the pavement with hands over their ears, covering children with their bodies. Samir saw one man — *musq'een, poor chap* — leave his little daughter and run for his own life. Moments later it was clear that a firefight had not broken out, and he scrambled back to her. Poor man, his pants were wet all down the front. She was still screaming, and he picked her up and hushed her. She buried her face in his neck, and Samir could see the resolve in the man's eyes, everyone on the street could see it: *Next time*, his eyes told everyone, *I will die first*.

From that moment, of course, he was a dead man, *poor chap*. But lucky, too, in a way, because the walking dead fear nothing, not firefights, nor parked cars, nor the slippery click of oiled metal.

Sam listens to the game in his left ear, and in a way he does not listen to it. It is there, that voice talking, talking, talking, and the talk so full of slang he gives up trying to understand it. No matter. The important thing is that the voice is always there, always saying something even when the crowd noise swells — *High fly ball to center field! Estevez is under it...and it bounces out of the pocket!*

With his right ear Samir listens to the counter girl in the Yankee Cafe, humming as she folds silverware into paper napkins. *Honey*, Cousin Jameel said to call her, or *Dear*.

More coffee?

Please, Honey.

How about more apple pie?

Thank you, Dear.

He loves to look at the back of the counter girl's neck when her hair is pulled up tight to show that place where the skull and neck join. Back home there were women who would pin their hair up like that for him, let him kiss them there. He hasn't thought about them in so long, and now look at how he is staring. This may be a good sign, he tells himself. *Sabr*, he tells himself, *patience.*

Meanwhile, there are times he will turn the radio up so loud that the high thin noise of it pierces his ear like a needle. Sometimes he will change ears because of the pain. But usually he keeps the ear piece in his left. The right, partially deafened anyway, tends to bleed. A forty per cent loss the doctors in Beirut had told him at the AUB University hospital. It was the car that had done it, the one on Rue Zokak El Hamra, as he was standing by his gendarme station. In two months' time he had with his own eyes seen two cars go up, and he had remained unscratched; this one he only heard. It happened more than a city block away, and it wasn't the explosion itself but the echo that deafened him. Sheltering him from the fragments was a row of buildings, one of which was a hospice for wounded children run by the Lazarine Nuns.

Samir had been walking next to a flat concrete wall but had stopped short when he heard the explosion off to his left. An instant later the echo struck from the right, knocking him off his feet.

"*Oreille de Beirut,*" the doctor smiled wryly, addressing the medical students in French. *Beiruti Ear.* "This gendarme was lucky," meaning Samir, "that he has not been deafened completely. More and more Beirut has been showing us an odd thing about echoes: namely, that because such echoes bring one closer to the sound," he explained, "they can have the same otological effect as the explosion going off inches from the ear." Then the doctor turned to the nurse who stood at his elbow with a notepad and spoke in Arabic: "*Idneyt Beirut.* Estimated loss: right side, negligible; left side, forty per cent."

Forty percent, and lately there are days it seems like more. Walking down Monroe Street and up Erie to the bus stop, there are whole days he can turn up the radio in his left ear, close his eyes, and there is only the radio. He misses the Monroe Street bus that way once. He hears nothing, opening his eyes only because he feels the hot blast of its exhaust pass over him.

When the tears begin, Samir is at work in the back room, sorting soda-pop empties into their crates. Coca Cola, Pepsi Cola, Hire's Root Beer — and out of nowhere he is sobbing. For days afterward the sobbing continues, on and off, bursting out of him just like that, and the cousins are puzzled. They decide, finally, that it must be homesickness, and naming it is as much a relief to Samir as it is to the cousins who are starting to feel embarrassed for him, all this blubbering that comes on unawares, that he must suppress and swallow and which finally sends him choking up the stairs to his room like a schoolgirl. Two rooms and a door he can lock, and only the mice and cockroaches to be disturbed by the weeping that ambushes him even during his ordinary daily tasks, toothbrush or toilet paper in hand. Homesickness, the cousins assure him. Some get it bad.

They barely know about the war in Beirut, the American cousins; they don't want to know. And who can blame them? It is 1975, late summer, and the world itself barely knows and does not want to know that three hundred are killed in what the radio announcer calls *the latest round of bloodshed,* that over a thousand more are wounded, one hundred and fifty kidnapped for ransom.

The Cincinnati Reds, the radio announcer says, *are closing in on the pennant race after winning sixty-four games at home this year. Little better than a .500 club on the road, last week they stole eleven bases from the Pittsburgh Pirates.*

What do you know? a fellow announcer exclaims.

Opposing Cincinnati in the World Series, will be the Boston Red Sox.

Boston last took the championship, the first announcer says, *in 1918 with Babe Ruth pitching.*

What do you know?

The first announcer knows that Highland Appliance in West Toledo is having a price-slashing sale on portable televisions, all with living color that will make the Series *Jump right out atcha!*

The television that Samir buys is not only a color set, it comes equipped with one of the new hand-held devices for remote control. He sets the *teefee* up on a low dresser which he has to move to the east wall to be near the room's one working electrical outlet. Since his bed is along the same wall he angles the dresser a little so that the entry door can be cleared.

Next, he takes his time positioning the *teefee* and the stuffed chair, adjusting for glare from the overhead bulb and reflections from the window. Finally, he settles himself into the armchair, opens a Budweiser, and puts his feet up on a crate, just like the picture of Americans in the funny papers watching *teefee*. He presses the button on the remote control device, and the first sounds to come out, before even the picture tube has warmed up, are unmistakable: an Uzi, judging by the low-caliber sound of its rapid bursts. Or possibly its American-made counterpart, the Ingram. Samir fumbles with the remote control device, looking for the off button but succeeds only in muting the sound. The tears begin of their own accord, and the first images he sees on his *teefee* are the blurred moving rainbows of colors.

In silence the picture snaps to a man running down a city street. The man is afraid. This is only a television program, Samir reminds himself. The salesman had certainly been right about the black matrix screen — the colors jump right out at you. Abruptly, the man drops like a top-heavy sack of flour. Only a television program, Samir reminds himself, but the actor too must have seen such a thing before. Because the body does not fall backward, arms in the air as in cowboy movies, but forward, in a heavy crumple; the weight of the human head and chest does this, even in children. Samir reminds himself to take a sip of his Budweiser.

Only when he thinks for sure that the tears will begin again does he switch the station. His hand feels stiff, his fingers tingly as if threatening not to press the buttons. And so changing channels on a remote control becomes an effort.

Channel Thirteen has a police program. Just a glimpse of the holstered .38 Remington at the detective's armpit is enough to make Samir continue pressing the channel button:

— doctors in an operating room...

— a slow scan of time and temperature...

— a rock-and-roll show...

For minutes Samir stares at the buttocks of the dancing women in full color and through the bright clarity of his tears. He turns off the mute button and presses the volume even louder because his left ear is acting up. The women, maneuvering to face the camera, grind their teeth in sexual smiles that say *Shu b'himni annah? Shu b'himni annah? What do I care? What do I care?*

On Channel Eleven there is a program in which a man named Mister Roger speaks calmly and so slowly that Sam does not even have to strain his good ear toward the set. Mister Roger speaks caringly, too, and just to Sam, until the tears subside. Then, in the middle of speaking just to Sam, Mister Roger begins singing, breaking into song just as Sam has seen announcers do on television programs in the Old Country. Only when the camera follows a talking trolley car to a land of puppets does Sam realize that this is a program for children, the poor things. Sobbing anew, he finds the off button.

The next day is a Saturday, his day off work, and it turns out to be a good day because all morning he watches cartoon programs. There is nothing else on the *teefee* — and the colors! — so what else can he do?

There are faces he recognizes from movie houses in the Bourj Plaza in Beirut, Popeye and Mighty Mouse and Woody Woodpecker, all of them speaking English now. Learning English himself, he mouths the salesman's words: *The colors jump right out atcha!*

In the afternoon there is a baseball game. He watches all three and a half hours of it, and when it ends he switches to Channel Thirteen and finds another game just beginning.

Evaporated. There was a news brief during the second ball game, and all evening afterward Samir has been walking to rid his mind of it, images of buildings he has stood before shattered, the car that caused it evaporated — the newsman speaking from Beirut had used that word, *evaporated* — and leaving a crater in the pavement. *Evaporated.* On *teefee,* the crater was strewn with all the different colors of shredded clothing.

America will change you, the cousins say, and Samir agrees, staying awake late into the night to feel himself change. At night Americans sleep or watch *teefee* safe in their houses, guarded by the large shut mouths of their garages. A song is played when the teefee finishes at night, the same song of America that is sung at the start of baseball games. The brave find a home in the land of the free, it says. In the Old Country he walked past ticking cars but he was not brave; here he will be brave. He is changing. They will see. Because he understands better than the cousins think: you must be brave to be this much free, to be this much alone.

Lately there are days Samir can plug a fingertip into the good ear and listen, and he can hear a dull, steady whir, like a fan going. Sometimes he hears faint voices form and echo out of utter silence, sometimes there is music in his head, the singing of Farouz or Abd il Bak'r of Cairo, and sometimes even his own. Then Samir must stop and remind himself that this is America, and here in America there is radio and here in America there is *teefee* and both are filled with the sounds of other people. Always, one can find a sports program in America, in the middle of the night even. There is an all-night radio station in Detroit that rebroadcasts entire Tiger games all week long. It is the American way, this, the cheering of great crowds in the middle of the night.

Shirley Goek-lin Lim

Immigrant Mother

How does one make a home? Sometimes I think too much is made of homes, as if because we equate having nothing with being nothing, we burrow deeper into the stuffing of sofas and beds. Too much can be made of homeland. Stories we tell often take their identity from a piece of soil, and the strongest stories may leave us still standing in the scene of our powerlessness.

Birth changes a place to a homeland: birth land, children, our childhoods, where our parents have buried our umbilical cords, where our children will bury us and will bear their children. There are homelands of the memory and homelands of the future, and for many of us, they are not the same.

Native-born children carry the cultural imprint of Americanism in a way that their immigrant parents cannot. If they become encum-

bered by nostalgia and regret, like their parents, this consciousness of another country cannot undermine the infant primacy of an American homeland. I wanted my child to possess the privileges of a territorial self, even as I had as a young Malaysian. "Out of the cradle endlessly rocking," the folding into and unfolding out of a social space and a people. While all citizens are guaranteed juridically their claim to a place in the United States, not every claim is unquestioned, nor is that place certain. Poverty, skin color, sex, disease, disability, any difference can arouse suspicion and exclusion. I did not expect my child to be safe from these discriminations, but I wished, at least for his infancy, the primal experience of bonding with an American homeland. In this desire, I marked myself as a U.S. citizen, and I finally began the process for citizenship.

Without relatives and with only my college colleagues for a community, pregnancy was a lonely, isolating experience. One morning I had to be in New York City for an interview with the Immigration and Naturalization Office. The train rattled through the underground tunnels into Grand Central Station, shaking its entire length. On any other morning I would have been absorbing its energy, bouncing with it, waiting eagerly to emerge into the day outside and to merge into the anonymity of coats and boots and shining shop windows.

Now, overcome with nausea, I munched furiously on saltine crackers. My seatmate pretended not to see the crumbs that fell like dandruff over my black winter coat. My stomach heaved and rumbled. It was aching to throw up, but there was nothing inside, only dry lumps of baked flour like wet cement chuting down to settle my hunger pangs.

The doors opened and everyone pushed out. I was a black fish gathered up in the net of bodies. The bodies carried me out of the train and up the stairs through other tunnels. I could not slow my stride; my legs trundled like part of a centipede's hundred pairs. I had no will in this morning rush hour's masses. Slowly my head was turning dark, and I felt myself lose consciousness. The centipede was rushing down a flight of steps toward the downtown Lexington. Just ahead the subway cars were spilling with other bodies, and a mechanical voice was announcing, "Keep clear of the closing doors. Keep clear of the closing doors." The feet rushed faster, faster down the steps.

But I could not keep up. I sat down on the steps, despite the press of bodies behind me. The river backed up, split open, then swirled around the boulder that was myself. I put my head down between my knees. The concrete steps were black and brown with grime. The dirt had piled up along the backs of the steps, bits of fresh candy wrappers still colored blue and gold, brown filter tips and butts with shredded tobacco falling out. I could see only a little piece of concrete. The rest was filled with moving legs, tan and khaki pants, blue dungarees, suede heels, frayed hems and silk-bound hems, unwashed sneakers split at the sides, white leather sneakers squeaking new, dirt-crusted workboots with soles like floors. No one stopped to ask why I was sitting on the steps of Grand Central Station. I was grateful for the city's impersonality: I could have been sitting by the abyss of the Grand Canyon listening to the rush of the wind among the bent piñon and ponderosa pines. The huge ingrained ugliness of New York's subways appeared as much a force of nature as the Grand Canyon's windscrubbed beauty; I was as invisible in the midst of thousands of hurrying feet as a hiker lost on the canyon's red-scarp edge.

On St. Valentine's Day, 1980, four months pregnant, I stood in a hall in White Plains and swore allegiance to the flag and to the republic for which it stands. There must have been about two hundred others there that morning, more white than brown, and there was a festive mood in the hall as the black-robed justice congratulated us. This is the crucible of America, the moment when the machinery of the state opens its gate and admits irrevocably those aliens who have passed the scrutiny of its bureaucrats — language tests, history tests, economic tests, social tests. Tests that impress with the enormous and amazingly indifferent power of representative Americans to deny you identity, tests that force you to compliance, tests for inclusion that threaten exclusion. So my patriotism on my first day as an American citizen was not unbounded. Scooping a piece of buttermilk pancake from its puddle of maple syrup at the International House of Pancakes where I had gone to celebrate my passage into American identity, I felt alien in a different way, as if my ambivalence toward the United States must now extend inward to an ambivalence toward myself. No longer a traveler, I was included in my accusations of America.

My morning sickness disappeared after three months. I swelled and swelled, fifty pounds above my normal weight, half as much as I was, a red plum tomato in my cotton summer frock. We had moved to Westchester County, fifty miles out of Manhattan, two years earlier, and while Charles commuted to teach in Manhattan, I fell in love with the Westchester suburbs for the first time. The May days were busy with Queen Anne's lace, day lilies, Dutchmen's-breeches, and flourishing sumac. I fretted over a strand of bright orange butterfly weed that had sprung up by Route 100, waving above the still gray water of the Croton Reservoir, just below our white-and-green colonial home. It was too exotic, an endangered wildflower, in plain view, with the red-winged blackbirds flashing among the sumac bushes. Sure enough in a few days the butterfly weed blossoms, winged like palpitating floaters that its milky sap invites, were gone. Some passing human had picked them, robbing the seeds that would have borne more orange wings for the years after.

We practiced huffing and puffing. The gynecologist's receptionist had me down as a *mater primigravida*. The term conjured the images of the Virgin Mary from those faraway convent days: the gravely tragic countenance, the graceful folds of cloak and robes concealing a thickened waistline. A pregnant woman oppressed by secrets, social isolation, poverty, married to a man not the father of her baby, that central story never told directly, the story of woman's delight in childbearing. The narrowing of the story to simply mother and infant, the man far away in the clouds or discreetly in the background…together with the oxen and donkeys. A celibate woman's fantasy, a revenge story for women harrowed by men's demands and commands.

I was lucky. Charles was tender and attentive, but all that deep breathing and panting came to nothing. At almost nine pounds, the baby had to be sprung out of my bony pelvic cage by a scalpel. As the nurses rushed me into the operating room, my temperature rising precipitously each minute and the fetal temperature mounting to life-threatening degrees, I focused on the life in my body. It, he, she was ready to emerge from the container which was myself. The event of childbirth is violent and bloody. As if experiencing her death, the mother cannot change course. She endures and, if she is able and wise, assists in the moment of expulsion. When the anesthesiologist crammed the plastic apparatus into my throat like a giant obscene penis, I willed my body to relax, to float like the lotus yielding its seeds to the light. At that moment I felt the cold swab of the anesthetic-soaked cotton like the curve of a scimitar across my abdomen and lost consciousness.

The nine months of pregnancy had been a slowly swelling swoon into domesticity, marked by giddy strolls through aisles of baby perambulators, crib mobiles, bath toys, terry-cloth books, hooded towels, fuzzy blue, brown, and white rabbits, dogs, lions, unicorns, Smurfs, bears and more bears, an instant cornucopia of infant goods for infant-obsessed Americans. But once my son was born, strenuously hungry and alert, it became clear I could not simply buy him a life.

I had entered U.S. society through the workplace, taking my seat in department meetings and at conference sessions as a colleague. My husband's parents were dead, he was estranged from his only brother, and all my brothers were in Malaysia. It mattered that we spent Easter, Passover, Memorial Day, Labor Day, Hanukkah, Christmas, and New Year's Eve alone, but it didn't matter that much. Occasionally a colleague invited us to a department picnic or a department brunch. But babies do not socialize through English departments. I was tormented by the fear that my son would grow up isolated, as I was, in the United States. I did not wish my son to be lonely the way we were. He was an American, whatever that was, and I wanted him to have the full plenitude of his world, not the shadowy existence of a green card holder.

The myth of assimilation became a pressing reality as soon as I brought my son home from Northern Westchester Hospital. A child's society is his parents': cut off from the umbilical cord, he is nonetheless tied to the company his mother keeps. Or does not keep, in my case. It may have been important for my imagination to maintain the distance of the resident alien, but I wanted something different for my son. Despite the absence of an extended community, I wanted for him to have a pride of belonging, the sense of identity with a homeland, that which I had possessed as a Chinese Malaysian for a brief time in my youth. I wanted Gershom to be able to run for the presidency of the United States if that was what he wished.

The passage of assimilation began at the earliest age. Anxiously I accepted every birthday invitation that came his way from the Montessori mothers. Together, Gershom and I shopped for Mattel educational toys, boxes with differently shaped mouths and blocks, cobblers' benches, multicolored xylophones, huge plastic contraptions that invited baby fists to punch and ring and pull and pat. I chose the opulent set, the more expensive version of a brand-name product, while Gershom sat in his thrift-store stroller, pointing at each large package within reach. We drove down numerous Yorktown and Somers circular dead-ends, clutching party invitations and directions in one hand. His bottom still padded with diapers, he waddled among pink-cheeked, blond, and blue-eyed toddlers. I sat with the mommies, an alien among a dozen or so white women, an awkward mismatch among the grandmothers furiously snapping Nikons at the cake and chubby faces and the fathers with rolling video cameras. A college teacher years older than the young homemakers with junior-executive husbands, I held my breath and sat very gingerly on the new sofas in these strangers' split-level ranches, where lavish bathrooms were cleaner than the shelters of billions of other humans. I could not afford contemptuous segregation or condescending kinship if I wished Gershom to have a full human connection with America.

Malls and department-store aisles do not discriminate. Everything is for sale to everyone. But women do. Mothers, keeping a wary eye on their scrambling pebble-picking children in playgrounds, do. Fathers, arriving to pick up their toddlers after work, loosening their ties by the Montessori entrance, do. If I could hope to have Gershom pass into Middle America in wall-to-wall carpeted living rooms, we never succeeded in the public playgrounds among anonymous whites.

Weekends and summers Gershom and I set forth to Reis Park, Leonard Park, Muscoot Farm, and assorted town fairs and parades. Cautiously I let him loose in the sandbox, retreated to one side where other mothers stood under the shade of birches and oaks and cast their eyes sidewise on the little spaders and grubbers. There were no homesteaders here, only transient visitors who might or might not return another afternoon. Was it the chip on my shoulder that sounded the alarm? I watched enviously as strangers veered toward each other and began exchanging intimacies of toilet training and bed-wetting. I imagined their eyes were already measuring their toddlers' compatibility, one pink hand patting another pink hand's castle.

My olive-skinned child had dark handsome eyes and thick dark hair. He was oblivious to social slight as he scrambled up the teeter-totter. There was no one to teeter with him. The other children had wandered away with their parents who strolled off deep in conversation. I called out to him, placed my weight on two legs so that my body did not pull the balance down, and planted the illusion that between us we could move the teeter-totter up and down, up and down.

Laura Kalpakian

Ethnic Cleansing

They are leaving. They stare out from the passport picture which is haphazardly glued to the nondescript little book, thick paper, coarse pages. Passport and photo are both embossed with the star and crescent. On this date in 1923 they declare officially that they are Turkish subjects, though they are not Turkish. Turkey is their home, but not their country, the land where they have lived for generations, for as long as anyone can remember. They are lucky to have lived at all. Their nationality is nowhere stated; they are Armenians. Eight years before, the Turks systematically decimated the Armenian minority living within their borders; they marched Armenian men, women, children off to desert exile, to death by starvation, or merely massacred them by various means, not all as quick and dignified as firing squads. Turkey is soon to be rid of a few more Armenians: the family of Haroutune

Kalpakian, his wife, daughter and a baby, they are leaving. They have lived in Turkey, which is to say survived, spared death and exile, but they are refugees nonetheless.

They do not want to look like refugees, that much is clear from the photo. The husband wears a tie, a high collar, a vest. The passport describes him of medium size with a round face, clear eyes, regular nose, normal mouth, a thin moustache, and no beard. His hair is visibly receding at 36. His posture, the sharp angle of his right elbow, his direct gaze all create an effect of pomp, of dignity, not in keeping with the iron bars in the background behind the family. Officially, the passport declares him without *qualité ou profession*. The child, four years old, looks skeptical. The baby, bundled up, asleep, no more than a round face atop a blanket and beneath a cap. The young wife, 22, her arms around the baby, looks stunned. Her eyes are not at all like her husband's. Her gaze goes behind the photographer, perhaps beyond him, through him. She seems to have seen everything and to see nothing. The iron bars behind them accentuate their differences of expression, and give a grim cast to this austere photo. The passport is stamped from the *4me Section* of the Constantinople police. It says so in French and Turkish.

Both my grandparents spoke French, but the commerce of their everyday lives in Constantinople, in any Turkish city, would have been conducted in Turkish. Armenian language was forbidden. For a while, during World War I, Armenian churches were closed. Armenian language, religion, culture, and identity — Christian in this Muslim country — had come to be a secret thing, confined to the home, to intimate discourse, familial exchange. It would not have been the language spoken here at the police station where stamps are affixed to their passport indicating that the fees have been paid. (There is nothing to indicate that the bribes have been paid, but they have.) The passport says their destination is *Amérique, Etats-Unis* and the point of their voyage, *chez ses parents*. This is a tidy lie. The ragged truth is, there are no more parents; they are either dead or dispersed. The passport is good for one year from today, 26 March 1923, the very day my mother, the sleeping baby, was one year old.

I doubt they celebrated her first birthday. From the *4me Section* of the police, the Kalpakians went home (according to this passport which only came into my hands after my grandmother's death in 1987) to the rue patchadji, No. 46, Constantinople. I picture it a noisy journey through a city still suffering in the wake of Turkey and Germany's 1918 defeat. The victorious Allies, the French and British, remain very much a presence here, even in 1923. The family's flat at No. 46 is three flights up. Two bedrooms and a kitchen. I imagine the latrine is shared, but there is no flush toilet. The kitchen has cold running water, but not hot. My grandmother would have set out the little plates, enamel, blue on one side, white on the other, cooked the evening meal, probably bulgur wheat and onions, and closed the shutters against the evening air (she had a horror of drafts all her life) and against the cries, nearing sunset, the haunting wails from the city's minarets calling the majority faithful to face East and pray to Allah.

My grandparents were of the minority Christians, now even more of a minority since the Turks had annihilated half of the Armenian population, about a million people (an estimate, conservative) during the First World War while the world's attention was on the Western Front. The war, as it progressed in Turkey, consisted of a futile Allied assault in 1915 on the Dardanelles and Gallipoli; from there, the Allies could have invaded Constantinople, toppled the Turkish government and forced their surrender. Gallant Australian and New Zealand, British troops died in horrifying numbers at Gallipoli, massacred, not merely by the Turkish army, but sacrificed to leadership entirely inept, and decimated by disease. Among the English losses, the poet Rupert Brooke, who with many others died in western Turkey (*there's some corner of a foreign field that is forever England...*), while in the mountains and desert regions to the east, Armenian men, women, and children were massacred as well. By 1923, it was all quiet on the Western Front, and at Gallipoli as well, and even in the eastern deserts where Armenian bones bleached unburied.

It was not all quiet in Constantinople, a panoply of voices and languages there, but I imagine the Kalpakian family after supper, the children got down to sleep, quiet in the kitchen. I see my grandparents, their hands folded. Silent. I can't imagine what they said. In truth, I can't imagine them talking at all.

This is not a failure of the imagination. It is not even a failure of language in that I have no morsel of Armenian language. This is pervasive silence, a silence which was not all quiet. My grandparents enveloped their experience in a veil of silence, shrouded it in silence, buried it in silence. In America, the uniform cry of their lives was *assimilate assimilate*, but their Armenian experience, or if you wish, their Turkish experience, died before they did, asphyxiated in the silence which in our family was thick and abstruse as smoke. Silence prevailed, became, in physical terms, not so much a gas like smoke, but a substance like ash, like grit, or lint or sand. In 1987, when my

Grandmother died, certain artifacts and documents (like this passport) came to light. They raised questions which could not now, not ever be answered, and they offered incomplete revelations, sudden illuminations, voices in the void. These documents — the passport, the ship manifest, the Declaration of an Alien About to Depart for the United States, the inventory of their household goods — are noisy documents. They seem to me chatty, rife with gossip, possibility, implication, if not understanding. From these official pages rose questions, definite questions, but by then my Grandmother had died, her silence unchallenged.

And who would have challenged her? Not me. Not any of us. She was a formidable woman. Not cold or angry or stolid as the word suggests in English, but rather, as the French use it, *formidable!* A tremendous force in her own right, a powerful presence, *formidable!* But until these documents and artifacts emerged, I had never really guessed at the extent of her silence. After all, little bits of anecdote had been broken off the silence, shaped and often-told. These few stories, perhaps four or five of them, all have their indelible, obligatory exclamation point at the end! If they did not, they would not be amusing! And if they were not amusing, they would not have become stories! You see the point in print more easily.

Here is one of these stories: Towards the end of the War, my grandmother Haigouhi (later to become Helen, *assimilate, assimilate*) graduated in 1917 from the Adana Girls' Seminary, a missionary-run school next to the Armenian Congregational Church. She was, by this time, an orphan earning her keep as a teacher at the school where she had been a student. Husbands for Armenian girls were scarce in those days, indeed, Armenian men, especially of draft age were rare altogether. All marriages were arranged and my grandmother had no dowry, nothing save for her looks, her learning and her purity to recommend her. However, a family who had known hers wanted to arrange a marriage for their son. According to old country custom, the prospective bride makes coffee (what we call Turkish coffee, beans ground to a fine powder, put on to boil, cooked till the froth appears and poured correctly into demitasse cups) for the mother of the prospective groom. If the mother says, *ah, this coffee is good,* negotiations can go forward; if not, everything is off. (It should be remembered my grandmother had lived for years in the school and so her housewifely skills would have been neither practiced nor exemplary.) In the parlor of the school's headmistress, Miss Grace Towner, the mother waited for her coffee which my grandmother prepared. The mother said, *Ah, this coffee is good,* and smiled. Haigouhi left the room and the mother talked with Miss Towner. When Miss Towner asked my grandmother if she wanted to marry the young man, my grandmother had only one question: could he read and write? It turned out he could not. *Forget it,* declared my grandmother, *I can read and write four languages and I will not marry an illiterate man!* Bravo, Haigouhi!

But there is no story with an exclamation point to tell us how she felt when she became a boarder at this school instead of a day student. The Turks ordered her family to join other Armenians about to make a forced march into the deserts to the east, to leave their homes and property (no small consideration) and go into exile. Miss Towner said Haigouhi should stay, board at the school, saving her life in effect by offering her the sanctuary of the American missionary enclave. And when Haigouhi left her parents' home, as she packed, collected her few things, did her mother cling to her? Silence. Did her mother help her pack? Silence. Did her father hold her one last time? Silence. Did they weep? Silence. Did she hug her ten-year-old brother? Silence. Did she know that she would live? And guess that they would die? Again, you can see in print how the silence engenders question marks, where the oft-told-stories oblige exclamation points. Never did my grandmother indicate — to anyone — anything of that leave-taking. She was about fourteen and went to live at the Adana Girls' Seminary. The rest of them vanished, off into the desert, to starve or be killed, to die in any event.

Her younger brother did not die. Haig was about ten or eleven and he survived. He watched his father die of starvation in the desert. He watched as the Kurds came and stripped the Armenian exiles (can one be an exile in one's own country? A refugee in the land one has always called home? Was it home? The tent in the desert where his father died, was that home?) took from them all their clothing, which was all they had anyway, left them naked. The Kurds took young Haig as a slave and shepherd boy. The others were all killed.

Haig's first owner had a daughter who taught him the Kurdish language as they took the cows to pasture daily. He ran away once, back to the Armenian encampment where he found unburied bones. Did he find his mother's body? We don't know. We only know the Kurd caught him, brought him back, sold him to another Kurd, a man with two contentious wives. He was a smart boy, Haig, a shrewd boy, so smart and shrewd that in time his relations with his owner deteriorated and one day the man tried to kill him, flung a knife at him; he carried this scar on his neck his whole life. Haig ran away, to the east, even farther east and he changed his name from the clearly Armenian Haig, to Ali. He spoke only Kurdish and he lived for five years on the run, cadging, begging, stealing, working, lying, living as best he could.

In 1978, in my parents' livingroom, Haig recounted these five years of his childhood, or rather, of his life, into a tape recorder. My grandmother was there. Late in his narrative Haig (who speaks in an even, hypnotic, a singsong voice) ventures near the unsayable, beginning to recount his return to the Armenian encampment where he found the unburied bones. My grandmother interrupts him: *That's enough. We've heard enough. I've heard enough. It does no good now. That's enough.* Then she adds, as both edict and observation, *You cannot put in words your feelings. You can only describe the conditions. But how you feel, you cannot say.*

Okay, Haig replies. *Okay* was his favorite punctuating phrase. As he tells his story that afternoon, he always throws in the contemplative *Okay, what I gonna do?* After he ran away from the second Kurd, he traveled two hundred miles to the east, begging, stealing, dodging Kurds and Turks and Arabs. He stumbled onto an encampment of Kurdish workers building a railroad for the German army. He spoke their language and they sent him, two tents down, to see the Turkish boss, to get work. Haig's telling of this tale indicates that Kurdish was his only language at this time — not the only language he dared to speak, but the only one he *could* speak, as though the other two languages, the home-language Armenian and the street-language Turkish, had both been eradicated from memory. He got the job, and slowly his recollection of Turkish returned, which delighted the Turkish boss because he needed someone to translate for him to his workers. He made this boy a sort of foreman, translating orders and told him to watch out when the Germans came around, to stay out of the way of the German officer in charge of the rail-building. He would recognize this particular officer because he rode a fine horse. Haig had a little dog (how or when he came by this dog, he does not say) and the dog had the bad sense to bite the leg of the German officer's horse. The Germans threw the boy and the dog into a tent which sufficed for a jail and told them to stay there. *Okay, these Germans, what they gonna do with me? Shoot me maybe.* (Haig tells his story like that, not saying what he felt, only describing conditions). *And I'm petting the dog, and I'm saying, you put me like this, you see, and I'm looking round the tent and I see nothing but dirt, and I went there, started digging and this dog just came over here and start digging, digging under the tent and we made enough room and slide under there — and run.* The dog too, says Haig. *But the dog left behind 'cause I didn't want to take care of him because I didn't have nothing to eat myself, what I gonna do with the dog?*

One wonders what he did with the dog. One wonders at their parting. But the dog vanishes from his story, from his life, which after that was *walking every day, one place to the other, looking for something, somewhere, looking for something, someplace that we live or do something.* He lies, cheats, steals, befriends another orphaned Armenian boy and under the name Ali works for a cook in the Turkish army, goes into town to change money for the Turkish soldiers. And finally, after World War I staggered to its terrible close, Haig was picked up begging on the streets of Dörtyol (so he had clearly worked his way back, westward towards Adana) where he was taken to the Foundling Home.

. The Foundling Home published all the names of the orphans, and a friend of my grandmother's saw his name and brought it to her attention. In about 1920, just as the British and French were withdrawing from the area and all the orphans to be shipped down to Jerusalem, my grandmother made contact with Haig and he went to Adana to join his sister and her husband. My grandfather paid Haig's fare, and the fees owed to the Foundling Home for his board and room, just as in 1917 he had paid Miss Towner for my grandmother's back-owed board and room. About fifty dollars.

Fifty dollars was a huge sum in those days. The Kalpakians, my grandfather's people, were merchants and bankers, quite wealthy, so it came down to us in little wisps, like lint, or ash, or grains of sand, it came down to us that they had money. Rumor persisted, but silence prevailed and we never were told anything particular, save that until the First World War, the Kalpakians had lived in a beautiful home in Mersin which was confiscated after they moved to Adana. (The house in Mersin was said to have been purchased with a single ring his mother owned.) Their flight was occasioned by political troubles, the arrest of someone in the family, but in Adana, they were not merchants and bankers. My grandfather worked as a clerk in a German department store. He met my grandmother when she and another young teacher came in to do some shopping for the Girls' Seminary.

My grandparents' was not an arranged marriage, but a marriage of love accomplished over the protests of Miss Towner (my grandfather was Armenian Apostolic, not protestant, and while this did not matter to my grandmother, it mattered to Miss Towner) and the objections of the groom's family who had no wish to see him marry a penniless orphan, even if she could read and write four languages. The newlyweds lived for a time with my grandfather's family, eleven other people, in an Adana apartment. His family have come down to us — albeit from my grandmother's lips, and on this she was not silent, not vocal either, but if you asked how they had treated her, she would tell you — they were a close and nosy bunch, ill-tempered, sniping, carping, and mean.

However, they were alive in 1918, all thirteen of them. They had not been marched off into the desert when my grandmother's family had vanished, so probably, they were wealthy, rich enough in any event, that money — or more likely jewelry — changed hands: from their Armenian hands into Turkish hands, bribes sufficient to keep them alive, if not safe. Moreover, once the crisis of 1915–1916 had passed and the War had ended, they were astute enough to see they could not remain in Turkey. My grandfather's family dispersed. Into the diaspora go the Armenians: a people with two thousand years of culture and no country; people with their own church and language, literature, art and architecture, and no home in which to build or create or practice. They dispersed like smoke. My grandfather never saw any of them again.

They wafted to Manchester, England, to Russia, to Romania, to France. The odd Christmas card arrived; in 1935 word from Romania that my grandfather's mother had died, in 1938 that his father had died. A half century after they had dispersed, my cousin Patty, a student then traveling in France in the early 1970s, followed an address to Marseilles, found in a filthy Marseilles backstreet, a hunched and horrible old woman, the widow of someone, a connection by marriage, some long-lapsed relative who was surprised to hear my grandfather had died in 1963.

I never really believed the story of the Kalpakian family's wealth. I thought the merchants and bankers were one of those gone-with-the-wind tales, because if you're going to lose everything, it makes imaginative, if not under-oath sense, to be rich and lose a lot. But now I do believe it. I believe it because they survived. I believe it because of what they declared on Form 139 as they were leaving Constantinople. I believe it from what they left undeclared on Form 139, what only emerged after they were both dead: a sapphire ring, a gold ring with three diamonds, a gold ring with two diamonds and a ruby, gold and diamond earrings, a gold oblong ring with many small diamonds. All this, the remaining personal property of Helen Clark Kalpakian, and no one in her entire family knew that she possessed these things. No one had ever before seen them. She kept them and her silence to the end.

The Kalpakians dispersed all over Europe and the young couple followed suit. Now, however there were four of them, my grandparents, their daughter, Angah and my grandmother's brother, Haig. They had buried an infant daughter, dead of scarlet fever, in Adana, and in 1921 went east to Syria, to Iskerundun (Alexandrette). My grandmother, in all her eighty-six years never spoke of these four months in Syria. Only at the end of her life when at my aunt's behest she wrote her "autobiography," she noted, succinctly, in perhaps twenty words, that they had left Adana "in the night and we were all hurried to get on the train, Turkish soldiers pushing us with bayonets to get on the train like a cattle car."

In any event, Alexandrette was a French-mandated city in those uneasy years following World War I. But what little we know of their time there comes from Haig in 1978. Talking to my aunt, he said that during these months, my grandfather took a journey alone, a boat trip to the Holy Land. Of what my grandfather saw, or where he went, or what he thought of it, we have nothing. We never knew he'd been to the Holy Land. A pall, the smoke of silence, hangs over their Syrian experience, save for Haig's unexpected anecdote of my grand-mother and the fortune teller. For half a loaf of bread, the fortune teller would read her palm. *Ah,* she told my grandmother, *You will move again soon and you are expecting another child.* It probably took no great foresight to divine either of these, but I for one, cannot imagine my grandmother (literal, hardworking, prudent, no toler-ance for nonsense of any sort) holding out her hand — much less half a loaf of bread — to a fortune teller.

When the French left Alexandrette, so did the Kalpakians. They boarded a ship, the *Bucovina,* in March, 1922, my grandmother hugely pregnant, and crossed the Mediterranean, westward towards Constantinople. They steamed through the Aegean blue sea, the Greek isles, along all those ancient beaches with all their ancient names: Rhodes, Léros, Samos, Patmos where Saint John the Divine was said to have written the Book of Revelation. Surely it must have seemed to my family, to Europeans everywhere, that the Four Horse-men of the Apocalypse had spent themselves during World War I. The *Bucovina* steamed up the Turkish coast, towards Gallipoli and the Dardanelles — *where there's some foreign field that is forever En-gland,* and New Zealand and Australia — where all those Allied sol-diers died in 1915. Did my grandfather stand on the steamer deck and wonder, as they passed the Dardanelles and all those foreign graves, how many Armenians might have been saved if the Allies had triumphed here? If the Allies had taken Constantinople in 1915 and effectively knocked Turkey out of the War? The Turks had accom-plished their systematic annihilation of the minority people — as Hitler was to do a generation later — behind the curtain of war.

If anyone wondered these things, it would have been my grandfa-ther. He was a dapper, learned, bookish man, shrewd, cheerful, and charming. I can't imagine my grandmother wondering any such thing. Speculation was never in her nature. Besides, one week after their arrival in Constantinople, she gave birth to my mother, born Pakradouhi Kalpakian, 26 March 1922.

One year later, 26 March 1923, their passports were in readiness, and if on that document my grandfather had been described as with-out *qualité ou profession,* nonetheless on June 7, 1923, when he pre-sented himself at the American Consulate's office (to fill out Form 228) he said he was a merchant.

This was true. He spent virtually the rest of his life behind one counter or another. In Los Angeles he owned a series of small grocery stores of the Ma and Pa variety, little stores with wooden floors and screen doors and chugging refrigerator cabinets. He sold groceries for a living, save for their first few months in Los Angeles when he worked in a kewpie doll factory while he was learning English.

Form 228 is the Declaration of an Alien About To Depart for the United States. My grandfather solemnly swore before Th. Murphy, American vice-consul there, that he intended to stay in America *for good*. He dropped the fiction of *chez parents* and said he was joining his wife's family who were already American citizens. He had the notarized voucher from his brother-in-law to prove it. He even had a destination: Pickering Pleasure Pier, Ocean Park, California.

On the Pickering Pleasure Pier, my grandmother's older brother owned a cigar stand. He was a naturalized American citizen now, sporting the name Arthur Clark, much as he might have worn a *boutonniere*, something fresh and decorative. Their family name, Kouleksezian (which Haig told my aunt means "the one without an ear," no doubt commemorating some ancient anguish) was a name they all dropped with a thud, and once they arrived in Los Angeles, Haig followed his brother's lead and became Harry Clark; my grandmother became Helen Clark Kalpakian. But, before he was Arthur Clark, Asdoor Kouleksezian had fled Turkey in 1907. He bribed his way out of the country and on to the steamer where his sister was a passenger. She was going to America to marry, in fact, Arthur's former English teacher (who also later filed down all the rough edges of his name to John Vanes Boyd). As a woman, she was allowed to leave, but Asdoor was male and of military age, and so, forbidden. Although Arthur managed to escape, the family suffered for his success. My grandmother spent two days at the Congregationalist minister's house while the Turkish police came and searched her family home and interrogated the rest of them.

There is a photograph of my grandmother's mother and her sister taken just before their parting in 1907, a stained and sepia, heartbreaking photograph. You can see in their eyes they know they will never meet again. They hold hands and stare forward, the girl's young face expressionless, the mother's brows twisted with sorrow.

This is the only photograph my grandmother had of either of her parents, one of perhaps three or four old country photographs she had at all. At the end of her life, writing at my aunt's behest, she said they buried all other photographs in Adana so that the Turks should not find them and know what the family looked like, pursue even those who had escaped to America. They buried their pictures in Turkey, but their bodies are buried in Los Angeles. This sister and brother were much older and died within months of each other in 1939. My grandmother and Haig died within months of each other in 1987.

But in 1923, Arthur Clark, his sister and her husband were prosperous American citizens and they vowed before a Los Angeles notary that the Kalpakians and Haig would not become a public nuisance nor a charity. They gave the exiles an address, a destination, a prospect of home: Pickering Pleasure Pier, Ocean Park, California.

So I imagine my grandparents and Haig, standing in endless queues, booking passage, filling out forms, paying the obligatory bribes, waiting endlessly at the American Consulate and dealing with men like Vice-Consul Th. Murphy (no doubt pale, dyspeptic, and bothered by the flies in this city). I imagine my family tolerating the endless delays and frustrations of getting their papers in order, all the while silently moving their lips around the unfamiliar syllables, *Pickering Pleasure Pier Pickering Pleasure Pier.* Did Haig, after what he had seen in his nineteen years, did he believe a pleasure pier could exist? Did my grandmother? The young woman in the passport picture clearly does not believe in pleasure piers. And when they returned at night to rue patchadji, No. 46, walked up the three flights, ate their evening meal off the four little plates (blue on the bottom, white on the top), their spoons clanking, did they wonder — the dapper husband, the haunted wife, the boy who'd been a slave — perhaps more to the point, did they dare to say, to speak, to ask: *do the waves rush under the high wooden boardwalk at the Pickering Pleasure Pier? Does the white foam swirl around tarred pilings where unlovely barnacles cling, slaves to the tide? Do electric lights reflect, bright and staccato, upon the water? Do the gulls soar high overhead and the moths zap themselves silly against the electric lights? And are there booths along the Pleasure Pier, their shelves all lined with rosy kewpie dolls, and nearby, at the dance pavilion, do girls in short skirts and high heels sway in the arms of young men with slick hair and cigarettes? And does the music from the tinny orchestra rise above the surf, breaking in long gray-and-white formations, rolling in below the pier, the salt-smell rising? Can you hear the music from the beach? Does Barney Google with his goo-goo-googly eyes? Does he? Is that what they do on the Pickering Pleasure Pier in Ocean Park, California?* Is that what they said? Were there words for such vanities? Amongst them, these people spoke Armenian, Turkish, Kurdish, French, English and Arabic; were there words for such vanities in any language they could possibly have spoken? Were there words at all? Or did the silence already reign?

By 5 July 1923, only one thing remained to be accomplished before they could leave for America: Form 139, to be completed before Mr. H. Brumley, another American Vice-Consul. This was the Declaration of a Manufacturer, Owner, or Duly Authorized Agent of Either, Covering Goods Shipped Without Sale. My grandfather swore (duly) he would not sell any of these goods; they were household effects only. The goods were to be shipped to my grandfather's cousin's in-laws (ah, the uses of the diaspora), rug merchants on Broadway in Manhattan. For a fee of $2.50 paid in stamps, H. Brumley believed him. (One wonders if the Americans picked up the casual habits of bribery; odd, how money is the truly universal language.) Everything in these three bales is carefully itemized, its worth noted in Turkish *piasters,* its value calculated by Mr. Brumley. Only two items had zero value: a small pack of photographs, and one *Diploma, American School.* This was probably the most valuable thing they declared (not that they took with them, but that they declared; there is a difference) because it meant my grandmother spoke English.

The inventory itself is three pages long, two columns each. The wonder to me, is that there was so much. They had only been married since 1917, had fled Adana in the night, and lived four months in Syria, one year in Constantinople, but they nonetheless had this much to pack, ship, and declare? The inventory itself supports my grandfather's oath that these are household goods: 60 collars for men (600 piasters), 41 pairs of stockings (30 piasters), one cap velvet (50 piasters), 1 brilliant bedstead belt (100 piasters), 6 pairs of gloves (70 piasters), 24 chemises, bodices and drawers (1200 piasters), 27 books (300 piasters), 2 paintings (100 piasters). I cannot help but wonder: what possible paintings were these, so cheap they cost less than the sixty collars for men and which 27 books did he ship? One package envelopes (30 piasters), 2 white curtains (75 piasters), 22 napkins, 1 tablecloth and 9 baby hats. They declared many things enigmatic to me: 1 impermissible for women? Two yards of tanjib, 3 tepsi, 1 petrole ojak, 2 tenjeres, 1 copying machine (60 piasters), 3 kelpetin and keser? Apart from those enigmatics, so much here is pathetic: one piece of sponge (20 piasters), 1 broom (10 piasters), 4 pieces of soap, some thread for stockings, one little box each tea and coffee, 1 kilo sugar, 2 kilos bulgur, 12 cups for tea and 4 little plates. These little plates, blue on the bottom, white on the top, are dented and chipped, but they do not break and they are still useful now, all these years later. The most valuable things the Kalpakians shipped were rugs. Many rugs. All three bales were wrapped in rugs and there were rugs inside the bales, and these old country rugs, itemized separately, totaled many thousand piasters.

But what is not on this declaration is any jewelry whatever. Not a single ring or pin or bracelet, though we know they brought such things because they gave each of their four daughters two old country gold bracelets on their wedding days. The jewelry remaining in my grandmother's estate after her death (those final salutes to silence) was all appraised as having primarily antique value and judged to be over a century old: old country, old workmanship, old stones, old everything, but not declared on this old inventory. However, they did declare 4 cache-corsets (100 piasters). I can imagine the uses to which a cache-corset might be put. Perhaps the Romanov women were wearing cache-corsets, when, as has lately come to light, they were executed, and the bullets ricocheted all over, astonishing their executioners. These men found on their corpses that Russia's royal women had sewed jewels to their bodices: jewels insufficient finally to protect them, or to buy their way out of Russia, or even to prevent their being shot, but enough to stun their executioners.

In my grandmother's cache-corset (never mind she was pregnant again), and, I suspect, sewed into her pockets and the seams of her clothing, were these rings and earrings, bracelets and brooches, the last few of which turned up, (undeclared), after her death. She was a very organized woman (alas, a trait I did not inherit) and before her death she parcelled everything out, arranged her will, all personal property as though she were going on a long journey. Everything but these rings. Everything but the last of the jewelry they had brought, undeclared, to help achieve their dreams. *Assimilate. Assimilate.* And they did. Within two years of their arrival in Los Angeles, my grandfather bought his own business, a cigar stand on Venice Beach. By 1928, five years after their arrival, he bought a grocery store. In 1931 they bought a house — cash — and a new Pontiac, this while Depression gripped the country. The little grocery stores he owned were all modest; my grandmother worked in all of them; sometimes the girls worked in them after school. They brought their four daughters up as Protestants — no incense and incantation for them (though my grandparents remained close to the Apostolic faith). The girls all had American names and clothes and friends and education: two went to USC, two to UCLA, all married men with Anglo names. My grandparents achieved their dreams, paid for these achievements not only with unremitting work, but with the goods left undeclared, the rings and brooches and bracelets. In the old country, bribery was the accepted, expected practice — and who knows, perhaps they found that true in America as well.

My grandfather sold some of the valuable rugs (never mind what he'd sworn to Mr. Brumley in Constantinople). But many of these rugs still remain in my home, in my siblings' homes, in my cousins' homes, cousins who (like my siblings and I) all have Anglo last names, Anglo first names, some even have fair hair and blue eyes. So assimilated are we, so ignorant of all that pall of innuendo attached to being an Armenian, even a "starving Armenian," that when a college acquaintance once remarked to me, in a derogatory fashion, that it took two Jews to beat an Armenian, I had no idea what he meant. No idea at all.

Clearly, they were not impoverished, but they came third class just the same. They sailed on a Greek ship, the SS *Constantinople*, delayed at sea (by weather? by mechanical failure?) arriving at Ellis Island, New York, one day later than scheduled, August 2, 1923.

There, disembarking proceeded by class, first class first, naturally. From Ellis Island they could see the Manhattan skyline and in August their clothes would have baked against their skin, despite the open windows, the high ceilings, the overhead fans creaking at Ellis Island. They must have watched with increasing horror as the passengers were processed, because by the time they got to third class, the quota had been filled and they were denied entry. Deported.

In the silence that surrounds my family's past, we hear no tears, no gnashing, no moaning, no wailing, no swearing over their being deported, not a single curse to register all that hope and effort expended into failure. We hear a funny story! The sole bit of this experience broken off, supplied with an exclamation point, and told to amuse the children was the story of my grandmother's being so happily surprised when she turned on the tap at Ellis Island — and out came hot water! Hot running water! Imagine that!

This — the hot running water! — is the sole anecdote to emerge from that experience: five people (five and a half if you count my aunt, born January, 1924) deported. The Kalpakians' was a one-way passport out of Turkey, so they could not return there. However, the steamship company had an agreement with the U.S. Government: they must carry back to the point of origin anyone Immigration deemed unfit to enter. (Usually this was the elderly, the lame, the mad, the criminal, or senile, but in the Kalpakians' case, they were the merely superfluous.) As the ship was a Greek liner, the Kalpakians went to Greece and their passport is duly stamped on 31 August 1923 to indicate they were provisionally admitted to Piraeus, Greece.

What the hell did they do in Piraeus? That's what I want to know. The household goods, three bales, had all gone on to New York City while they lived in Piraeus and did — what? Walked the harbor? Walked the beaches? Camped in a hotel room while my grandfather stood in more queues, perhaps offered more bribes, parted with more of his cache (because they were not allowed to take money out of Turkey, and now they had to live in Greece) while he bought new tickets, booked new passage. Second class. No more costly economies. On 13 September they boarded the *SS Canada*, a French ship, to make one more sweep across the Atlantic, trying to get to the Pacific, to the Pickering Pleasure Pier in Ocean Park, California.

My family next appear to me on the Manifest of Alien Passengers for the United States Immigration Officer at the Port of Arrival, Providence, Rhode Island, October 1, 1923, page 90.

This manifest is a wonderful document: noisy, convivial, intimate, expressive, evocative. There are eleven people on page 90, women mostly — Armenians, Jews, Greeks, Romanians. There were the fiancées, two Greeks and an Armenian, young women in their early twenties, Sourpig Hartounian to marry a man living at 207 East 29th Street, New York City; Helene Karakassi to marry a man who lives in Toronto; Androniki Manolakaki to marry a man whose name has already been anglicized to James Michael, in Rocks, Pennsylvania. Androniki is illiterate, as are the two Romanians, a mother and daughter, Mathilda, 39 and Rona, 65, going to join Mathilda's husband, Maier Zammer at 1208 Adams Street, Brownsville, Texas. In an official hand it's noted that Rona is senile. Was she? Or did this merely mean that Rona gibbered in Romanian, that she could comprehend nothing, no sign, no instructions, that she wept without reason, looked confused and was elderly? Also there are two Jewish sisters going to join a brother in Montreal, Refka Cohen, age 36, a teacher, who, the manifest tells us, speaks English and her sister, Cencha Cohen, 25.

This manifest momentarily breaks the silence. I know what Mathilda and Rona and Refka looked like, at least I know their height and coloring, their complexions, their eyes and hair. And I can hear their voices: the babble of second class, where Sourpig could speak Armenian at last without fear of reprisal, where Refka might have practiced her English with my grandmother, where Rona might still have sung in Romanian despite her having come most recently from Smyrna, Turkey. Perhaps all these women, whatever their language, helped to amuse my mother (now a toddler, nineteen months) or my aunt, a sturdy five-year-old, amused them in the way that children can be, without language of any sort, with rag dolls, or shadows on a wall. Perhaps the fiancées compared fiancé stories (how different will Rocks, Pennsylvania be from Crete?) and perhaps young Helene Karakassi flirted with Haig who was 19. Perhaps my grandfather told Mathilda his parents had gone to Romania, and perhaps all these people patched together their brief, forced camaraderie in any language that came literally to hand — gestures, or expressions, smiles, laughter. Or, it might also be these women were not given to laughter, but like my grandparents and Haig, were human debris in the wake of the First World War, exiles, refugees, looking *for something somewhere, looking for something, someplace that we can live or do something.*

After they departed the *SS Canada*, these voices disappear into another kind of diaspora, the North American diaspora, and now, of course, seventy-plus years later, all of these women have gone to that last country from whence no one returns. Perhaps they, like my grandparents, kept their silence to the end, but here on this manifest, their voices rise off the page, ascend out of the past and I hear everything: the hope and fear, leaving home and going home, all at the same time.

Helene Karakassi told Immigration she had $8. Sourpig Haroutunian had $35, and each of the Cohen sisters had $50. Androniki had $20 and the Romanian women between them had $300. My grandfather had $735. Where did this money come from? I am especially intrigued since they could not take money out of Turkey, so it must have been exchanged in Piraeus. (A ring, a bracelet, something removed from the cache-corset?)

Immigration then asked them the name and address of their closest relatives in the country from whence they had come. All these women have long, chatty answers from which I can discern enough to imagine the homes they left behind. After the Kalpakians' name, there is a pathetic, *Nobody.* They had no one in Greece; they had only the Pickering Pleasure Pier which must have beckoned and winked at them, the possibilities now so close as they processed off the *SS Canada.*

Question 26: Have you ever been deported from the United States? All the women say *No* but my grandparents say *Yes, August 1923,* and no doubt my grandmother's schoolgirl English stood the test of explanations, how they had been deported because of quotas and not for any of the reasons listed below: had they ever been in prison, insane, or supported by charity? *No.* Were they anarchists? *No.* Were they polygamists? *No.* Did they believe in or advocate the violent overthrow of the U.S. Government? *No.* Were they deformed or crippled and if so, the nature and length of time and cause. *No.* Question 20: Whether alien intends to return to country whence he came? *No.* Question 21: Whether alien intends to become citizen of the United States. *Yes.* Question 22: Length of time alien intends to reside in the United States. My grandfather replied *indefinitely* and in the line behind him, the fiancées and the Cohen sisters took his cue, and by their names it is also written, *indef.* But when the immigration officer asked this question of the Romanian women, both illiterate and one suspected of senility, two women en route to Brownsville, Texas, their reply is a heartbreaking, *always*.

No one was going as far west as Ocean Park, California. No one had the ineffably romantic destination of Pickering Pleasure Pier, but first the Kalpakians took the train to New York, to the cousin's in-laws on Broadway to pick up their three bales of household goods all wrapped in rugs. They stayed in a hotel, and from these first few nights in the new country, the only anecdote that emerges, trussed up with its exclamation point, again has to do with the plumbing. In the hotel we're told how impressed my grandmother was with the bathtub and the hot running water! Hot water and a bath tub right there in your room! We're never told how she felt when she finally closed that bathroom door, ran that hot water in the tub and took off her heavy traveling clothes from her pregnant body, the cache-corset with all the goods they had failed to declare, the rings and brooches that had bit into her flesh and caused her to cry, with pain, fear, with anxiety, to cry now with relief, with joy, to cry for the ones who were left unburied, for the siblings she was going to see after fifteen years, for the husband and brother and two daughters brought to this safety, for the child she was yet carrying. Did she turn on the hot water, and let it thunder into the tub to cover up the sound of her weeping? In all my life I never saw my grandmother cry. At my grandfather's funeral, she alone remained dry-eyed.

The silence ends with their arrival in Los Angeles. In their new home there is lots of talk, all in English — *assimilate assimilate* — and many snapshots and occasions and anecdotes and relatives with whom they could alternately be convivial and quarrel. Wisps of the old country penetrated, punctuated with exclamation points, but no one ever told us the unvarnished truth, and as I said, I grew up not knowing that it took two Jews to beat an Armenian. So I was very surprised when, at the age of 19 I attended a class, or a tea or some such college event at the home of a professor. I was a typical California university student of that vintage, standing by the fireplace awaiting my ride. The professor and his wife had a foreign student boarding with them and he came home, into the livingroom, spoke to me cordially, and I replied in kind. He was a nice enough young man, a graduate student in agronomy, well mannered with an odd accent. I asked where he was from. *Istanbul,* he replied. I said my mother had been born in Istanbul. *Ah,* said he, brightening, *are you Turkish? No,* I replied, *I am Armenian,* and instantly — like voltage applied to my hands and feet and temples — immediately I knew enough to loathe him, and to know that he despised me. No more was said.

What had transpired between us had to do with the Allied defeat at Gallipoli, with the German and his horse; it had to do with Haig watching his father die of starvation and his mother stripped naked before she was killed; it had to do with Miss Towner saving my grandmother's life, offering her sanctuary at the Adana Girls' Seminary, and my grandfather paying $50 for her hand in marriage. It had to do with leaving home in the middle of the night, pressed with gun butts onto a train heading to Syria, and to do with the *Bucovina* plying the Aegean toward Constantinople, where my mother could be born. It had to do with this precious passport, now in my hands, stamped by the Turkish police, allowing the Kalpakians to leave the country where they had lived all their lives and yet remained foreign, where they had a language they could not speak, a religion they could not practice, and two thousand years of culture they had to shroud. It had to do with the haunted look on my grandmother's face and her refusal, till the day she died, to admit she was haunted. It had to do with carrying what you could not declare, not only literally — the rings and bracelets, the last few of which still clanked and rattled after their deaths — but metaphorically, spiritually.

It had to do with events so monstrous and cataclysmic they could not be silenced, and if for my grandparents, their old country past existed only to be ignored, denied or repudiated, nonetheless it dripped down, the past did, silent as the intravenous bag beside the patient's bed, the bag itself out of sight, the fluid going directly into the vein. I have inherited things from the people in this passport photo, things besides their olive complexions, their dark eyes, dark hair, their facility for languages. Instinctively I define myself in opposition to what's around me, a foreigner's reflex, not a native's. I carry that thin strain of sadness I sense in every other Armenian I have met, like an extra chromosome in the blood, that sadness, as though we somehow all have knowledge of events in which we did not participate. I keep secrets.

Can the past be cherished if it is not preserved? Can it be preserved if it is not cherished? Can it be either, if no words are fastened to it for shape and texture? I would say probably yes to all those questions. I would say for my family, the notion of homeground was not at all solid like the real estate they bought in Los Angeles, but home ground up, carried like sand or lint or ash, something gritty and secret, caught in your clothes, in the seams and pockets, under your fingernails, in the cache-corsets of your mind, the undeclared regions of the heart, clinging there indelibly, no matter how much hot water you use to wash it off.

Pakradouhi Kalpakian, the author's mother, became a naturalized U.S. citizen in 1943, changing her name officially to Peggy. Laura Kalpakian took her mother's maiden name when she began to write.

LAWRENCE DiSTASI

HOME NOT HOME

i am home not home. sitting in my aunt's kitchen in the cold light of a late winter morning. her long, upstairs flat is quiet with the others gone — my sister and cousins at parochial school, my uncle downtown to his insurance office — with here my aunt ironing from a huge pile of underwear and sheets and white shirts, humming softly as she sips every now and then from a cup of black coffee and eyes zi'giorgina, great spinster aunt with a pot between her rolled-stocking knees, snapping beans to clean into a colander. she looks at me oddly now and then, the old lady, and for a minute i fear it's with something like knowledge; not my kind of knowledge — i am doing my latin assignment, trying to learn the imperfect of the fourth conjugation — but hers. the italian kind that understands shame. the shame of my being here for one, my aunt waiting on me hand and foot, while in the night, i keep trying to slip into her daughter's bed; who shrugs me away as soon as she wakes but i keep trying, i am obsessed with trying. and ashamed. of it. of the traces of it maybe on the very sheet she's ironing. of my very being.

   here. i am living here; boarding here; my sister and i both. charity cases, because we have no home. or rather, our home, the one we have always had albeit in different places, has come apart. my father's construction business — of which he knows nothing, construction — has come apart and he can't make the bills. can't even pay the rent on our apartment. two houses custom-built, but neither customer will pay because of problems. the doctor's house on lake forest, a seven room all-on-one-floor ranch style beauty, has turned sour. wet. water keeps flooding the basement, from that *porca miseria* of a lake my father curses. we have even tried living there, my brother and i, for a week trying to keep the place dry long enough to con the doc into making the final payment but it hasn't worked. sump pumps, bailing cans, mopping, caulking, nothing worked. the water kept seeping in and so, like water unstoppable, the doc came to inspect, went into a tirade about amateurs building houses, and refused to pay. now all the subcontractors are suing too, my father's partners are bailing out, and he is left with the albatross — a custom house with no customer, nothing to pay the subcontractors, the rent, nothing to support a family of five children.

"what the hell are we going to do," i could hear my mother wail each night. "don't worry about it, damn it, i'll take care of it," he roared. and he did. "we go live in staub's house" he was smiling it two nights later. "it'll be like camping. we take the kids and we live in it till he pays. *fa'n cul'*. the sheenie won't pay, we live in his house."

"are you *pazz'*? how are we going to live there? on what? we can't drop a crumb in the place or it'll never get paid for! and besides, this one has to go to harding, how the hell is he going to get all the way across town?" it took three days for a solution: "we just take the three — gino's going to bassick so it's nearby — and elena and the baby — and stay there. the kid and rose can live with my brother a while. it won't be long. guaranteed. it'll be like camping out."

that's what baby tommy had yelled. "yea! camping out. we're going camping!" and he and elaine had danced to that. not me. me and my sister were being parceled out, and she too had taken up the idiot cry: yea. yea.

what yea? you mean we're splitting up?

"it's not like that," my mother soothed. "it'll be fun. for a few weeks only. you practically live there anyway, half of last year you spent there — what's the big deal?"

it was true. i had come to live with my aunt for several months

last year because i was so skinny the doctor said i needed protein. so
my aunt and uncle said let him come, we love him, the kids love him,
he'll fill out in no time. i didn't mind a bit. their house, unlike ours,
was almost normal. my uncle dressed in a tie every morning to go to
work. my aunt, american-born, stocked american goods: ice cream;
peanut butter and jelly; ginger ale! and for me it was extra helpings
all the time. have more steak. have more pork chops. have more corn.
i did, and it was paradise.

but this was different. this was broke, broken, with no fix in sight.
besides, i was in high school now. it was bad enough the razzing i got
for being small; skinny; buck teeth. what would chernicki say if he
ever got wind i was so poor i had to ship out with relatives? christ.
what would the girls say? the chewing gum girls i was always longing
after, and who sometimes turned to me and smiled that funny "are
you old enough?" smile, and now wouldn't.

but i couldn't say any of that. because my mother was already crying. and my father had slammed out the door to go for "a few brews."
adding the finality of it: "we're moving next week. period."

i couldn't make it worse. all i could do was contemplate this final
humiliation, and remember all the others.

we'd moved every two years ever since i could remember. he was always coming home, it seemed, working us up about "what do we
need this shitbox for? can you tell me that? what do we need this?"
she could never say. she would just sigh, and continue stirring a pot,
or folding the diapers. and wait to hear what he'd found this time.

the first time i remember it came shortly after my second sister
was born. i think my mother was barely home from the hospital
when he started in about the damn landlord. *cafones.* with their
cafone of a chow dog. we're getting out.

out? leaving? it was the only home i knew: the big stone porch on
the corner of salem and madison, in bridgeport's north end where
mostly italians lived. with uncle hector in a nice flat only a couple of
blocks away. with down the street the corner drugstore, owned by a
bald jewish guy who said *che si dice?* as we bought licorice cigarettes
in those little capitol boxes, a penny apiece. and a block further we
bought our clothes from mr. schul in his store that always smelled of
new clothes and mothballs, and faintly of something else, maybe cab-

bage, with the clothes boxes piled high on shelves everywhere, and spilling as he pried one out to show her, saying the same thing every time, "this, mrs., *this* is a material, pure corduroy, it'll last forever." and she would say something about it being too expensive, but would usually buy it 'cause times were pretty good with the shop in the front of the flat where my father did ladies' hair and it was easy for her to slip in to do the manicures or dye jobs he would never do. and down the street, on salem, the house of the mayor — bridgeport's most famous citizen, jasper mclevy, a few doors away. which my father didn't care he called him a cheap scottish bastard and a socialist besides who won every election being cheap. "god put the snow there," my father would mimic him, "let god take it away." cheap sonofabitch. but i didn't care. i was only in first grade. king of the playground. fastest runner. smartest in the class. toughest in my gang. it was the golden age as far as i was concerned; salem and madison, stone or no, was the age of gold.

not to him. "what do we need this shitbox for?"

she didn't say. so we moved, to fairfield, sunset drive — the first of our homes with a street that sounded like magazines. which to me was like outer space. in first grade and doing splendidly, after we moved i hit my first failure — a "u" in math. making up my own system, the teacher said, perfectly consistent, but wrong. still, it was only a small failure, and we had a whole house for the first time we were growing into, and me not lamenting much the passing of the golden age. there were other things to think about like older kids with slingshots who could make you do anything they wanted including feel up your own sister while they watched. and pigs squealing at tobacco road places down the street and mckesson and robbins across king's highway with guinea pigs and rabbits big as dogs in their lab, their eyes so big you almost expected to hear them rant, as he did: "what's keeping us in this shitbox? caged up with *cafones* like this?" she didn't say, but we all knew what was coming.

stratford. another fair name on the other side of bridgeport, the northeast side though i didn't know that then. to me it was but another foreign, floral universe — rosedale lane. and another school. and another teacher. and a fife and drum corps my brother and i joined to play in memorial day parades. and other neighbors in bigger houses. whiter. ranch style. american. with the war on and him railing about that goddamn roosevelt and his goddamn war and what's wrong with mussolini, at least he got the trains running on time. and our doberman trained for war who wore a path around the house doing guard duty. though i didn't care about war. what i cared about was walking to school a mile or so and in the fall watermelons to pick in nearby fields. which one day we picked several of and dawdled eating to get to school just as the bell was ringing us late! terrified to enter. so my big-mouth brother formed a plan: "we don't go. we come in after lunch. say we were sick." younger, mike and i agreed. but my teacher only smiled funny: just bring a note from your mother, she said. who wouldn't do it — my mother: "*you* told the lie, *you* get out of it." the worst was, the others told the truth so they got off free. me, i stuck with the plan and had to stay after all the next week to make up every bit of time. hard lessons in betrayal. better lessons in the basement lab. watching his quest for the permanent wave getting closer. cleaner. clean in that basement the house was nearly new, his partner young the nights late the fumes in beakers exotic why not stay? we're on the way to finding the permanent wave, the non-toxic one a little cleaner and we'll be rich, why not stay? "because i don't like this two-bit dining room that's why. why wait? why live in a two-bit place like this that's no bigger than a railroad flat?" but it's ours; there's no problem paying the mortgage; why go into something bigger? because it's time that's why. the time being 1945. which i know because one day he came home happier than he'd been in a long time. "the sheenie finally croaked," he said. he meant the president. who wasn't a sheenie but who died in his sleep. and my father drank a toast. and we all danced in the street with our neighbors across the street who didn't like him either. dancing roosevelt's death: it's the last thing about that house i remember.

soon as we got into the next place though, nobody complained. it was our best house. cleveland avenue, a real street name again, presidential, though to me at the time it just sounded like leaves. trees. which it was. the house big, eight rooms with full dining room and sun porch and a backyard a mile long with cherry trees. and the rooster river running rampant during hurricanes nearby. with a white bridge over the street you could hide under playing ring-a-lievio at night, and a rat-infested culvert nearby leading off beneath yards to a vacant lot blocks away. terrifying. we'd get torches and pick our way through hearing the scurrying of furry things that scared us to pissing our pants but compelled to do it, explore, somehow get through. and my grandfather pissing out the upstairs bedroom window when he'd wake in the night drunk on wine. which one night killed him i guess. and i heard grown men, my uncle and father, crying for the first time. death. it had reached me finally, reached mine. even so that house was the best. ice-skating on the country club pond in winter. trick or treating at the big houses nearby on halloween. caddying round hot, golf-course fairways for sleek, blond ladies in summer.

it was also the worst, a whiff of the end. my mother fell and broke her back; took half the year to convalesce; the elders meanwhile doing the cooking, the cleaning, the taking care of the kids. she recovered only to be followed by him. felled by a heart attack: the old ticker. we had no idea what it meant except that there was worry. the mortgage. him recovering on the phone all day trying to score a hit at the track to catch up. it didn't work; only got him further behind. before long, it was the old refrain: "what do we need this for? we get a rental, get caught up, then we'll be on easy street."

louisiana ave. it was called, which did in fact have "easy" in it and i wondered how he knew. not that it mattered; it was a garden apartment that never seemed quite ours; like the new ford he got easy on credit that was soon not ours either; it was repossessed. still, there were woods nearby, beardsley park with its zoo nearby, my aunt's house nearby, and stick ball and softball and roller derby on the smooth macadam sidewalks and summers in the woods exploring with girls growing swells never seen before, and my cousin after piano lessons whispering about hair there, and how her friend had it too, and did i? sort of, i lied. and we explored. and i couldn't get it out of my mind: hair. there. incredible, unlikely hair. it seemed like home.

it wasn't. her hair wasn't home, and her house wasn't home, and i knew it somewhere as i knew in some shamefilled, awful way that the end had begun and i would never — despite one more move — get home again.

i don't know how i knew, or if i really knew it all then. i don't know. maybe in that morning kitchen all i knew was that *she* knew — the old lady. because she was in the same boat. this was her home now, after living with us forever she had been farmed out too: "we've had her all these years, had ma and pa and her too," my mother had stamped. "let someone else take her for a while." and though i never heard her win an argument with my father before, this one she won. maybe because he'd had another heart attack. maybe because with our home about to come apart he couldn't fight it anymore. maybe because he was tired of the old lady too.

whatever it was, she was living with my aunt when i was shipped back and something told me she knew what was coming. for her and for me. no home in this world, never mind this bread-warm kitchen, never mind the steam puffing from my aunt's iron in comforting panting rhythm, never mind the panting rhythm of my desperate breathing as i roamed those halls hot and obsessed at night — it wouldn't be long.

and her beans snapping seemed to tap out the refrain: it's never too long.

"not too long before lunch," my aunt was smiling fatly over a white sheet she was folding. "i've got some roast peppers from last night, how 'bout those on some nice bread?"

"sure," i smiled, not looking up. because in those hungry days i could eat lunch here, and then during gym wolf down the sandwiches she'd given me, and then say 'sure' at five or so to a snack before supper. and then do some homework and maybe help my cousins with theirs and end with a bedtime treat and wait as my breathing got tighter for lights out and my shameful ingrate roaming would begin. unhoused. unhomed. as i was now, and ever would be. still not knowing what awful knowledge i had imbibed in that morning kitchen, but knowing only that somehow, now, i knew.

home was not something you left like odysseus leaving for troy, and after weeping on beaches and exploring with goddesses and going through hell and back, finally got to return to.

nor was it the village left in italy my father never stopped tantalizing us or himself with, and swore each year to return to, but never did.

in bridgeport, in my time, home was what left you.

Russell Leong

Paper Houses

Last year, on a whim, I went to the fabled Malibu retreat for an after-noon meditation held by Thich Nhat Hanh, the Vietnamese Buddhist teacher and monk. I told my lover, Jandro, who was driving a Toyota: let me count the number of BMWs and Volvos in the parking lot and I will tell you the composition of the audience. I was skeptical, even cynical as a new Buddhist, but Jandro, being Catholic, let out a big laugh. "Incense or censer — everything looks the same in all that smoke and mumbling!"

We were not the first in the dusty parking lot. A convoy of pastel-colored BMWs, Mazda Miatas, and other imports had preceded us. Couples walked ahead. They were mainly white, with a few mixed white/Asian couples — average age, thirty-eight. The men were mostly blonde Nordic types: long-sleeved white cotton or taupe linen shirts rolled back to the elbows, thin expensive watches, tan slacks, and Birkenstock sandals. The Asian American females — Japanese and Chinese — were lean and toned with shiny black hair cascading over their gauzy Indian tunics and tight body leggings. No obvious makeup over their glowing New Age complexions. The half-dozen

African Americans that attended were black males accompanied by white fe-males.

Jandro and I ran into Pama, a Thai friend of mine. The three of us made our way to the grassy knoll and set down our blankets, pillows, and jackets. Clusters of people around us were al-ready munching on granola bars or swilling bottled water. Many were wear-ing crystal *malas* or sandalwood rosaries around their necks along with New Age healing gems of amethyst, rutilated quartz or topaz dangling on black leather cords.

We had forgotten about preparing food and had bought a large bag of barbecued potato chips, carbonated drinks, and hot dogs at a roadside stand. As we opened our paper bags the people around us began to stare. Others had brought wholesome vegetarian dishes in plastic containers — tofu and grains in assorted forms, cut apples and carrots, and fruit drinks. Here we were, perhaps the only Asian threesome out of three hundred people, eating the most processed food. Pama stared back at them, but soon embarrassed, she slipped the greasy hot dog out of the bun and ate the bread and relish alone. Jandro and I thought to hell with the vegetarian voyeurs and noisily chomped down the rest of the hot dogs and salty orange-dyed chips.

The meditation retreat and lecture began when French and American monks and nuns wearing traditional gray Vietnamese garb took their places around the dais. The French were from Plum Village, the monastery Thich Nhat Hanh had established in France to do his work outside of Viet Nam. The monks and nuns gave a pitch for supporting the work of Plum Village, and then they spoke of the significance of Thich Nhat Hanh's worldwide efforts for peace. (He was nominated for a Nobel prize.) They seemed sincere, yet obviously they had spoken these sentences many times before. After a sitting meditation led by the French nun, Thich Nhat Hanh was introduced by an American male aide. He was a slight, smiling man in a brown robe who appeared direct in manner and unencumbered by his fame or retinue of French and American devotees.

Thich Nhat Hanh began to speak. I remembered only one thing that he said out of that hour: his story of flower and compost. He said that many admire the beauty and fragrance that emanate from flowers. Yet flowers by their nature decay finally: leaf and stamen, filament and anther, pistil and petal lose moisture, crumple and fall to the ground. I glanced at the nape of Jandro's smooth neck, imagining my hand caressing it. Jandro loved flowers, buying them, arranging them, bringing them as gifts to others. Listening to the monk at that time, I had not yet experienced that family, friends or lovers could also flourish, wither, and die. I could not know then that

Jandro would leave this world, and me, a few weeks later.

Perhaps it is not surprising that I was drawn to Thich Nhat Hanh, because he was a Vietnamese. Viet Nam had figured strangely in my life as a young man — in the form of Tet, which is the Vietnamese name for the lunar New Year celebration, and which was also the Vietnamese Communist Offensive during the war a quarter of a century ago. I remember, as an American college student, protesting the Vietnam war, because I could not understand killing women and men who looked exactly like my own relatives. But even before Tet and Vietnam, as a youth in San Francisco's Chinatown, I had found myself locked in conflict.

I remember the smell of that day clearly, as pungent as the sun on the asphalt of the basketball court beside the Chinatown alley a few blocks from my family's apartment. As the basketball bounced and landed outside of the fence, I ran to retrieve it and looked up. From the alley, I could see TV antennae and United States and Chinese flags at the corners of the painted balconies unfurling in the breeze.

My white T-shirt was damp with sweat. I loved the body I inherited, the stockiness, muscular legs, and even the large forehead over my darting black eyes. My parents, who worked hard, believed that boys like me who fought right, won at cards, and played fair could fend for themselves. Sisters were another act altogether.

We played in the Presbyterian church courtyard, because in this Asian barrio of four-story walk-ups and small shops, open space was at a premium. Some of us believed in the Father, the Son, and Holy Ghost. Others came just for the space, the friendship, or to check out the girls who came on Sunday for the morning worship. We were second or third generation offspring of working-class Chinatown families descended from Cantonese peasants in Pearl River Delta.

The head of this church was a burly American reverend of Germanic descent, who was a "father" to us, especially the boys. He followed a long line of "Jesus men" — the Reverends William Speer, Otis Gibson, Ira Condit — who had come to Chinatown a century before to teach "heathens" how to pray. For these white missionaries, many of whom were previously stationed in Shanghai, Ningbo, and Canton, the Chinatowns of America were the last Chinese settlements left to conquer. Churches and mission houses duly dotted every third block of my neighborhood: Baptist, Congregational, Catholic, Adventist, Presbyterian, and the True Sunshine Mission.

The reverend ruled his Chinatown roost in a baritone voice. He had a special way of explaining the variations of love to us with Greek terms: *philia, agape, eros.* He'd take us into his office, a wood paneled inner sanctum lined with bookshelves and knickknacks, and explain doctrine and desire to us patiently. There were stories of fishermen who dropped their nets on the sand to follow Jesus. Fallen women picked up their lives and children again after meeting him. Monkeys and goats, tigers and donkeys in pairs, gingerly stepped onto the giant wooden ark fearing the violent sea beneath them. Being saved, in essence, was a matter of faith and grace that could only be accepted, not earned.

After basketball that day he called me into his office. He whispered *agape* in my ear. It was not his paternal smile or familiar words that disturbed me this time. It was another feeling that I could not name. Suddenly I felt his body — twice as wide and whiter than my real Chinese father — pressed against mine.

His litany worked its way slowly under my skin, soft shrapnel designed for a war I could not win.

"How doth move a missionary's hand?"

"Save me with your hands on my chest and legs. Promise not to tell in the name of him who died to save us all."

Were these my words or his?

"Who moves inside me, plucks ribs, forks intestines, enters esophagus, takes tongue?"

"What is a mercenary's hand doing here?"

I grasped the fingers of his hand.

"Where is the shame, what's in a name?"

"What's this evil game?"

My body tailspun like a basketball out of court. I cried foul. The invocation continued....

Flesh versus spirit.

Age versus Youth.

Christian versus Pagan.

Occident versus the Orient.

Colonizer versus the Colonized.

No one could sense my fear behind the mashing of mah-jong tiles and the buzz of sewing machines in the Chinatown alley. The litany both infuriated and intoxicated me. Mekong machetes sliced their way through bamboo. My legs ran of their own accord, but without a map I was lost. Under his irreverent hands my body slipped.

My T-shirt was sweaty and dirty. Even after I showered and washed the shirt, I could not rid myself of the nameless love and hatred that rose and stuck in my throat. I was estranged from the person I once was. Condemned to silence by the Father, Son, and Holy Ghost, I never said a word to my brother, my parents or friends. Like a chipped Chinatown roof tile unloosened, I fell from the eaves to the ground.

Ornamental figurines graced curio shops in the form of plastic mock-ivory statues of Confucius, Buddha, or Kwan-Yin — goddess of mercy. None of them would lift a hand to save me, an ordinary boy of no consequence. They were one and the same to me — interchangeable icons and images that could be bought, sold, used to decorate home altars, the top of television sets or the mantels of cramped Chinatown apartments. If Christianity betrayed my generation, Buddhism was no less alien to my nature. Buddhism was something that only white poets went to Japan or China to do. They grew beards, wore cotton robes and sandals, and made pilgrimages to Nara and Nepal between bouts of the drugs and sex of the '70s. They had no relation to me. For the most part, they regarded Asians like myself who were born in the Americas as inauthentic and immaterial. Our complex history in this country contradicted all their spiritual or aesthetic notions of orientalness.

The middle-class Mahayana Buddhist temples in Chinatown were filled with slick gold icons, red carpets, and well-dressed Asian Americans who attended services on Sundays. I sometimes visited our family association temple, with its lacquered gilt statues of Kwan-Kung, the warrior-guardian of borders and of the seas. The clicking of joss sticks and the sweetish burnt smell of incense in front of ancestral tablets on the wall hooked me in their narcotic way. But whatever moved through me was as intangible as smoke. When I left Chinatown, I did not want any more to do with religion or Asia.

During the next two decades smoke and sex obscured my life. I drifted, craving the dusky embraces of women and men. I steeped myself in alcohol, and believed, wrongly, that through another's love or loneness, I could be desired or diminished. One day desired, the next day abandoned. New York, Seattle, Taipei, Hong Kong, Naha, Tokyo, Kyoto, Los Angeles. Streets meshed and merged in five languages, then lost me again. I wandered, searching desperately for an identity and a home more hospitable than the one I had left.

In these countries so foreign to my upbringing, I gravitated to temples or gardens. Outside of Kyoto once, I was standing alone with the old granite stones in the garden at a small Zen temple, the Ohara. I realized the temple was closing for the day. Even the brown-robed monks had overlooked my silent presence, and they smiled when they discovered they had almost locked me in for the night. Maybe I should have stayed there then — joined the ancient noble family of stones — and never left. I even now remember that stillness which was not entirely empty. The dusk was filled with the summer noises of shifting branches and evening doves.

Later, and further South along the archipelago, Formosa emerged like a green turtle from the sea. Taipei, its capital, was still under martial law. No matter, I was a U.S. citizen, invincible, like all arrogant, young Americans those days. Like the Chinese and the Japanese and the French in Indochina before me, I was but the latest American colonizer of native brown bodies. One evening I remember climbing up the bamboo scaffolding of an unfinished three-story brick building with a friend. The floors were piled with dust and debris, and there were no stairways connecting the floors yet, just bluish pockets of air. We abandoned ourselves to lust, our feet and slim arms dangling over the edges of darkness. The buzzing of cicadas covered our breathing. Afterwards, we climbed down the scaffolding into that Asian city alive with streets, stairs, and signs that led home. But not to mine. There was "no place like home." Anyway, I never wanted to go home again.

I found love in other places: in alleyways, between palm trees at dusk, in barely-furnished rooms, on worn floors, and tatami mats. Sometimes I could not tell the sex of my companions, under their powder

148

and paint, until I pressed myself against their legs. I would walk towards or away from people. Other times motorbikes and their drivers would pick me off the streets and carry me to shabby alcoves in pre-World War II Japanese houses. The mama-san would leave a bucket of cold water, soap, brush, and towel for customers. I would wash and lay naked on the wooden pallet and close my eyes until I felt a stranger's breath on mine.

Some days I would take the bus. On Hsinyi Bus No. 10, I would reach the old Taiwanese section of the city, Yuan Wan, where preserved serpents in glass apothecary jars lined the storefronts of herbalists. Working girls in Japanese wooden and paper houses vied for my money and happiness.

Alongside the bus, Mormon missionaries pedaled on their bicycles, their polyester shirts soured by their large pink bodies, damp with the sweat of faith. As part of their missionary training they had to spend a year or two in a foreign country, in Asia, Africa, or Latin America. They, and the Seventh Day Adventists, competed for the island's brown souls: Taiwan mountain aborigines, innocent country folk, unrepentant bar girls. For a hundred years, as precise as German clockwork, Western soldiers and missionaries seemed to follow one another in war to Manila, Saigon, Seoul, Taipei.

In the late afternoon before the dusk cooled the streets, outside some of the older Japanese houses young girls of no more than fifteen or sixteen would dust the cobblestoned alleys clean, preparing for evening. After dusk fell, many of these same girls would smear their lips red and anoint their cheeks with rouge, and in their thin, cheap cotton dresses pull and tug at the shirt sleeves of any local man who passed through the alleys, urged on by their mama-san who took most of their meager tips. The brothel madame was usually a middle-aged, heavyset woman in a floral print dress, a brightly made up apparition who cursed at her indentured girls.

One time, I had gone up with a young woman to her reed-matted cubicle, lit by a single bulb. She dipped a white hand towel in a tin basin filled with an astringent mixture of water and vinegar, and told me to pull down my pants. I did, and she cleaned my body with the towel before she pulled up her blouse and placed my hand on her small breasts the size of half-tangerines. I tried to kiss them, but I could not get excited by her naked body. Not because of her sex, but because of her age. She looked away from me without smiling. I apologized, hurriedly put on my clothes and left ten dollars on the worn mat.

Anxiously, I paced the cobblestoned streets. I was a character in a film rewinding upon itself over and over again. Yet, I could not escape those slender white arms that tugged and pulled at my short sleeved shirt, at my chest and waist. Painted faces were the ghosts of children entangled in their bondage. They laughed at me in disdain when I ignored their pleas and the harsher cries of the older women who owned their bodies.

I found myself stumbling into a small side-street doorway, partly to escape them. It turned out to be a shelter for sailors and seafarers, to Tien Hou, goddess of sailors and protector of the seas. I fell, my knees scraping the worn brick floor of the temple. Tears began to blur my vision. I was no different than those teenage prostitutes. They also had learned to perform acts of love against their feelings.

I, too, was floating on the sea of desire with no sign of harbor. When would I return to myself? Where was my community? In Asia? In America?

As a young man in Asia, I could support myself easily in the company of older men or women. Only after I had run out of money and love and was no longer as desirable, did I return to the United States. I found odd jobs here and there: in a radio station, as a shipping clerk, newspaper assistant, and so forth. So I ended up here, in the City of Angels, as a middle-aged man, forty-four in fact. Old ways of living stayed with me, though with a twist; now I inexplicably sought out the company of much younger men, like Jandro.

Such desires diluted my prayers to Buddha, who had entered my life relatively late. It was around the time of the L.A. riots, driving down the Interstate Five freeway. The sky was smoky from days and nights of bonfires and rampage. I sought refuge in a Vietnamese Buddhist temple that a friend had introduced me to in Westminster, called "Little Saigon" by the locals. There the monk seemed to understand my wordless despair, not only at the state of the city, but at the state of my self-destructive life. The burning flames, the temple monk told me, could lead to both ruin and renewal. He told me to look at the world and myself, clearly, without judgement.

Once home, in the mirror I literally examined my body. No longer lean or agile, it was flaccid like that of the nocturnal madams whom I had encountered in red-lit alleyways years ago. I ran my hands over my shoulders, chest, belly, cock, and thighs. Sweat seeped from my skin. The trapped, stale smells of vinegar, sweat, and sex unfolded in the folds of memory. I reached for my bottle of vodka. It was already emptied.

I recalled the pummeling of the small hands of nameless girls and boys whose bodies were sold by others. With the palm of my hand I struck my face, the stinging bringing warmth suddenly back. But their bruises remained hidden within me, buried beneath the skin's surface. At least with this body, older and tougher now, I could shield each face and hand from further pain. Even the pain of a lover's death.

For shortly after the Malibu retreat that Jandro and I had both attended, he died unexpectedly, followed by the brush fires and the earthquake. It was as if the moment I turned my face away, he, the mountains, and earth changed into dust.

I returned to the temple I had fled to during the L.A. Riots. The monk allowed me to have a forty-nine day mourning service for Jandro. The forty-ninth day was the Buddhist day of reckoning for the soul of one who has died. At dusk I drove for an hour in the rain to meet his family at the temple. His mother had brought tropical orchids and incense for the altar, a three-foot cardboard and paper-mâché replica of a two-storied house, and square packets of facsimile gold and silver money to burn, as some Chinese from the old country still did. Two of the temple women took the paper items to the patio and set them ablaze with a cigarette lighter.

"Jandro will be richer in his next life," his mother assured herself, and me. But no words came to my mouth. I looked into the darkness and light. Smoke, ashes, and darkness engulfed the space. A single, lime-green orchid danced against the orange flames, separated by the thin wall of patio glass. I felt suspended in the shadow and embrace of opposing energies. Pain, pleasure, and prayer melded in that blazing transformation.

All homes in my life have now vanished: paper windows and walls gone up entirely in smoke. A return to home or childhood unsullied by loss and experience was no longer possible. Home was no longer origins, family, or friends. Neither was home the transient refuge of another's embrace or the strong arm of religious belief. I glanced down at my two bare hands. Brown skin held intact the veins, bones, and blood. I would let go of the past. I would no longer crave the future. I would live in this moment.

Sandra Scofield

Grudges: A Memoir

Two weeks out of three my grandmother came to the schoolyard at the northeast corner of the convent grounds. Those weeks she worked graveyard. She couldn't come the week she worked days, so on the Friday before she always gave me a dollar, bunched up, her hand to mine. I never told her I had trouble spending it. There was nothing to want, and no way to get it.

I was in eighth grade, a student at the Catholic academy. When I was six my mother had converted to Catholicism during one of her stays in the Catholic hospital in town. She never tired of telling me how lucky I was. The nuns, she said, were devoted to God and education, and I, a bright girl, would benefit all the way around.

My grandmother had been coming to see me in this way all year, September to April, since my mother took my little sister Faith out

to Ronan, where my father had been working for more than a year. I hadn't gone. The nuns begged my mother not to take me; I could live with them for nothing. My piano teacher said I would have a private recital this year. (I had learned to play, had practiced for two years, on a baby grand in one of their polished parlors.) My class teacher said there was a diocesan composition contest and I was a fine writer. My mother did not put up much of an argument.

She only said, "I'm afraid I won't know you anymore." We all knew that west Texas was like a Saudi desert, vast and gritty, cultureless and heathen. What was there for a fine-boned, dark-eyed sensitive wisp of a prodigy like me? How softly my mother sighed. She looked off as though there were mountains on the horizon, and she said, "I suppose you might as well stay."

It was as if heaven had opened a side door and let me enter. Convent life was full of secrets and ritual, smells of incense and wax, the creaking of a building already seventy years old. I didn't think I would miss my family. My father lived on the edges of my mother's family, always remote. My sister, pouty and plump, was four years younger, hardly a person at all. My frail mother spent her days in bed. I had already discovered Dickens, and the thick, rich soup of London life made my own existence seem hopelessly dull. It was the ordinariness of life that I minded.

Boarding school took me to higher ground, with its air of orphanhood, the Sunday hailstorms of lonesomeness, the cool, spare rituals of an ordered life. The nuns were strict but almost never scolding; I craved their approval. I rose in the dark with one or two older girls, to attend 6:30 Mass and kneel in front of all the sisters. Before school, I practiced Bach and Grieg in the front parlor. I wrote joyously, no matter what the assignment, and read like a starved child gobbling bread. I committed to memory everything that seemed to matter at all.

And there was the relief, that I wasn't really leaving my grandmother. She lived across the city in an overstuffed house in which I had spent more years in than out. With this arrangement, so sensible given her work at the mill, I would have weekends of pure pleasure. She would drive me to the barbecue place for chipped beef on a bun, and make Red Velvet Cake with cream cheese frosting. I would watch television while wrapped in one of her quilts beside her on the couch. Everything I did was important to her, laden with a special, double meaning. I might say, "We started a new art unit on perspective," and she would reply, "Your mother was always drawing as a child." I would say, "We're studying World War II now," and she'd dig around in a chest and come up with a stack of news clippings she had saved for just such a day.

How confused I was when the Mistress of Boarders, Sister Sebastian, told me gently that my mother had left explicit instructions that I was not to go to my grandmother's house. I was not to see her at all. Sister said this had already been explained to my grandmother the day my mother delivered me to the convent door. Sister added, kindly, that she had talked to my grandmother herself, on the phone. "She is very happy that you stayed with us," Sister said. Her face shone, as if sympathy were a glaze; she knew that things always happen for the best.

I saw immediately that I was left afloat, suspended between that mother and daughter who had been kicking quarrels between them for as long as I could remember. I'm not sure I thought there was anything odd about it; it was all I had ever known.

There were seven boys and twenty girls in eighth grade. The boys sat in a row along the side of the room, under the windows. They had their recess in a separate part of the grounds. This was their last year in Catholic school; the high school was for girls only. I was glad of this, although I thought to myself that girls would know how to act in public schools; boys, I had no doubt, would revert to something wild and sinful.

The girls fell neatly into two groups, one of twelve, and the other, mine, of eight. The larger group was rowdy and sometimes mean-spirited; they played tag and kickball, often bickered and threw someone out; they punched one another on the arms like boys, and teased others of us when they got the urge. In class they had to be called by name to get an answer. My coterie was of finer stuff, tender girls who tested one another's Latin declensions, exchanged scraps of art, wondered endlessly about the secrets of Fatima. Most recesses, we played Convent. We laid out our rooms with twigs and stones, and circumscribed an altar with great care. We were a contemplative order, we said; that meant we could not speak. Whole recesses went by without a word. We moved about in the Chinese shuffle of old nuns, our palms together, our heads bent. There was a young novice assigned to guard our play. She sat on a small iron bench under one of the sycamore trees, and watched us. If I looked up, she smiled. I never thought she was amused. I knew she smiled with pleasure, seeing us, like her, with our minds on God.

One of the hot, bright noons of September, Mozelle Chambers said, sibilant from behind clenched teeth, "There's this old lady watching us by the fence." Jennie Lennon said, "Shhh! Don't look!" but the spell was broken. Everyone had to turn and see.

I knew who it would be before I saw her. The cyclone fence came to a height just above her belly. She gripped the smooth top bar as I walked toward her. When I saw the look on her face, when I remembered how she loved me, I knew why I had not worried about my mother's strange proscription. Nothing would keep my grandmother from me.

She asked how school was going. I told her I was taking French with the high school juniors, and algebra with the ninth grade. She shook her head in disbelief. "I hope your mother is good and happy," she said. I reached over the fence to grasp her hands. "I'll be here tomorrow," she said. I hugged and kissed her and ran back to my friends. One of them was pretending to be the priest, passing out Necci wafers as Communion. The novice was watching.

I understood that my grandmother would come every day that she could, and I depended on her for my emotional life. We exchanged kisses. She asked how I was. (I never thought to ask her.) At first I tried to think of something special to report each day, an accomplishment from the morning's school work. I reported test grades and writing topics, and mentioned what I was reading. I told her I was the best student in eighth grade. Slowly, over a number of visits, I realized that my grandmother did not care what I said. I might have recited Sanskrit for all it mattered. After that I spoke of simpler matters. We had a toilet overflow and run into the boarders' dormitory. We found the tooth of an animal while we were looking for rocks. A pattern for the rest of our lives was set. Our dialogue was a communion rite, and not conversation at all. I did not yet realize that quarrels could take the same shape.

Our winters were characterized by bizarre fluctuations in temperature and condition. Rain turned to ice in an hour. I said to my grandmother, on one of the first cold misty days, that I had left the basement where the kids were playing, but someone would surely notice. And it was cold. If she had said, "But you must! If only for a moment!" I would have braved any weather for a quick cold clutch of mittened hands, but instead she said, "When it's too wet or cold, watch for me. If you need me, you can come out and wave and then I'll stop." At first I was baffled, but all soon came clear. My grandmother drove her pea-green Chevrolet slowly around the block. I could run from this window or that to catch a glimpse. Every few seconds she waved.

The novice watched. Neither of us mentioned it. She was bound by rules more stringent than I, and what she could ignore she surely could not deny. The whole conspiracy was a smudge on my soul; disobedience is a sin. I had pondered a life as a Carmelite. I now saw I could not bend my will so easily to authority, not even for a surer route to heaven, not even for a chance to die young of holy love.

Sister Frances, my music teacher, said to me one day in April, "The day is set, and you must call your grandmother." I was seated at the piano. The notes of my sonata seemed to wash down the page like ink in a rain. I had stopped thinking about what the nuns thought of my noon meetings; obviously, they were not going to put a stop to them. But now my chest burned with resentment toward my grandmother. Didn't she know how she pulled me from the way it was supposed to be? She didn't just ignore my mother's wishes, that was the least of it; she made me know myself as willful and sly, and not the pious child I pretended to be at all.

Sister meant no reprimand. "She can't know how talented you are if she doesn't hear you," she said. When I stood up she gave me a dime. "You can use the pay phone in the basement."

I went downstairs as soon as my lesson was done. It was five, and my grandmother would be home. It was her week for day shift.

Her voice cracked like something dry. "Oh my, oh my," she said. I strained to make her understand. The date. The time. "My mother sent money for a dress. Sister Mary's sister is making it for me, white lace and a crinoline." My grandmother was crying in little gulps, like hiccups. I was suddenly eager to flee. The phone might burst into flames. Someone might come down the stairs.

"Mommy, please," I cried. "Please come to my recital."

"I can't, baby, oh, oh," my grandmother said. She was weeping now. "Your mother forbids it."

My mother was more than three hundred miles away. "She won't know."

"I can't go against her. She's your mother. You don't understand. She has the say."

I wrote my mother, saying nothing of the recital, and asked if I might spend a weekend at my grandmother's house. I had not asked her at Christmas, when I was home. She had been in bed most of the time, with a pillow over her head. Now I told her I was lonely on the weekends. Other girls went home. I told her we ate cold suppers. Once I was the only girl left. (It was wonderful. I ate with the sisters, and then later, a novice walked with me up the street to buy a hamburger. I learned to play backgammon. Nothing like that ever happened again.)

My mother wrote back in her elegant hand that a visit was out of the question. "You're too young to understand how wicked she is," she wrote, "but I won't have it anymore."

We had lived with my grandmother off and on all my life. Only the year before, when my aunt took my sister, and my mother was in the state hospital for half a year, my grandmother and I lived together wonderfully. She traded shifts so she could work days; I rode the bus back and forth to school. I had never noticed any wickedness. I could not bear to be so ignorant.

"What did you do?" I asked my grandmother the next time I called. Now I knew it took only a dime and a few furtive moments below the dining hall. I could say things, there in the dark, over the phone, that could not be said at the fence.

My grandmother was offended. "All I ever did was try to keep us all alive."

"I don't understand!" I had been left out.

"It was what they did to her, or what she thinks they did. As if we had anything to say."

"Who? What?" I had to know.

"In the hospital." I knew she was shutting me off. She did not like to speak about painful things. "She had to blame someone, they told us. She never really got well, despite their treatments. She begged to come home." Now her voice faded. "What did we know?" she whispered. I could not speak. There was so much to know, or not to know. I held the phone, and waited. In a moment, my grandmother spoke bitterly. "Not Charlie! It wasn't *his* fault. He's never responsible for anything. It's me she chose to hate instead."

I thought of the little red leather wallet my mother brought me from the asylum. She had punched holes around the edges, and then pulled through strips of leather to bind the pieces. When I said I loved it, she said, "I don't ever want to see it again."

The week before the recital I stood on a chair in the music room while Mrs. Sayres pinned my hem. The dress scratched and crackled as I moved slowly around. I thought of myself on stage. Who would come to hear me?

Sister Frances said there would be parents of other students, and music lovers from the town. All the nuns would come. When I said my grandmother would not come, Sister Frances called her. "Who would turn her away?" she said.

I felt my heart unclench. I had thought there would be nobody who loved me to hear me play "To Spring." I tried to thank Sister. She put a finger to her lips.

The afternoon of the recital an orchid was delivered to the door. Sister Frances pinned it to my dress. It was from my grandmother. An hour later another arrived, this one from my parents. I skidded off into a child's confusion, and began to cry.

Sister Frances said she would put my mother's flower in the refrigerator, and I could wear it on Sunday, to Mass. "It will be very nice, dressed up for God."

My grandmother did not come. There was no surprise in that. We never mentioned it. On Monday she was at the fence. I leaned across and kissed her. Her cheek smelled of flour. "I didn't make even one mistake," I said.

She nodded. "I never thought it would be otherwise."

For the diocesan composition contest, I wrote an essay about Maria Goretti, a recently canonized saint. She had been a girl hardly older than I, who had died defending her purity. I suggested that Maria's holiness lay not just in her virginity (after all, I was a virgin, and hardly holy at all), but in the clarity of her perception, as though she carried her own light in her eyes.

Understanding, and then accepting — that was how you learned to do the right thing. Even if what you understood left a lot unknown. Somewhere in the balance, acceptance became faith. That was what I said.

A boy in my class, Patrick McMurtry, wrote an essay about the vocation of fatherhood. He knew quite a lot about the subject, being the third in a family of seven children. He told me that his father sat up with him talking after all the rest were in bed. He said he wrote the essay so he would not forget what his father said. His essay won first in the boys' elementary division. Sarah Applewhite wrote about the religious vocation — she was going to be a Carmelite — and won first high school girls' division. The principal of our school said I might have had first — should have had first — but the judges could not believe I had written the essay without help. When she assured them that I had worked quite on my own — after all, I lived at the school — they said I must have had a wonderful memory; my essay must have come out of a sermon I didn't remember hearing, a book I didn't remember reading.

"But Patrick is the one who had help!" I cried. I didn't envy him his family, only the prize.

Sister touched my face with her long cool fingers. "You must try to see this as a special lesson in humility. As your special opportunity."

I had lately learned that it is easy to be misunderstood, and misjudged, and that bad things can happen to you even if you try to be good. My awareness was like a great tumor, something greater than the thought of my mother dying out in west Texas. I could feel a weight in my center. This is what it's like to be grown-up, I thought: to see that nothing stays the same, that nothing changes, that these two things can both be true at the same time.

I received a letter from my father, the only one I would ever receive. He said they had moved to Odessa and had rented a house. Since they were in a city now, he said, I might want to go to school there. Mama was getting worse. She needed my help with my sister.

In a few days school would be over. I didn't know if anyone had told my grandmother I would not be back. I couldn't say it to her.

I was in study hall, conjugating reflexive verbs. I excused myself to go to the bathroom, and crept down the stairs to the front parlor, where I could look out the windows on two sides, at two streets. I simply knew I had to do this, that my grandmother would be there.

She was parked at the corner. She wasn't looking at the building. Both arms rested on the steering wheel, and her head lay against the window, to her left. I scratched at the pane where I sat. I whispered her name. She did not move, and I went back upstairs. I was afraid she had died there. I knew someone had to die, ever to resolve the differences that boxed in my life. It was a question of who, and when. I knew it would not be me.

Naomi
Shihab Nye

My Brother's
House

In the guest bedroom at my brother's brand-new house in the north
Dallas suburbs are four sets of electrical sockets with no cords coming out of them. The possibilities feel overwhelming. My brother
could plug in appliances I haven't even heard of yet.

Our 90 year-old house in inner-city San Antonio sports intricate
ugly tangles of extension cords and multiple power outlets. I am always stuffing them back under the skirt on the bed. I have heard it is
not good for one's electromagnetic field to have electrical cords criss-
crossing under your sleeping place, but have not yet learned how to
activate my reading lamp and alarm clock without them.

My brother's house smells of fresh paint and packaging — those
foam bubbles and peanuts that come in big boxes. It smells like carpet no one has ever stepped on. I cannot imagine the bravado of
white carpet. My brother prefers if you
remove your shoes at his front door. So
do I, but no one ever does it in our
house.

We have dusty wooden floors and
raggedy little rugs from Turkey and
Libya. We have throw rugs hand-knot-
ted in Appalachia in 1968. We have a
worn Oriental carpet that once belonged to my friend's reclusive father, a
famous science fiction writer. He lived
on an island all by himself. Our house

smells of incense and grandmother's attics in Illinois in the 1950s and vaguely sweetened shelf paper pressed into drawers.

My brother and his family are the first people to live in their house, which is part of a generically-named and very expensive subdivision — something like Fair Oaks (but there aren't any oaks, so it couldn't be) or Placid Plains or Rampant Meadows. They made some decisions about finishing details, deciding which wallpaper would go in the bathrooms and the shape of the pool and the color of its tiles. They chose a lion's head to be spitting water into the pool from beneath the flower bed. Even the curb beside their front sidewalk is sleek.

Our house with its high ceilings and columned wraparound front porch was built in 1905 a block from the San Antonio River by a French family that started a "Steamship and Travel Company" downtown. Their agency still exists, mailing out travel tickets in blue envelopes imprinted with elegant, floating steamships. I visit their offices, scribbling checks under the watchful portrait of the man who built our house. His eyes say, "Can't you ever stay *home*?"

Later the house belonged to his son and daughter-in-law, named Ruby, who left her screened windows open in summer, as everybody in the world used to do. She outlived both her husbands. Her rusting wedding gifts — a hand-cranked ice cream freezer, a giant oval platter — remained in their original, crumbling wrapping papers stacked out in the chicken shed, even after she moved. She did not want them back. The old-fashioned gift cards with fluted edges said, "Salutations! We wish you years of happiness!"

Ruby listened to a rectangular radio on her kitchen table. It was the size of a box of saltine crackers. She served me Coca-Colas in squatty old-fashioned bottles when I first visited her here. I asked where she bought bottles like that, but she never answered. Maybe she had been saving them up under the sink for decades. To this day, sometimes we call this her house.

She raised one son in this house, as we are doing. More than once I have caught a brief echo of her boy's feet running across the floors right behind our boy. Maybe he's leading him, or they're traveling side-by-side. I like the fact that in ninety years our house has known only three owners and two little boys.

My brother's house is made of pink recycled bricks. Recycled bricks are more expensive than new red bricks. Someone told me that. They make the house look organically weather-beaten, but only slightly. The other houses on the street, very similar in design to my brother's, with high-pitched roofs and enormous windows and exalted dormers, are made of redder bricks. Most of the families have planted beds of petunias and hibiscus as borders.

These are words that could apply to my brother's neighborhood: manicured, impeccable, formal, aloof. There are others: cookie-cutter, master plan. Words that could apply to ours: offbeat, down-at-the-heels.

Our house used to be made of old wooden boards, but a few years ago we had our carpenter take the old boards off, stuff the thickest insulation he could find inside the walls (try facing west through a blazing Texas summer), and apply new boards. Then he painted them white so the house looked just like it used to look, but felt substantially cooler. Our neighbors thought we were crazy, wasting our money. Why didn't we put the old boards back on?

My husband said they were too thickly mottled with old paint. It was hard to make the house look fresh when the paint was so lumpy. Plus, some of them were rotting. Our neighbors raised their eyebrows. Our neighbors, we think, lead mysterious lives themselves.

Gigantic pecan trees cast their shadows down on all of us. We suffer collective web worm invasions. If you walk barefoot in the grass, fat nuts poke your feet. During autumn, various citizens — skinny black men in baseball caps, Latina *abuelas* in long, full skirts — appear in the city park across the street from our house with plastic bags and long poles, for poking the towering trees. Nuts shower down and they collect their bounty. I imagine them strolling home to their kitchens to make pecan pies more easily than I imagine them standing in line at the pecan cracking plant down the block (We Buy — $ .50 a pound).

My brother has six fancy bathrooms in his house. One offers two toilets in separate closets and two gigantic gleaming sinks. I think I would dream about Dutch cleanser if I lived there. His bathrooms have fan vents and special mirror lights for putting on makeup. I opened a sleek drawer under his sink and found 1,000 miniature bottles of hotel shampoo.

We have one old-fashioned bathroom downstairs tiled with blue flying birds from Mexico. We hauled those tiles home in our car after visiting the hand-painted tile factory in Dolores Hidalgo. I was drinking Coca-Cola from a squatty Mexican bottle when we spotted them. Of course, we hadn't measured the bathroom back home, so we had to guess how many to buy which is why a plain navy blue border lines the bottom and top. We filled in. Our bathroom wall still features an ancient, ornately-scrolled gas heater that we are afraid to turn on, but like to look at.

We have another bathroom upstairs with a claw foot bathtub. I found the tub on the front porch of an elderly lady's house on Maverick Street. I knocked on her door. "This is very brazen, but the fact that your bathtub is filled with — leaves — makes me wonder if it is essential to your life anymore or if you might consider selling it." She took twenty dollars on the spot.

Four men almost died hoisting that bathtub up to our second floor, which used to be the attic. We have a metal spiral staircase heading up there, but the tub was too wide for it. So the men had to build a scaffolding in the backyard and haul the tub up with ropes. I wasn't home, but my husband says there was a moment they lost control of it, like a slippery bar of soap. We would never have voted for that tub if we knew the risk they were taking.

My brother's kitchen has a ceiling that vaults like a cathedral over two ovens, two sinks, and two gleaming dishwashers. A commune could live there, a whole Girl Scout troop, or an entire division of Simon & Schuster. My brother has a trash compactor and a bread machine that cooks bread even while you are sleeping and a giant refrigerator and a couple of garbage disposals and a dozen cabinets filled with chips and kiddie cereals and Dallas Cowboy beer mugs. His stove is electric and has a memory, I think. Or maybe it's his ovens that have memories. They have memories but not much to remember, since they are so new.

Our stove (a red Magic Chef — people are always commenting on its unusual color) was purchased by our parents when I was two. My brother wasn't born yet.

I was in love with it. I thought it had a face. Teeth. I thought my dreams were stacked inside the double-boiler and the steamer pans. There's a silver door on the left where the pots live and an oven on the right that long ago gave up being true to its own temperature. Every baked good is a gamble in our house. The enchiladas come out like *flautas* sometimes, thoroughly crisped, and the birthday cakes — well, we gave those up. Now we buy angel cakes and cut up fresh Texas strawberries.

As a child, I begged my mother to save this stove for me so I could have it when I grew up. This was a real burden for her since she had to store it in somebody's barn while we lived overseas, then have it hauled all the way down to Texas. It waited for me to grow up. I have also managed to preserve an archival, turquoise refrigerator from the rocky days of the late '60s when my parents plummeted back into the United States and had to start keeping house again from scratch. It has bungee cords in the door for holding the mustard and ketchup in place, instead of real shelf fronts anymore.

Sometimes I feel like a hobo. Just camping out.

Our refrigerator's freezer compartment is, intelligently, at the bottom instead of the top. *Why don't you buy a new refrigerator?* our parents ask me. The front panels of the vegetable drawers are cracked, the rubber door seals dubious. But I feel attached to it. What could go better with a red stove than a turquoise refrigerator? Anyway, isn't there something to be said for waiting till things truly *give up the ghost?*

The main thing I admire in my brother's house is his closets. Anyone who has lived in a 90 year-old closetless house will appreciate this. My brother and his wife could entertain guests in their closets. Children could have sleepovers in there, surrounded by racks of color-coded shirts, fringed rodeo sections, neat shelves of shoes. My brother's daughter and son have their own giant, well-lit, walk-in closets too. I think my brother's dogs have their own closets. Even the Christmas tree ornaments have their designated hideaway.

At our house, we have a few antique wooden wardrobes, items of furniture which should never, ever be romanticized. They don't hold much and they don't hold it very well, either. Also, they take up a lot of room. My husband has never yet figured out how to close the door to his, so it is always standing slightly open. Mine came off a British train. The drawers are efficiently labeled: underwear, shirts. It has a little trough for "collar stays" too. Very useful in the 1990s. The drawers are still lined with the British newspapers they held when we discovered it.

When we turned part of our attic into an upstairs room, we built in a single closet, but failed to air-condition it which means, in the summer, its contents are held at approximately 200 degrees. Also, it is four feet tall. One must ask, *Is it worth banging my head and sweltering to find that old velvet vest?*

When we added a workroom for me, we added another (too skinny) closet that has turned out to be just perfect for a few T-shirts and strips of (unlabeled) 35 millimeter negatives. Nothing else. Our son has no place to put his clothes but on a toy shelf with his Monopoly game and his Star Trek phasers. Is it any wonder the boy has not yet mastered organization? Is it any wonder his pajama pants pile up like Mount Hood in the center of the floor? We will buy him a wide set of drawers to inaugurate the new school year. We will say those magic American words: *this goes here, that goes there.*

When I spend the night in my brother's well-organized house, I wake up thinking, *but there are no one else's legends lodged in these walls.*

He likes it that way. His wife likes it that way. They are the main characters.

I stand in their narrow front yard staring up into the sky, which always feels like the real "terrain" of suburban neighborhoods.

The first years they lived here, no birds came. I thought — well, there are no trees. Maybe the sky is too well-divided for birds.

These days, when we sit by their pool, I catch a few blurry flashes above our heads, which feels heartening. Over the investment experts and interior decorators and corporate executives, the birds are once again lifting their wings. Just as they do in our own neighborhood over barbers and hospital maintenance workers and security guards and retired alcoholic mechanics and mariachis in silver-studded black suits.

I think the roots of old houses go deep down into the ground before we were born and the roots of new houses go out into the atmosphere, into the disembodied visions of developers and the crisp edges of dollar bills rolled up at the bank.

The houses in his neighborhood are palm trees with very short roots.

I realize the same kinds of things must go on in both our houses: people eat, clean up, converse, pop videos into the television, take showers, make love, and occasionally plow through old family photographs with a forlorn sense of lostness. *Who were those people? Did I really look that good, when I thought I was looking bad?*

People say things they don't mean to say. *Not now! Later!* People lie around on beds or couches planning their next moves out into the world. My brother's children have dogs, cats, and newts. Our son has a cat, nine hens, and newts. Where did all these newts come from?

I would like to go nowhere. I would like to stay home, learning slow secrets, harvesting the earthworms that live in a ventilated composting tub on the back deck, pruning the lanky Don Juan roses at the correct moment.

I would spread new hay on the bottom of our chickens' coop as the hens butt me like young goats for the juicy prizes they think I carry. I would take all day about it, collecting the dried corn cobs and watermelon rinds, recycling them into the worm tub. One thing could go on becoming another.

For years I've had a title in my mind: *Still Waiting for a Dull Moment.*

I would continue my ongoing (extremely gradual) excavation into the deep recesses of the storage sections of our jumbled attic to find the handwritten air letter sheet that Graham Greene, the British novelist, mailed to me in 1971. He professed recurrent doubt about his work. He hoped I would never locate a copy of his first book — a collection of poems. I know his letter is pressed up against the large stack of square, white envelopes from Stella Kerouac, last wife of Jack, which I rubber banded together long ago.

But this is what happens: every time I get up into the attic, I find a box or bag of baby clothes, little pants, small T-shirts rippling with sailboats, and have to smooth out each one dreamily and refold it or put it in a stack to give away.

This takes eons.

The air whistles through the spinning air vent in the top of the attic while I am musing.

The buses steam past along Main Avenue and the boy who will never be so little again goes on clacking away on his computer downstairs. I could be a squirrel trapped in a wall.

My brother and I grew up in the same houses together, in St. Louis, Jerusalem, and San Antonio, three cities as dissimilar as pretzels, *hummos,* and salsa. So how did we become such different people? Our parents had Egyptian wall hangings, camel saddles, Moroccan hassocks. Such cultural exclamation points may still be found in both my brother's and my residences.

Our St. Louis house, a square, unassuming box with few distinguishing features on the outside, has now been swallowed up by the redbud trees my grandfather planted when we were babies. It is startling to consider how trees grow, while objects constructed by people stay the same or disintegrate.

This house once had a forest green, screened-in back porch which was all we needed to feel wealthy. How much air we owned! We could sleep out there on cots in the summer. We could follow the moon rising up over the vacant lot behind our house.

Recent owners have removed the porch. I knock and ask what's cooking. I don't know what comes over me, but it's the first thing out of my mouth. "Potatoes," the woman says.

"We lived here once."

She does not say "Come in" and I do not suggest they rebuild the old green porch back where it used to be. She is black and I am — sort of — white, and for one moment we stare past each other's eyes.

My brother has never been back to that house.

Why do I burst into tears beside the blue mailbox across the street from our house where I mailed my first letters? I knew there was A Larger World out there. The scent of pine nuts and garlic sizzled in olive oil clung to my clothes. In Jerusalem we lived in a stone second floor flat eight miles north of the holy places. In those days, I thought a lot about what makes one place holy and another place not. Homes were holy. My brother was happier in that house than I was. Gypsies camped in the stony meadow beside it. I wanted to go live with them.

We could hear the guns in Israel firing from our own bedrooms. The soldiers were practicing. Newspaper headlines back in the United States always pretended Israelis were just "keeping the peace" — after they'd stolen the land. Songs burst forth in my head. "Liar, liar, pants on fire." When our refugee father talked about being "back home," he referred to all of Palestine, not just our new address. Finally, in 1967, the situation exploded and we flew as far away from it as we could — to Texas.

In San Antonio, our parents bought the first house they looked at.

It had a tree in the backyard that seemed to whisper "yes" if you leaned against it long enough.

We were teenagers there, hot-blooded and melodramatic, and my brother got so mad at me once he kicked a hole right through my bedroom door with his pointed cowboy boot. The hole outlived us in that house. No one, of course, could remember what had made us so mad.

If people grow up together, eating the same whole-grain cereals, under the same mapped ceilings, how do they end up so different? College students discuss this as "Human Nature vs. Nurture." I have no conclusions.

When my husband and I married, I visited the local department store to "pick out our plates." I looked and looked through the fine chinas, the bone-thin frills, and elaborate floral glazes, and selected the thickest variety (gray with a single navy stripe and vertical sides, like a baby would eat from) called "Less is Enough." Why is less enough for some and not for others?

Am I holding myself above my brother? Do I judge him by his house? He has told me what his monthly mortgage payment is — or maybe our father has told me — it is so large whole parts of our house could fit inside it. He could be eighty and still paying. Something like that.

He told me once, with a note of sadness in his voice, "It's like a carnival ride — if you're on, you can't just jump off. "

We have no monthly mortgage payment. Our modest house was paid for long ago. The mortgage company stamped the receipt in red — PAID IN FULL. We used it as a centerpiece with flowers for a while.

What surprises me is this: my brother sometimes says he imagines a slow going, rural-tinted existence. He mentions stepping down, leafing out, taking the chance. Anyone who has worked more than a decade for a major corporation must carry these little bubbles inside. He delights his family with a weekend at a rugged bed-and-breakfast ranch in the Texas hill country. His son collects fresh eggs and his daughter washes a horse. He imagines having less and being happy.

I sit on the steps of our front porch in the evenings. Our son scrawls a picture on the sidewalk — blue chalk man with a runny nose vast as a volcano's eruption. For him this feels like spectacular, nasty fun.

Across the street, women and men walk arm-in-arm around the quiet park, under the yellow lamplight, as they do in Mexico. What are they thinking of? I imagine they carry the days when their own sons and daughters were small tucked deep inside them. When other children shout at dusk, swinging wooden bats or skidding onto the gravel jogging path on their bikes, something in them still shouts, *Come back, come back! It's time for bed! It's time to go home!*

My brother and I used to answer to a call like that. His skin smelled like pennies, the faint coppery twist of pockets and salt inside a fist. He kept his little cars all lined up in shoeboxes and would flip the doors of the milk truck and the fire truck open now and then before going to bed, just to make sure everything still worked.

Robin Hemley

Family Legends: It's Impossible to Please the Gods and Relatives

I was in a strange, contemplative mood the day of my brother's wedding in 1980 — seeing Jonny married in an Orthodox ceremony, married to a woman he'd met through a matchmaker. At the wedding, men danced with men and women danced with women. Not more than four years earlier, Jonathan had been as non-observant as anyone in our family, and none of us quite knew what had changed him. My great-grandmother Hannah had been the last one in our family to keep kosher. I'm still not sure, and I doubt there's one answer, but on that day I knew that the change in my brother was a profound one. The conventional wisdom in my family was that this

was a phase he was going through, a phase that he's still going through sixteen years later — and even though I doubted from the beginning that this was a phase, I still hoped it was.

To me, Jonny had always been a genius, fluent in any language he chose to study, brilliant in math and science as well as literature. At the age of 15, he'd founded a literary magazine called *Lotus* that published some of the most important writers of the day, many of them family friends. The first issue, published in 1968, contained the first chapter of Isaac Singer's memoir, *A Passage to America*, poems by Stanley Plumly and Denise Levertov, a novel excerpt from Josephine Herbst. After my father's death in 1966, Jonny, who is five years older than I am, took over the role of father figure in my life, and I, adoring little brother, followed his every step, received advice (some good, some terrible) on love and sex, modeled my sense of humor after his (sardonic, absurd, world-weary), followed his politics (decidedly liberal). One day in the early '70s, our great uncle Morty, sitting at my grandmother's kitchen table, accused us both of being "Commie Pinkos." We wore this appellation like a medal. The only path down which I didn't follow my brother was the path of observant Judaism. Our relationship has never recovered. He — always strong-willed and uncompromising in his beliefs, even when they were completely the opposite of those he holds now — views me, perhaps, as a disobedient son.

On the way back from the wedding, I rode in the company of my great-uncles Morty and Bill and my aunt Carrie from New Jersey to Long Beach, where my grandmother Ida lived. At that time in my life, I thought I could do without most of these relatives. I only wanted to know the legends. Our greatest family legend is Houdini. He was the nephew of my great-grandmother Hannah, or something like that. No one in my family knew him, though my mother once went to one of his performances. But we all bask in the trickle-down glory of Houdini. As a child, I entertained my family by breaking old belts with my stomach muscles the way Houdini broke chains. I'd suck in my stomach, tighten the belt, and waddle to the dinner table, where I'd announce, "Look, I'm Houdini," and then I'd exhale. Pop. For a second, I was Houdini. A return to a golden moment in my family's identity.

To me, my great-uncle Bill, who had come all the way from Hollywood for Jonny's wedding, was a living legend. He was the most unfamiliar, the most distant of my great-uncles and -aunts, so of course, he was the one I idolized. He was an actor. His real name was Harold, but as a child he looked particularly cute, like the kewpie dolls that were popular at the time. Billikin was another name for kewpie dolls, and that's what people started calling him: Billy. The name stuck.

Even his name had a legend surrounding it.

Whenever anyone in my family referred to Bill as an actor outside of his earshot, it was as a "ham actor." To them, he was never a success, except for the time he won a new car in a fishing contest. That impressed them.

His stage name was Bill "Tiny" Brauer. He played bit parts in everything from Three Stooges shorts to The Dick Van Dyke Show. He was in more Three Stooges shorts than any other actor besides the Stooges themselves, and in the last year of his life was flown to Philadelphia by the Stooge Fan Club to give their keynote address. Bill had grown up with the Stooges in Bensonhurst, and Moe had married a cousin. In my lexicon, Moe was synonymous with the word "legend." I still count among my prized possessions a signed autograph from Moe that reads, "To Cousin Robin." I met him when I was ten, at another uncle's house, and I cannot tell you what he was *really* like, except for on that one day, from the perspective of a young boy, when Moe answered the door and my grandmother said, "Robin, do you know who this is?" All I saw was an elderly balding man.

It took some convincing for me to believe this was Moe. He was quiet, didn't poke me in the eyes, and didn't have the proto-Beatles haircut that was his trademark.

When we returned from the wedding, we sat on my grandmother's porch, and I listened to the collective nostalgia of my great-aunts and -uncles and my grandmother. The only interruptions in their stories were from the occasional low-flying jets, leaving or coming into JFK airport, 30 miles away. Of course, it was of Hannah, my great-grandmother, dead for thirty years, that they spoke. I never met Hannah. She died years before I was born, but I've been hearing of her my whole life. On this day, Morty told me that Hannah was the first person in our family to fly in an airplane. She wanted to go to her brother's wedding in Cleveland. Morty suggested that she go by plane, but he wasn't serious. She took him up on it. He tried to dissuade her. She had a heart condition. Morty went to her doctor ("Everyone in the family was furious with me"). Morty smiled when he said that — a remarkable occurrence, that smile.

The doctor said that the high altitudes *could* affect her heart. So the doctor called her up, with Morty standing beside him. Hannah was polite but asked the doctor to speak to her son. "You can tell the doctor to go to hell," she said. She dressed in a completely white flowing dress for her flight to Cleveland. That same day, a plane crashed in Albany and everyone was killed. On the plane everyone was frightened except for Hannah. A woman gave her child to Hannah who held it the whole way. When she arrived at the wedding, they made a bigger fuss about her than the bride and the groom because she was the oldest person to fly in an airplane.

Hannah was born in Lithuania. According to family legend, her mother died in childbirth and Hannah was suckled by a she-goat. I don't know why the she-goat is an important detail, but I never heard the story without this detail. I suppose Hannah herself was the one who first related it. According to my mother, she was a born storyteller. When I think of Hannah being suckled by a she-goat, I always think of Romulus and Remus, the founders of Rome, being suckled by a wolf. I know that's a pretentious comparison, but in my family, Hannah has more importance than Romulus and Remus. My cousin David says that this side of the family is always inventing myths about itself.

Hannah grew up on her father's farm, had wild red hair, rode bareback on horses, and ran away from home when she was a young woman because her father and stepmother wanted to marry her off to some old gentleman in the city. She ran away to England where she joined her older brother. Her first job there was in a sweatshop where the owner's son was constantly making advances (as my mother puts it). No talk of sexual harassment and no recourse from it back then, except for homemade remedies. In this case, Hannah arranged her brooch so that the pin stuck outwards, and the next time the owner's son advanced upon her, she clasped his hand to her breast, fervently murmuring, "Oh Shmool," and stuck him through the palm.

From the sweatshop, Hannah made her way into the Yiddish theater, and traveled around much of Europe. In Holland, Hannah met her future husband, whose name I don't even remember. I could find out with a phone call to my mother, but it's not important. He's a foil to Hannah's story, a necessary plot complication, and the only thing that makes him interesting is that he, too, has a legendary attribute — namely the supposed fact that he was the shoemaker for the Queen of Holland, and he made such good shoes that the Queen rewarded him with a family crest of his own. The crest, of course, has been lost.

Hannah left the theater for her shoemaking husband — Jacob, Isaac? — and their first child, Anne, was born in Holland. After her birth, they moved to America, to Brooklyn, where they settled in Bensonhurst. In my family's estimation, Hannah remained heroic in all the stories (or most of them) told about her, even after her arrival in America. But maybe my great-grandfather should have stayed in Holland because his stock in the family legend steadily declined. Until the Depression, he was a wealthy man, but then his business partner embezzled their money and ran off. My great-grandfather could have declared bankruptcy for his business while retaining some of his personal wealth, but he didn't believe in that, and insisted on paying back all of his creditors with his own money. Hannah, apparently, never forgave him, and my mother remembers him towards the end of his life, weak and perpetually coughing, standing by the radiator, Hannah upbraiding him for his wheezing. "You lummox," she'd say as he coughed. "Stop making that noise."

Hannah could be cruel, certainly, and she was also vain, always talking about her beauty and her red hair, but she was also adventurous and bold, and nurtured her children and their artistic sides. Hannah's cruelty to her husband makes her less heroic but more human. Can a person be a legend and a human being at the same time? I'm not sure. There's a deep judgmental jealousy that runs through my family like a filling in an otherwise good tooth. My family takes offense, and I'm including myself here, at the whiff of an insult. Not so much from strangers, but from each other. So while, on the one hand, we're building up the legends of our dead, we make sure to tear down the living. In the end, we barely talk to one another.

After Morty finished telling stories of Hannah, he and the others did something very uncharacteristic — they taught me various Yiddish curses. Until then, I'd never heard one of them say a single word in Yiddish.

It's impossible to please the gods and relatives.
Go to hell and bake bagels.
Lie with your head in crap and grow like an onion.
What does a pig know about noodles?
We shouldn't know about such illnesses.
A big boil should grow on you.
Tuchus licker.

You should give birth to a trolley car.
I have you in the toilet.
You should have a couple of beds and a fever in each.
Get luck from your children.

The sayings that stand out for me from that list are "It's impossible to please the gods and relatives," "We shouldn't know about such illnesses," and the only hopeful one, "Get luck from your children." A couple of years after learning that last one, I used it as a toast at a friend's Episcopalian wedding reception, in Yiddish, as though I'd grown up spouting such cute Yiddishisms. The first saying strikes me as true of my family in particular and all families in general. The second seems slightly mysterious to me. What illnesses? We shouldn't know of what illnesses? I'm sure there's a simple explanation, but none of the relatives who taught me these phrases is still alive. I don't remember the tone they used. I have to rely on my imagination. Maybe the saying was meant ironically, as in the case of a pregnant woman, perhaps carrying a child out of wedlock, suffering from morning sickness. "We shouldn't know of such illnesses," I imagine Hannah saying. Or even more ironically, someone winning the lottery. We shouldn't know of such illnesses. Or perhaps the saying is meant superstitiously, as though knowing about the illness might inflict the speaker with it. Or perhaps, it really was meant literally, not knowing about such illnesses that might strike us as vulgar — syphilis, for instance. I imagine for my family at least, the saying really means that we shouldn't know of illnesses that aren't illnesses at all, but simply a part of the human condition. Anything that makes a person complicated, that breaks down the legend, that can't be caricatured, can't be reduced to a simple story. My brother's religious awakening, if you want to call it that. Other stories, other problems, that are more difficult to explain. But I'll try.

My mother says that she always felt closer to her father's side of the family, the Gottliebs, rather than her mother's side, the Brauers — with the legendary exception of Hannah. The Gottliebs, she says, were the artistic side of the family. Her grandmother Fanny had written a novel when she was 17 or 18. The novel was about Fanny's grandparents, one or both of whom came from Bohemia. The only thing my mother remembers about them is that Fanny's grandfather was a stained-glass maker. The book was written in the 1870s and has long since disappeared. But after she wrote the novel, she took the manuscript down to *Harper's* and showed it to an editor who said he liked it very much, but he asked her to go home and rewrite it, using only one side of the paper. She told her father what the editor had said, but he forbade her from returning because *Harper's* was on the waterfront, where nice girls did not go.

Fanny's husband, too, had artistic talent. He'd been a tap dancer on the Vaudeville stage, part of an act called The Golden Boys. My mother remembers him as a man in his seventies, still able to click his heels together three times in midair.

My mother's father, Nelson Gottlieb, was born in 1886 and wanted to be an illustrator, but was shepherded by his tap-dancing father and his nearly-published mother into something more practical. He started out at 18 selling malt and hops for his uncle Fred, who was a flautist for the Baltimore Symphony, but made his fortune selling beer supplies. Then Nelson sold stationery for a while, and finally became a podiatrist/chiropodist. My mother, though, still has a number of his drawings from the turn of the century, accomplished sketches of men and women turned out in high-Edwardian fashions, sketches that would have looked at home in any of the popular magazines of the day.

At the same time, my grandmother Ida Brauer was attending school to become a teacher. She played the violin (she eventually became a music teacher), and according to the boundless vaults where our family legends are stored, she was something of a musical prodigy. At the age of six, some musical gentlemen, who will forever remain faceless and nameless, somehow heard her play the violin and tried to convince her mother to allow them to take her to Europe and hone her skills at the feet of the masters. Hannah said no — it wasn't the right thing for a nice Jewish girl. But it was enough to be asked. It was enough to be known as a one-time child prodigy. This is something I knew about my grandmother from an early age. I can't remember ever not knowing that she'd been a child prodigy. Of course, we know nothing about the gentlemen who said she was a prodigy. We don't know how many child prodigies they asked to come to Europe with them that week.

I suppose I could stop here, leave the family legends more or less intact, leave Ida and Nelson playing pretty duets for Uncle Fred, say love blossomed, that nothing ever went wrong in my family, that the only things to remember are the good things.

But other things nag at me, family resentments passed down from one generation to the next, the unspoken anti-legends. Nelson and Ida married against the wishes of his family. Nelson's family looked down upon Ida's family because Hannah and her husband were Russian Jews — actually from Lithuania and Latvia, which as my mother says, "isn't strictly Russian." But the Gottliebs were Hungarian Jews, from the Austro-Hungarian Empire, and as such, thought of themselves as superior to their unfortunate brethren from the shtetls of the Jewish Pale.

Nelson's parents boycotted the wedding. This high-handedness is something intangible that I can't explain rationally. The distinction between Russian and Hungarian Jews was moot to any outsider. Certainly, gentile Russians and Hungarians would have simply lumped them all together as Jews, neither truly Russian nor Hungarian. This schism between the Jews of Europe has been well documented, and is part of the reason why many of the Jews of Germany stayed in Germany until it was too late for them. They thought of themselves as Germans first and Jews second. The Nazis, of course, disagreed. In America, the German Jews, who had already established themselves here by the time the waves of Jewish immigrants from Russia started arriving at the turn of the century, were horrified by their Russian cousins. They immediately started Aid societies for the immigrants, not so much out of a philanthropic sense of duty, but so they could make the new immigrants respectable in a hurry so as not to reflect poorly on Jews as a whole.

If I could ask Fanny what she had against Ida's family, what would she say? "Low-class Jews," I suppose.

And so I am part low-class Jew and part high-class Jew. The war between Fanny and Hannah still continues within me. At the heart of every person, there are two families warring. One side is always diminishing and destroying the legends of the other. Or believing more in one than the other.

My brother, Jonathan, boycotted my wedding because I married a woman of Scotch/Irish/German descent, not Jewish. A couple of weeks before my wedding, a rabbi from L.A. called me and told me he was an emissary from my brother. He wanted, he said, to fly to my home and spend a day with me to "tell me the great spectacle of Jewish history."

I thanked the rabbi and told him that the spectacle of Jewish history, while interesting, I'm sure, would not affect the outcome of my marriage. Finally, the rabbi gave up, but before he left me he extracted a promise that I'd tell my brother that he'd tried. For some reason, he also seemed intent that I remember his name, which I repeated three times, like something out of Rumpelstiltskin, and promptly forgot the next day.

Within a few years of their marriage, my grandfather and grandmother had separated. My mother blames Fanny, who lent them money to buy a house and exacted a brutal repayment schedule from the struggling couple. Ida and Nelson had two children, my mother and her younger brother, Allan. The separation was a legal one. My mother remembers being in court as a young child. The tensions between the Brauers and the Gottliebs became so great at one point after the separation that the Gottliebs kidnapped my mother and Allan, and brought them several blocks away to their house so they wouldn't grow up under the debilitating Brauer influence. The Gottliebs wouldn't call my mother by her given name either. Each grandmother wanted my mother named for her own mother. So she was known to the Gottliebs as Sylvia, her middle name (Fanny's mother was named Sarah; close enough), not Elaine, her given name.

When my mother was six, in 1922, Nelson died in his sleep of a cerebral hemorrhage. He was 35. He and my grandmother were in the process of reconciling, and the struggling young family had gone away to the Adirondacks for a retreat. My mother remembers him carrying their luggage up the mountain the day he died.

What's important here is not his death itself, though this year (I'm 37 now) I had a strange moment when I was driving my car and suddenly realized I had lived longer than my grandfather. What's really important is the legend surrounding his death. A year earlier, he'd visited the Everglades and had gone up in a plane for a joy ride at a fair. The pilot had lost control and the plane crashed in the swamp. The pilot was killed instantly, but Nelson survived with various broken bones, still managing to swim around for hours before being rescued. A doctor told my mother years later that the accident had perhaps caused an embolism that went undetected and eventually killed him. The story of his survival in the swamp made him heroic. It makes him a legend, the type of story I loved to hear as I was growing up.

As a child, I somehow mixed up my grandfather Nelson with his father, the tap dancer with The Golden Boys. I imagined him dying as a wing dancer, clicking his heels over the Everglades…once, twice, three times, and then over the side of the plane into the infinite spaces of my family's collective memory.

I guess, when it comes down to it, sometimes I'd rather believe a beautiful lie.

Jonny and I went different routes even in the way we explored our lineage. Jonathan was strictly a Family Tree sort. For years, he wanted to find out who our earliest known ancestors were (Family legend on the Hemley side says that we're related to Atila the Hun, but we can't prove it), and he even contacted the Mormons for help, since the Mormons keep the largest records of this kind in the hopes that they can convert everyone retroactively to Mormonism. A couple of years ago, a cousin sent me a family tree, and I've probably looked at it twice. Family trees don't interest me. I want to hear the legends.

Perhaps these legends are a salve. They keep us from truths that we can't or won't face.

My brother called me up. We hadn't spoken in a couple of years, but his voice was familiar — we have the same laugh, we have the same walk, our sense of humor is still the same. He told me that he'd been to a rabbi who said that it was all right for my wife Beverly and my kids to visit now. After eight years of avoidance (he hadn't spoken the names of my children or Beverly, at least not to me), I didn't know what to say. It seemed very late, but I said "Thanks," weakly. He had always said, through the mouthpiece of my mother, that it was nothing personal, this refusal to acknowledge my wife or children. He didn't even know her, he said, so how could he dislike her? But that didn't make the rejection any less painful. I told him — through my mother — that that argument, "nothing personal" didn't matter to me. It was a chilling excuse, the kind of argument that rationalizes any discrimination.

But I wanted to reconcile. I wanted, at least, for his children to know me, even if he didn't want to know mine. I didn't want this family rift to continue, but I wasn't quite ready to forgive. This was my version of the Gottliebs versus the Brauers, Hungarians versus Russians, and who knows how many other anti-legends, the stories no one wanted to recount. I didn't want ours to be that kind of a story. It's not simply a split between assimilated and non-assimilated Jews. That suggests that all Jews who are not as orthodox as my brother, or who marry someone who isn't Jewish, want to disappear, want to blend in and lose their sense of Jewish identity, and that's just not true. There are different ways of celebrating one's identity. The exclusion of others does not make one more of what one already is.

Within a month, Beverly and my kids and I were on a flight to L.A., our tickets paid for by my mother, who was already going to be visiting my brother and wanted to be there for our "reconciliation." In my extended family this event received about as much attention and promotion as a heavyweight title fight. We arrived on a Thursday, but had to wait until Sunday to meet Jonny and his family because of the Sabbath.

That Sunday was unbearably hot. For the past couple of weeks, the temperature had been creeping around the hundreds, and where did Jonny want to go for our reconciliation but an inland desert lake, Lake Cacitas, an hour and a half drive away. The ocean was much closer, but apparently (according to my cousin David), Jonny couldn't take his family to a beach where there would be nearly naked women in bikinis — a corrupting, secular influence. I don't know if that was true or not, but no one could swim in Lake Cacitas — it was a reservoir.

Our initial meeting was brief. Jonny and the other eight members of his family showed up in an old station wagon, got out briefly to say hello, and then I followed them in my rental car with my family and my mother. On the way to the lake, I let off steam by criticizing my brother's fast driving and the way he kept changing lanes without letting me know. Here I was, following him again, as always, hardly able to keep up. His seven kids, half of them crammed in the back of the wagon, waved at us and we waved back. There was a bumper sticker on the back of his car that read, "Put the brakes on Loshon Hora," and I wondered what it meant, but I was afraid to ask.

I figured it was some right-wing slogan having to do with Israel, probably the West Bank. It probably meant the peace process. Put the brakes on the peace process. But I didn't know for sure.

Lake Cacitas shimmered in the dead heat of the afternoon, and we drove for fifteen or twenty minutes before we found a spot where my brother wanted to picnic. The picnic area was on the edge of the parking lot. Jonny's children piled out of the wagon and were handed sacks of groceries — all paid for by my mother, the Don King of reconciliation. With seven kids one can't worry about details, so no one seemed to mind that the kids were dropping more hot dog buns on the parking lot than they were successfully ferrying to the picnic tables. They were cute kids, adorable even, and I felt an immediate attachment to them. It struck me that day that it was almost fifteen years to the day of Jonny's wedding. Maybe it was the intense heat of both days that reminded me. Most of the old relatives gone in those fifteen years, receding into memory: Morty, Ida, Bill. Replaced by new relatives: my daughters Olivia and Isabel. And Jonny's children: Asher Lev, Adina Leah, Shmool Chaim, Sarah Chaya, David, Hannah, and Ariela. Another Hannah, this one only five years old. What stories would she tell? My kids alongside my brother's kids. Their names alone told part of the story, but they got along.

Beverly hung back, uncomfortably, and decided to spend her time with the kids at a playground near the picnic area. She'd been dreading this afternoon even more than I. She felt hurt and insulted by my brother in a way that one picnic couldn't erase. "You don't understand," my mother told me later. "He's coming around. He's softening. This is a big change in him." When I mentioned this to Beverly, her response was that she didn't understand why we had to jump as soon as my brother decided that the presence of her and the children wouldn't poison his family.

Beverly had come for me and I had come for my mother. Everyone expected Jonny and me to talk, to discuss our estrangement, but we didn't. Instead, Jonny immediately hunkered down by the grill. First, he piled the charcoal on it, then he poured most of the bottle of lighter fluid on the charcoal. Then he set the hamburger patties and hot dogs on top of the grill. Then he lit the charcoal. "Jonny, you can't do it that way," I said, but he wouldn't listen. It was the funeral-pyre version of cooking out. The flames leapt up dangerously close to Jonny's children, singeing the meat, and died down again. Jonny poured more lighter fluid, the flames danced, Jonny barely moved.

Beverly later told me that watching Jonny cook in this manner made him look kind of stupid, hunched over the grill, soaking the coals with lighter fluid. And she'd been surprised because I'd always told her what a genius Jonny was. Her saying this shocked me, not because it was untrue or ungenerous — I couldn't expect her to be generous — but because I saw that another version of my brother existed, maybe many. If Beverly ever told a story about my brother, this would be it, this schlemiel-like picture of a man scorching hot dogs and hamburgers. It seemed somehow unfair, unnatural, despite my ambivalent feelings towards him at that moment. To her, he wasn't Houdini. Not Atila the Hun. Not even Moe...maybe Moe.

Jonny never mentioned my children that whole day, nor Beverly. The only reference he made to her was when he shouted over to me, "Does she want a hamburger?" Jonny's wife, Sandra, tried to make conversation with Beverly, but Beverly, shy under most circumstances, didn't feel like talking. Later, Sandra asked my mother why Beverly was so quiet. The answer, to me, seemed obvious. After being ignored for eight years, she wasn't in the mood to chat as though nothing had happened between our two families.

Jonny eventually ran out of ammunition, and so it was decided that he and I would go into the nearby town of Ojai to pick up more lighter fluid and some more buns and soda. I suppose we were expected to talk, and we did, but again, it wasn't about anything important. Jonny told me about the writers in the religious community, like the thriller writer, Jonathan Kellerman, who had made it big. I told him about a few developments in my writing, and he told me about a children's book he wanted to write. That was about it, as though *we* had no issues between us.

Only after the meal, well into the day, did we finally talk — maybe not what needed to be discussed, but what we felt comfortable with, in the old way, our own way, by telling stories, by remembering, even though our memories might be completely false.

We took a walk along the lake, just the boys, my brother, me, Asher

[handwritten marginalia: No sense of pre-existing connection that needs healing]

184

Lev, Shmool Chaim, and David. As we walked, Jonny told us stories about me.

"I was telling Asher Lev about that high school you went to for a semester and then transferred. And they didn't take your name off the roster, and you still got "A's.""

"What?" I said, and I laughed.

"Some students who knew you'd left put your name up for class president and you won."

"What are you talking about? That never happened."

"Yeah," he said, "it happened." Even though it was my life, he was sure.

I felt embarrassed because I thought I knew the source of this story, though I didn't remember the story itself. As I was growing up, I was always telling my family stories, exaggerating them to make my brother and sister and mother laugh. Once, I transferred in high school from a large impersonal school of five thousand in South Bend, Indiana, to a small boarding school in Tennessee of less than two hundred, and I'm sure I told Jonny, who was away at college by then, that the old school had made me into a legendary character. I've heard of things like that actually occurring, but they never really happened to me.

"Do you remember going to that psychic in New Hampshire with Nola (our older sister)?"

"I wasn't there, Jonny," I said.

"We were all there, and the psychic said I was a Hebrew, and that Nola and Mom were Egyptians, and that you had been a French doctor in the 19th century." Jonny laughed. "Can you believe that? She called me a Hebrew. And this was long before I became religious."

"I wasn't there, Jonny. That thing about being a doctor, it's a dream I told Nola once."

He looked at me doubtfully. He remembered me there.

A little further along he said, "Do you know your dad and your uncle saw a ghost once?"

"There's no such thing," said Asher Lev.

"Didn't we?" Jonny asked me.

I nodded. This one I couldn't deny, though I was only five at the time and he was ten, and in all those intervening years, who can say what we really saw? Or if it's just another legend I've learned to believe.

We sat down at a picnic table and rested. The kids started asking me questions about where I lived, and they wanted to know if I lived near the ocean. I told them I lived near Puget Sound, and they wanted to know what a Sound was. I explained it as best I could, and then the discussion went on to other bodies of water. They wanted to know the difference between a lake and the sea and the sea and the ocean and where rivers came from. In each case, I tried to answer as best I could. Jonny stayed silent, looking down at the ground.

I looked at Jonny and wondered why he was allowing me to do this, to play the sage for his children. To me, it was his most generous act, to allow me to speak for myself, to be whoever I was going to be in their memories — and to match those memories to the stories he had told them about me, about us. I saw that it was only through these stories that we could still find a way to love one another.

Before we left, there was something I had to know, what that bumper sticker meant. I asked Jonny's daughter, Adina Leah, about it.

"It's kind of a bad pun," she said, and laughed shyly. "Put the brakes on Loshon Hora means you're not supposed to do it."

"I...think I understand that it's a pun," I said. "But what does Loshon Hora mean?"

"Oh, it means talking bad about someone. We're not supposed to do it, but sometimes it's hard not to."

Legendary status isn't something that one can or should strive for. Legends are imperfect memories and have lives of their own, like the people they supposedly portray. Sometimes I think we need to expect less of others and more of ourselves. And forgive. What makes us so proud? It's pride that makes us tell these stories and pride that makes us claw at each other.

My brother and I will never reconcile completely. We'll never talk about the issues that are central to our relationship, because I'm not even quite sure what they are anymore, how to unravel them, twisted in years of real and imagined slights, slow burns, rationalizations. Loshon Hora. To my brother and many others, the marriage of a Jew to a gentile breaks a line, a direct line of thousands of years, a tradition. But who is really to know how unbroken that line truly is. Who really can say when most of us don't even know the histories of our own grandparents? Keeping alive the stories of one's grandparents is another way of celebrating one's identity. The word "legend" connotes an old, almost magical story, rooted more in myth than fact. But really, there's no law that a legend can't also be true. It's just exaggerated, or reshaped, depending on the teller. The facts aren't as important as the overall impression of awe that one receives from the telling of the tale, or the embedded moral lessons. Secular legend is as important to me as sacred legend is to my brother.

I would argue that Jonny and I don't really need to reconcile because we are linked in other ways. My brother believes we're linked through religion, ethnicity, family trees, and while I don't deny that, I'd say that the stronger links are the stories we tell our children about each other, stories about the old neighborhood, nearly-forgotten sayings. To me, this is real communication, real reconciliation. As long as we don't stop telling stories about each other, we're getting along in some fashion.

Frank Chin

Bulletproof Buddhist

"They like to carry the 9mm handgun," Officer Roy Moody says. He's talking about Lao and Cambodian gang kids. "And, of course, they do like the semiautomatic rifles like AK-47s, even though we haven't seen an AK-47 in awhile."

He looks like a big kid, I mean an enlarged robust four or five year-old kid, ready for some fun. He looks like Bob the Big Boy in front of Bob's Big Boy coffee shop with a flat top. He goes out of his way, a long way out of his way, to make you feel he's not as big and danger-ous as he really is. He talks in the tone of voice and rhythm of a dog handler talking a strange ugly dog out of a corner.

"You know, we get threats on police officers. Some definitely wouldn't hesitate shooting anybody, *ANYBODY* now. So it's defi-nitely changed.

"The things that have happened to these communities didn't have to hap-pen. You know, it's just, I think, in the 1970s early '80s, our whole system just wasn't prepared for that mass influx of refugees. And the police department definitely didn't know how to deal with them."

I don't want to be mistaken for a dangerous dog. I glance around the framed photos and citations on the wall of his office and learn his father is a retired San Diego cop. He's thirty-five. He's married. "As a matter of fact, I'm married to a Southeast Asian lady. I was not in the service. As soon as I turned twenty-one, I became a police officer."

He answers every question in even, whole, and complete sentences in words you know he's deliberated over before letting me hear them. He also weighs me, in a glance, and measures me and gives me a complete physical, frisks me for weapons, and knows more about me than I know about him.

On his desk, among the Polaroids of guns confiscated off of gang kids, is a nasty little Mac 11. From the back end of the receiver to the end of the muzzle, it's only 11 inches long.

"Basically, with Southeast Asian gangs I started in 1989. I was working a beat that had a very large Lao population on it. So through a period of 1989 to approximately 1992: patrol. And then over here as Indo-Chinese Community Relations Officer.

"Cambodian gangs tend to copy the Hispanics in dress and tattoos. The Lao gangs are a little bit more upscale. They like to get dressed up a little bit more. They've been known to wear jacket and tie, yes.

"When I first started working with Southeast Asian gang members, I'd pull them over. I was very polite. They said, 'Yes, sir; No, sir' — did exactly what you wanted 'em to do, and you go away feeling, What a nice kid! But, you know, this guy could have been the worst kid in the world. And so they play that game.

"You know, they try to come across, especially if as a policeman, you don't know, they'll come across as, 'Well, I stay at home. I'm a hard working student.' When, in fact, he hasn't been in school in two years. A lot of times you can't identify them by their dress. You've got to know this person is a gang member by being out there all the time.

"Most people don't know the difference between an immigrant and a refugee. An immigrant was mentally prepared to come to this country, where a refugee didn't have any choice. And a lot of these refugees that came — and moreso in the Lao and the Cambodian community, didn't think that they would be making the United States a permanent home. They were always thinking they were going to go back. But the reality is that there's not much to go back to now. So the reality is that most of them are here for good."

Southeast Asian Gangs: The Beginning
ROY MOODY

"Basically, Southeast Asian gangs were first documented in the early '80s, but the violence didn't really get started until about 1989, between Lao and Cambodian gang members. The shootings started — that's when they started getting all the attention."

Shootings attract attention.

"The shooting between the Lao and the Cambodian gang members happened in the beach area. Prior to 1989, they were pretty much fronts, because they could identify with each other.

"Maybe I should go back to the very, very beginning. What happened was when they first came over here, they were put in lower economic neighborhoods where there were already established gangs. African American and Hispanic gangs. And so as they were going to school, because they were different, they were constantly being teased and picked on. And with Cambodian gang members, more so than with the Laos, back in the early '80s they started doing that New Wave style.

"I don't know if you remember the hair and whatnot. And so they were teased even more. And they were picked on at school, after school. And so they came together. And they found that by coming together, they were stronger. And then they started fighting."

"Who did they fight?"

"Pretty much everybody."

Yeah, that's Asian, I think.

"When they were at school, you know, they were Asian, they identified with each other. There wasn't a lot of problems amongst themselves. And so they started coming together to protect themselves.

"They went to Crawford, Horace Mann, Gompers, Lincoln, Kearney High School, Linda Vista.

"We're talking about three main areas in the early '80s. And recently, we're talking about a fourth area. In the early '80s we're talking City Heights, Southeast Division in San Diego. And Linda Vista. And then lately, Mira Mesa has been getting a lot of Asian gang activity.

"When they came together they found that they were stronger, to protect themselves. But one of the things that occurred then was they'd say, 'Well, let's go look for so-and-so, because he used to pick on us.' And so they'd go out like after school or on the weekend, and then a lot of these guys, they were already gang members, and all of a sudden, they're starting to get shot at. And they're thinking, 'Oh, man! We'd better get guns to protect ourselves.' And so there was a slow progression.

"School officials did what they could. Police did what they could. But actually, because of a lack of communications, a very serious lack of communications, they were pretty much — you know there weren't a lot of resources — and they were pretty much just left alone.

"You have never had such a mobile group of kids as you do with Southeast Asian kids. You could be talking to 'em, in the daytime here, and then eight hours later they're in San Francisco, or they're in Long Beach, or they're in Fresno, or they're in Las Vegas. Or they're in Texas. So they're very, very mobile. A couple of years back, I stopped a thirteen year-old girl. And she was a runaway from San Diego. She'd come back to San Diego. But in the course of a year, she had gang pictures from Florida, Boston, New York, Chicago, and Michigan. And this was a thirteen year-old girl. And there's kind of like a built-in circuit. And they make the rounds.

"You've gotta remember, for Southeast Asian gangs, this is new. This is something that's only been around for thirteen, fourteen years, at the most. In San Diego, they weren't full-fledged gang members till six or seven years ago, when they actually became a gang under the Attorney General's guidelines.

"The Attorney General's guidelines say you have got to have two or more members who associate on a regular basis, who claim an area, who are engaged in criminal activity. And that they claim a gang.

"We don't have like…It's anybody's guess what's going to happen next. We don't have a history to go by like we do with the other, more traditional, gangs.

"What we have is that we're starting to see kids as young as ten years old saying that they're OKB or OBS. So up to the early twenties.

"What we have is that they get gang members that come in from Boston to San Diego for a week. If they commit a crime, they're back in Boston. It's so difficult to solve these crimes."

The Crimes of Kids

Are we talking about real crime or kid stuff?

"Crime," Roy Moody says, and gets specific. "Well, mainly for Laos

and Cambodians, it's auto thefts. Auto thefts are their bread and butter."
Do the thieves have a favorite car?

"Honda Preludes," Roy Moody says with a nod. "They love their Honda Preludes and Toyota Supras. Definitely! Absolutely! Back when I was in patrol, almost once a week, I was arresting 'em for stolen cars. Kids. Southeast Asian gang members for stolen cars. And almost every time, it was a Honda Prelude or a Toyota Supra.

"Stolen car parts. Stereos. You know, for the Vietnamese you can get into more of organized crime type aspect. They haven't really reached (the organization) of organized crime as we know it. But yet, they're, you know, between street gangs and organized crime.

"In Southeast Division, there used to be a Lao pool hall. And we heard stories about older Vietnamese males going into the Lao pool hall there, saying '*I need a.…*' placing their order. And the first one that gets it gets two or three hundred dollars. And so there's definitely a correlation between…"

He doesn't say the words "gangs," "auto theft," and "Asian fix-it shops." He's a cop, used to talking to people and the press.

"And then, from a period of 1989 to 1992, Southeast Asian gang membership grew three to four hundred percent. Tremendous growth."

"Numbers?"

"Unfortunately, I'm not allowed to give out those numbers. But it's tremendous. Just to give you an example — and I won't identify which group — but one group of Southeast Asians has a hundred something kids. Two are in college. Their gang membership is over 200 citywide.

"They come from all different types of families. It's real popular to say these kids are gang members, because they come from dysfunctional families. But a lot of these kids come from very, very good families. And some of these families are very well educated. You know, I think it's a combination of a lack of communication on the parents' part. Whether that be because they don't speak English too well, and geography, where these kids grew up. One of the things that we see is that geography plays a very important role.

"If these kids grew up where the gang members are, you know, there's a better chance of them becoming gang members. But not all the kids that grew up in those particular neighborhoods became gang members. So there's other reasons for it."

Bounhong Khommarath agrees about the gang kids' favorite crime: "Auto theft is their number one. They say that Toyota is a lot easier to get in, so any sport-looking Toyota and late model, that's their preference. For joy riding, they just take any car that is available, from A to B and then if there's no gas. They just use the vehicle as an escape tool."

Bounhong Khommarath is Project Director, UPAC, The Union of Pan-Asian Communities, Pan-Asian Youth Project. UPAC is a storefront office, started in 1973, and the youth project started in 1991. He counsels kids and thinks up ways to keep them out of gangs.

Bounhong Khommarath continues the list of the favorite crimes of Lao and Cambodian gangs. "Then the next would be home burglary. They keep on watching almost a week before they break in. The other type of break-in, let's say that I have a kind of kid that's acting up. And then he knows your son, your daughter's that's also gangs. And then they rob their own parents when the parents' not home. But this one is kind of minimal.

"Then armed robbery. The kids from Orange County come in here and know a couple of gang kids in here that used to run away, and they associate and they just go over and rip armed robbery, but this is less number.

"For the home burglary, armed robbery, these, they target their own people. Their own Asian people. We have heard that especially the family that's on welfare, they know that the family do not keep the money to the bank, they're just hiding it at home. So these do pop up news here and there. And again, if they're on welfare, they tend not to report to the authorities."

Middle-class Asians?

"That probably be the Filipinos and Vietnamese. For the Vietnamese, they're the ones that came in here in 1975, '76, '77. Those are the ones that are the elite group that escaped right at the fall, and then relatives leaves. So we could see here lots of physicians, store owners. Residential areas would be in the Rancho Penasquitos, those areas. The lower ones, the late arrivals, the new arrival here tend to live in the lower social economic areas mixed with the other so-called poor."

The Legend of Ith

A French philosopher said, in the absence of myth, people will create myth. On the street, even in the storefront, where no stories of heroes of your own kind were told to you, you will create stories of heroes to tell your blood and kin. Though he tries to neutralize the heroic effect of the story of the founder of the Lao gang, by avoiding using his name, the good officer's omission is a form of respect and deepens the legend and mystery of Ith Chernivase, the first Oriental Killer Boy.

"One thing you gotta remember is that these were *kids* that started this," Roy Moody says. "There was very little adult influence when they started these gangs. Take the Laos. They used to call themselves the 48th Street Crips. Most of the neighborhoods that they came into the African American gangs were Crips sets. Crips sets were supposedly the biggest and supposed to be the meanest.

"There was a kid that was a couple a years older than most of the other kids. And he was in high school. And he came along and said, 'Okay, no more. Nobody's gonna protect you anymore. The school's not going to protect you. The police aren't going to help you. I'm going to help you.' And anybody who said anything bad about them, or picked on them, he would attack 'em. He would physically attack them. He was big. He was very aggressive. And so, all the kids, they loved him.

"And he's the one that formed the main Lao gang here in San Diego

"So these kids said, 'Well, we're a Crip set too.' So the Laos in the Southeastern Division used to call themselves the 48th Street Crips. But then the leader, when he was arrested the first time, he went to jail. He was eighteen, came out at the end of 1988, and he told everybody, 'We're no longer the 48th Street Crips.' So something happened in jail for him. He didn't want to have any association with Crips. And he said, 'We are now the Oriental Killer Boys.'

"And they would idolize this guy. They would do anything for him. They would break into cars. They'd break into homes. They would even do shootings for the guy. Because here was somebody that finally would stick up for them, when they saw that nobody else would. And this person, incidentally, was shot and killed in a gang-related shooting in 1990.

"Ith (pronounced 'it') was one of the first nine of the OKBs. Ith made everyone feel like they were his best friend. Some boys remember Ith told them not to hang out with him, to stay in school, and stay home. Ith forbid his sister to go out with gangsters, and kept gangsters away from her. He made sure she stayed in school. He took care of her," Roy Moody says.

"She loved her brother very much and it devastated her when he was shot dead by a rival gang. Just devastated her. Young men cry when they speak of Ith's death. If he were still alive, the OKBs would have continued to grow instead of splitting and fragmenting.

"I actually believe what kept everybody together were personalities, individuals, who said 'This is it!' And of course, these kids growing up, most of them live in lower economic neighborhoods. And they see that maybe the gang members driving a nice Honda Prelude, with all these stolen parts on it. A nice car. And he might have a few dollars in his pocket. Some girls are attracted to that element. And so they see the pretty girl and his arm. And so these young kids growing up think that's success. Even though they're used to traveling to other cities and whatnot, they go from one Lao community or Cambodian community right into another. And so they're very limited in knowing what opportunities are out there for them. So they see that as success. It's very hard for them to picture themselves as a doctor, as a lawyer, as a police officer."

Storytelling in Portland

In the early '80s, I was in Portland high schools telling Chinese and Japanese stories in the morning and loaning out bilingual Chinese fairy tales and comic book novels of the heroic tradition at noon from two milk baskets. Every day, in every high school, Asian immigrant kids took all my books at noon and brought them back at nine the next morning.

I was surprised to learn most of these kids had reached high school and were ready to graduate without ever having been told a kid story while they were kids. Not just the Asian kids, the Chinese and Vietnamese and Lao and Cambodian and Thai children of boat people. The big black kids in their letter jackets, punching each other for fun, the squirrely white kids with more hair on one side of their heads than the other, didn't know "Rumpelstiltskin," "Sleeping Beauty," "The Tar Baby." So I told them their own stories before I told them stories from China and Japan. And another surprise. All these angry kids listened. They were kids again. Their childhoods had been on hold.

I was the marketplace storyteller. In one school, an Asian kid walked up to me, smiled, opened his jacket and showed me a gun, because everybody liked the storyteller. A gun! A revolver. .38 caliber. I looked him in the eye, smiled, and told him to get out of here, be a good boy, go home and not come to school with that thing, and saw him out one of the big front doors. Whew! The power of the story.

In another school, the teachers told me a couple of white kids jumped a couple of Asian kids talking their Asian language to each other at their lockers. The next day, before school, five or six Asian kids jumped the white kids and beat them up. At lunch time, the Asian kids jumped the white kids and beat them up. After school the yellows in numbers beat up the two white boys. It went on for weeks. They wanted to know why.

"Because these kids are small and speak a language that's funny nonsense to young white American ears, the white boys think the yellows are easy pickings," I told them. "These kids were born in countries that have been in a continuous state of war for four hundred years; to get here, they had to escape war, the Communists, pirates, small boats, and gang warfare in the detention camps in Hong Kong. They have seen, or been a part of real war and murder while these kids were doing kindergarten. To these kids, life is war. Unless you are willing to kill them, don't mess with them. Beating up bullies is the easy part."

But that was back in the eighties. San Diego is another time. Another story. Here the Lao and Cambodian kids of today's gangs never saw the war. They remember TV, not boats and camps. They are the children of the children who escaped Pol Pot, the Pathet Lao, the Khmer Rouge, the Cultural Revolution.

ROY MOODY

"You see, with these kids," Roy Moody says, "they were very, very young when the wars were on in their countries. And you know, Cambodians suffer very high post traumatic stress. But you don't see the violence attributed to post traumatic stress in the adults. You see it in the kids that aren't suffering from the post traumatic stress.

"Why they tend to be so violent at times is because of their physical size. Somebody insults them. You know, Asians tend to be smaller than Occidentals, or Hispanics, or African Americans. And so what they do is they always take one more step of violence. They're not going to go toe-to-toe with somebody. They might pick up a chair and hit the guy, but they're not going to trade punches with somebody that's physically bigger. There are a few that are exceptions to that rule. But they always take that step further. If someone they know is a gang member throws something at their car, they're not going to get out of the car and confront them. They'll go home get the gun and come back and do the shooting."

BOUNHONG KHOMMARATH

"The hard core, this kind start from anywhere age nine, ten and so on. They misbehave in classrooms and express themselves with anti-social behavior, talk back to the teacher, disrupt the class. The teacher maybe sends them home for two, three days suspension. Now, kids enjoy freedom and get more acting out at home. So parents don't know what to do. The bad kids just band together with the bad kids. And, of course, they do not choose to fight with anybody. So they always have fights with the other ethnic group that already band together as a gang. So that's why we seen that no matter when we look at Hispanic, African American, Lao, or Cambodian. They just fight among so-called gang type. But they just do not go after any normal blacks or any normal Hispanics to treat to the fight.

"There's the same thing with African American gangs. They just do not go around and beat all the Lao kids. But they just have with the eye contact. That triggers the conflict. And if you are gangs, the chance of fighting would be like 90 percent. But if you are a decent black student and a decent Lao student, you could make friends easily. So, trouble kids tend to have problems with other trouble kids. We see rarely that innocent either black or Lao have fights with another innocent.

"We do work here with drug and alcohol prevention. Our community, the parents, do not see, it is invisible for them. But gang kids, runaways, truancy, misbehave, or acting up and do not obey parents — that's a very visible problem for the parents. That's how they refer their children to us.

"The kids that are referred here by police or probation to do community work, to do counseling, have some kind of activity and linkage among themselves, but speaking about the numbers of kids in gangs, the police, they take records, they take pictures, they probably have a better sense of the numbers. But for us, when we talk to a kid, he says, 'No, no, no! I do not belong to a gang!' But he knows friends that commit shootings, or commit burglaries, or auto thefts, and so on. So why you come here? 'Oh, I just joyride with my friends, you know.'"

Storefront Police Station
ROY MOODY

"This is a very mixed neighborhood. City Heights. But this Storefront, even though we're located in City Heights, would be citywide services. It's just that this is more the center of the city.

"The Storefront was established in 1987 because the San Diego Police Department knew that there was crimes being committed in the Asian community, but the crimes weren't being reported. And so it was designed to be away from traditional image of police stations so we could get more people in.

"We have our community service officers that come from the community here in San Diego. We go to all the events. All the activities.. We've gone out and built a relationship between the community and the police department. And people come here they can report crimes. This acts pretty much as a central referral system for the Southeast Asian community. They can go to a phone book if they don't read and speak English. If they need help, they come here and we'll find the answer for him. We don't turn anybody away. We try to find the answer for 'em. It might not always the answer that they want to hear, but we'll get 'em an answer.

"They come with problems with their kids, husband-wife problems, the landlord, crime. They ask us to mediate neighborhood disputes. It could be a host of things. There's a lot of fraud in the community, so when they get ripped off, they come in and say, 'Hey, what happened?'

"So this Storefront is pretty much a catchall for anything and everything that can go wrong in the community. Currently, we have nine community service officers. We're budgeted for thirteen. We're in the process of hiring. And the breakdown will be five Vietnamese, three Cambodian, two Lao, two Hmong, and one Ethiopian, which serves the Ethiopian community out of here.

"Back in the early '80s we had extortion here. A lot of communities were afraid. But the last few times that we had extortion groups that came into San Diego, we were notified. The police department was notified. They were set upon. They were arrested and they were convicted. So San Diego's gotten a very good reputation in Asian communities, across the United States, that San Diego's the place not to come to try to set up an extortion ring.

"Most extortion that occurs now with the shopkeepers is under $5 type of extortion. You have a gang member who walks in who says, 'Hey, I don't have any money. I just want a pack of cigarettes. I'll pay you back next week.'

"'Well, you didn't pay me back for the last twenty packs of cigarettes.'

"'Well, yeah, I know, but I'll pay ya back. And besides, it's better that you lose a pack of cigarettes today than to pay $500 for that broken glass window tonight.'

"And the shop owner's thinking to himself, 'If I call the police on the two dollar pack of cigarettes, first of all, will the police really arrest this guy?'

"Yes, we will arrest him.

"But he's also thinking about, 'My window's gonna get broken by his friends. That's $500 that I gotta pay out right away. And if I arrest this guy, I'm going to have to spend a whole day in court, probably several days in court. Who's going to take my place here in the store?'

"So, you know, before they call us, it's gotta be something that's worth their while to call. It's very difficult to get them to call on shoplifts. Most of the extortions are under $5.

"One time we had some Cambodian gang members that were doing door-to-door extortion. 'Hi, so-and-so. Do you have $5 I can borrow? Oh, it's better to lose $5 now than for somebody to break out your car windows.'

"You even have cases of kids extorting their parents. We had a thirteen year-old gang member kid who admitted to his mom, *'yeah, I need money for rock cocaine.'* And she told him, no. He wanted eight bucks, and he broke all the windows in the house. He was arrested.

"Our residential robberies have gone way, way down. We've been very aggressive here, attacking the Asian gang problem. We have our detectives who know who the players are. This Storefront has definitely opened the doors of communication between the Asian groups. So the communication's going back and forth both ways. Asian gang members can no longer operate in San Diego like they did in the past, without being identified. We know who they are. And if they commit a crime, we will arrest them.

KENJI IMA

Kenji Ima, twenty years on the Sociology faculty at San Diego State University, is a paper activist, "not a street person," out to turn kids away from gangs. Dead kids get to him. He writes the grant applications for UPAC. He connects with San Diego Police Department on Asian gangs.

"The Black Jacket Boys used to dominate Madison High. Chinese Viet. Low profile and retired," Kenji Ima says. The bad boys grew up and entered the middle class. He feels funny about that, because, "they were involved in an unsolved homicide. It was done inside a restaurant on Convoy Street, which is a very busy street. People knew who did it. But no one was able to come up with the goods on them. The police are kind of frustrated over it, because no one would testify. They killed somebody, and because nobody would appear to testify against them, nothing was done about it. I feel that you did it, you should…but for them, life just goes on. The gang retired, and they have jobs now and are just living their lives.

"You know, it's water under the bridge to them. As one kid told me, 'Well, they really didn't mean to kill him. It just happened.'

"That caught your attention, huh?"

"It sounds very Chinese."

"Those who lived through the Cultural Revolution and survived and came over here affect many people over here as ruthless. Do you know the word *schnorr*? A *schnorr* is someone you don't invite to your wedding, but shows up and eats up all your food."

It Wouldn't Hurt for the Good Sociologist to Read a Few Comic Books

Kenji Ima believes there's something in the culture, a certain ruthlessness, common among Asians from the continent.

He doesn't know the source. It wouldn't hurt the good sociologist to read a few comic books. The culture comes to the kids in the stories that shaped their childhood. He doesn't know Sun Tzu, the strategist, or the comic book versions of *The Book of 36 Stratagems* published in Korea, Singapore, and Hong Kong, or *Romance of the Three Kingdoms* or *The Water Margin*. The Chinese and Vietnamese gang kids do.

A gang kid in New York introduced me to the *Outlaws of the Water Margin*, by pointing to a poster of the 108 outlaw chiefs standing on the Golden Shores of Mt. Liangshan on the wall over his bed. "Recognize them?" he asked.

It was a test and I'd flunked. The kid was surprised and offended I didn't know what every kid knew.

Mao Tse-tung tells the world through Han Suyin that his favorite books are *Three Kingdoms, Water Margin, Monkey's Journey to the West*, not to impose his will on the masses but to identify himself as one of the people.

These are the works that have dominated the Asian childhood and Asian folk art and opera since the Ming. All the works of the heroic tradition, including the fictionalized legend of Ngawk Fay, the tattooed general, feature Kwan Kung, the god of war, or a fictional descendant of Kwan Kung as a blood brother.

Three Kingdoms is comparable to The *Iliad, Water Margin* to *Robin Hood, Monkey's Journey to the West* to *The Odyssey*.

Theravada Buddhism: Big Wheel-Little Wheel
ROY MOODY

"You gotta understand Theravada Buddhism. Let's just take the small country of Laos, where conflict is something that's to be avoided at all times."

Does the righteous Buddhist repugnance for conflict explain why a relative handful of aggressive, cruel Pathet Laos could take over the entire country of Laos? No, Officer Roy doesn't want to go that far, sounding very diplomatic, or very Lao. He is saying that, because of that attitude to avoid conflict at any cost, some Lao and Cambodian parents are at a loss dealing with their children raised in the American soup of conflict.

"Here in America there's always conflict. Everybody's in conflict, it seems. And they (the parents) don't know how to deal with the kids who aren't minding, because, where they come from, there are no street gangs. When the parents sent kids to school, they went to school. You know, they learned! But here, kids go to school, but they don't learn. They ditch. They do what they want to. And their parents are having a very hard time coping with that.

"This thing with the gangs is they see a transference of power between parents and the kids. Parents who might not speak English, who can't read English, they have to depend on their kids to get 'em through everyday life here in America. Read bills, read anything that comes through. So there's a shift of power. All of a sudden, these young kids have all this power. And pretty soon, it's like, 'I'm going to do what I want to do, because you don't know.'"

BOUNHONG KHOMMARATH

Bounhong Khommarath sees Buddhist avoidance of conflict as a strategy instead of an inhibiting dogma, an advantage and not a handicap that has helped the Laos and Cambodians settle in San Diego. "Because that's the way guide me to respect other people, no matter what they believe, and accept another way of life. Also, I have the sense, because I have these kids, that's why they give me reward that my kids doing well, so that urge me to help more people in my line of work. America is the land of opportunity, and is a materialized world and a lot of TVs and automobiles. And then, if I don't have the sense of Buddhism to refrain me, I would maybe try to get a Mercedes, or BMW, or whatever. So if people have that, that's the opportunity, that's what they should get. So I'm just happy what I have here.

"I think the young couple that maintains traditional ways and then tries to also adopt the new ways would be manageable to continue their lifestyle here. So the traditional ways have a lot to play in their lives. They cannot be American totally. They cannot be Asian totally, but maybe have a sense of awareness of both worlds and then try to guide them through."

It sounds like Monkey leading the pilgrims west through strange country, strange people, strange ways to India to recover Buddhist scripture.

A Story Grandma Told Me
BOUNHONG KHOMMARATH

"Personally, I'm forty-six, going to be forty-seven. I'm a refugee from Laos, came to this country in '78, June '78, and with the agency ten years, shuffled from project to project, depending on the funding and the program design.

"My grandma. Father's mother. I recall my grandma. I have less interaction with my mom and dad. They're real busy. Grandma is always there at home. She's just like...not babysit, but also give nurturing and guidance.

"Mostly the story that she told us is like the Bible story is in the Buddhist Bible, let's say. The good manners is always the winner, but at first the bad the evil win first. But at the end the good manner is the one that the winner. Teach us about how to behave. Teach us about to pay the gratitude. Respect the elderly, respect the teacher, respect to the boss to feel proud of your job or whatever you have. Do not jealousy other people have more that what you got. So that I think that's applied to my life now.

"I know that. Because my family is not that in the upper level. We are in the upper level of the lower class. Let's say, we were not even the lower level of the middle class.

"We live in the neighborhood that are local gangs already there, and kids tend to acting out like among ducks want to be a duck. And also because working with this agency I see a lot of what happened, and then my job also to go out and teach all the parents, so I'm equipped with a material resource to teach my own kids. That's why I say lucky. If I'm working in, let's say, in auto mechanic field or sales, I'd probably look at money, money, money and I'd have no time to interact with my own family.

"Everywhere that I have time to mingling with the group that my staff bring here, I told them a story."

"Tell me a story."

"There's a boy that's in the poor family, and mom and dad just go out gathering the food. Just like a version of the Jack and the Giant? And the same kind of story. Very parallel. Family very poor. Mom and dad try to get rid of him. But he managed to stick with the family. Finally parent escape to manage to leave him in the woods.

"Later on parents kind of becoming stable economically and want to get the boy back. When they reach to the jungle now, the boy all grow hair, becoming like the monkey or something. The story end that way. The boy is a monkey. And they say that because the parents have sinned in the previous life, and then they're so poor, and after that they teach kid to behave well. So when you have your own child he will not become like a monkey in the jungle.

"So, when you're a kid, just preparing yourself, and you become a parent yourself. And at the same time, we tell kids, because your parents probably do good in the previous life, they could raise you, becoming stronger in yourself, and you'll get older, just go back and take care of them. If you do not take care of them, your next life will become having poor parents and then your kids will be in the jungle.

"Those are the sort of stories that we were taught."

It's Kind of a Catch 22 for the Parents
ROY MOODY

"We had a meeting here at our Storefront with Cambodian gang members, then we had a meeting of the Lao gang members at the Lao temple. First they say that they came together for self-protection. But the biggest thing they say is, 'Hey, it's fun! I'm having fun! I'm having a good time. I like the freedom. I like excitement. I'm having a good time.'

"You know, a lot of kids don't ever associate with gang members. They stay at home. They go to school. Nobody comes along and forces you to join a gang.

"You know, we've heard stories that people are pressured. Like we had one, where a father's oldest — and I think he had four or five kids — his oldest son who was about thirteen or fourteen was claiming a Cambodian gang. And what happened was, his father told him not to not to, and he still was. And one day he saw him hanging out with the boys and came home. And the father, 'Why? Why're you doing this?'

"And he goes, 'Well, if I don't hang out with them, they'll beat me up.'

"And so for this Cambodian father, what he's thinking is, 'Are you going to be more afraid of them? Or are you going to be more afraid of me?' And so the father beat him, and beat him real bad. And CPS (Child Protective Services) came and they took all the kids out, and the father wasn't beating this poor child, you know, because he liked it. He saw that as his only option to save his son. Because, we're getting calls all the time from parents who ask, 'What can I do to get my kids to quit hanging out with gangs?'

"And the reality is, there aren't any systems set up to help parents in this situation. We gotta wait for the kids to break the law to get 'em in the criminal justice system. Or if you beat 'em up, then we can have CPS come in and take the kids away. There's nothing in between to force these kids into counseling. There's nothing to force these kids into any type of program that will help 'em. So it's kind of a Catch 22 situation for these parents."

The Snake and the Mongoose
VITOU REAT

Vitou Reat and his older brother saw their father taken and thrown to the ground in front of them and tied up. He was eleven and his older brother twelve. The Khmer Rouge wanted to kill the boys, but they were too young. Their father was taken away and killed. Vitou is twenty-six now, working as a Cambodian Counselor at the Southeast Asian Project. Occasionally he works at the Old Temple Cambodian language school as a substitute teacher. He thumbs through a book of Cambodian folktales, points to the pictures and tells me his favorite, "The Snake and the Mongoose."

"The crane lives near the snake, and every time the crane has children the snake eats the children. So the cranes get together and have a meeting, and one of the cranes has an idea. 'I know the mongoose. The mongoose can eat the snake.' The problem is how to bring him here to eat the snake. One of the cranes says, 'Just leave a trail of fish leading to the snake's den.' The cranes drop a trail of fish and the mongoose comes along eating the fish, finds the snake and eats the snake and sees the baby cranes and eats them too!"

He's a kid again and laughs, sees I don't quite get it, and explains the story. "They like to warn the children that if you thinking, you have to think all the way. Like what's going to happen next? The cranes didn't think what the mongoose would do after it ate the snake. They want the children to think long, not short.

"My English is so young. I hardly able to tell you the story. From Cambodia. No just me. I got married. A chemist San Diego State. I speak Russian. In Moscow six years. I just go to college there. I don't English before I came here." He's been here a year and a half.

"When Pol Pot there, nobody left the country. The border closed. My father, Pol Pot killed, just like that. My mother in Cambodia still. One younger sister, and one older sister, and one brother older than me.

"Yeah, Pol Pot kill my.... I don't want to talk about that story."

He turns away, holds back tears. But more of the story comes.

"They want to kill all the men you know, that was their plan, but I was too young. Eleven years old. After my dad run away, I run after them and they want to take us too, and they have gun on us and everything, so we just run away."

Outside the temple, Pematokyryasmey Chunn, an SDPD Community Service Officer, offers me a can of soda pop. The women who come to the temple with food for the monks got soda for us. It's Saturday morning and children from six to eighteen years old come into the temple yard for Cambodian school. The boys wear white shirts and khaki pants. The girls wear white blouses and blue skirts. The morning is cold and rainy. No one complains when the kids show up with all kinds and colors of sweaters and jackets over their uniform.

"I am not a psychologist," Chunn says, "I do not know psychology. But the psychologists say the kids go into gangs and shoot and violence because they saw nothing but violence, and murder escape from Pol Pot. Look at these kids here. They are all born in America. What do they remember from Pol Pot? The oldest ones, they are two-three-four-year-old babies when they escape. What do they remember?"

"I remember," Chuun says. "I am not doing violence. I am not gang. I hate them gangs."

This guy hurts. All the Cambodians twenty-five and over hurt bad. They all have bad memories that won't let them go. Memories about Pol Pot, the dictator taking daddy away and shooting him dead.

Chuun looks at the children hunched over their books, pencils in hand, and the memories come back to get him. Cambodian grammars are hard to find, because Pol Pot killed all the teachers and killed all the books, all the writers, all the artists and intellectuals and lawyers and college educated and with them effectively destroyed the culture, the very language of Cambodia. In San Diego, at this Old Temple, for these girls in blue skirts and white blouses, and boys in khaki pants and white shirts, and odd sweaters and jackets — the death of all the teachers and artists, writers, intellectuals, and college educated means the books of grammar, the book of folk tales, the book of proverbs, the books of manners and history were all written here, in San Diego, from memory, by hand and photocopied, hundreds of times, by those who had the memory and the hands.

"We escape Pol Pot, we cross the minefields, cross the mortar, we cross the river, come to America to save the children, and still we lose them. They become Americanized and go with the gangs. The violence, the gangs are American, not Cambodian. The psychologists are American. I don't care what they say. The psychologists don't know."

The first grade has a mix of little kids and not so little pubescent girls and boys. They take their seats under a plastic awning. The first grade is meeting in an open carport. And the second grade is meeting in a garage, with the garage door open.

The kid teaching the first grade looks thirteen. He's nineteen and a half. His name is Sophea Ross. He uses the nickname "Tommy." He says the police regularly stop him and refuse to believe he's not thirteen and too young to drive his car. Escaped Cambodia at two. In a camp in Thailand for four and a half years. Ten years in the United States. Three younger brothers. Two younger sisters. He learned Cambodian here, in this school, with these homemade books. He was a monk here at the Old Temple for six months in 1990. Shaved all his hair, his eyebrows, and wore the robes. He's in San Diego Community College now, and is the editor-writer of *Cambodian Now,* a Cambodian language monthly magazine with a print run of 2000. They print 5000 for the month of Cambodian New Year. Tommy Ross's friend, Woody Mean, is the publisher of *Cambodian Now;* he's also the printer, and owns the print shop. Tommy hates gangs, has never been a part of gangs. But he dresses like gangs. "Style," he says. It's style, not content.

The enrollment at the weekend language school is increasing. Parents and the teachers and the temple are talking of expanding, building another building for more classrooms. For some of the young, the adventure of rescuing Cambodian civilization, language, and literature from the ravages of the Cultural Revolution and Pol Pot out of the memories of old learned men in America, and Xerox machines, is more attractive than drugs, gangs, and guns.

BOUNHONG KHOMMARATH

The Union of Pan Asian Communities is the umbrella organization that serves the Korean, Japanese, Chinese Lao, Vietnamese, Cambodian, Filipino, and Hmong communities and all the ethnic groups from the pan Asian community.

"This program I'm in charge of, High Risk Youth, got funded from the county of San Diego, from the Alcohol and Drug Prevention Services. And we focus to serve children nine to thirteen, and their family members, for drug and alcohol education and prevention.

"And the focus of the services is targeted in the schools in this area, of course; for the Filipinos, it's in National City and Chula Vista. We organize a after school program, recruit students from the schools and we talk to the counselor, district counselors, and Principal, so they open a classroom for us, for kids to come in with the parents' authorization to participate in the twelve-week session for controlled competency training curriculum, include the students to learn about their own home culture. So students would have a better understanding of their parents' culture. And in addition to that, we teach them about life skills, like communication skills, problem solving, anger management, and include a big piece of alcohol and drug education. What they should be aware of and what they should know. So when they grow up they should be equipped with these knowledges."

The English he speaks is original and strange to my ears. A strange mash of baby talk vocabulary, shipping expediter verbs, and bureaucratic gibberish that works on me. The grammar is a mystery to me, but it always was. Understanding what he just said sometimes comes as a delayed reaction. There's a lot of impressionist art in the way he makes himself understood in English. I wonder what the French thought of his French.

"To me as the counselor or somebody that provide advice, they do not identify themselves, 'I am here from the dragons or Crips' or whatever. They don't indicate those numbers or identify themselves as gang members here."

Numbers of gang kids? Up or down?

"It's kind of grow up and rising. Then six months ago stable. And three months now, I do not hear anything that increase, seems to be a quiet moment. But kids are kids and always they are just like a time bomb. If something clicks, they would gather friends and then another fight, another shooting occur. But for the time being, for the last three months, it's kind of going down a little bit. Six months ago: stable. But nine months before this, it's kind of really high.

"This is the fourth year of the program now, and we serve close to one thousand kids. And we do not count the family members — dad, mom, and maybe sometimes sisters and brothers, but just individual kid that we register and we open the case file for them.

"Mixed gender in prevention work. Intervention, kids referred by police and probation, 90 percent boys. Less than five, girls. Runaways, referred by probation, that associate with joy riding, auto stealing."

Cambodian gangs fight Lao gangs, he says.

"I have working with some Cambodian kid, he said, 'I don't hate Lao kid. I only hate Lao gangs.' For the Lao also, you see Cambodian walking by, doing the same thing they are doing.

"And I have one time another gang Linda Vista area, dress red. Red cap. Red shoelaces. Red T-shirt. And another one we do an interview here, and another one come in for counseling. Blue, and he's from this area.

"Oh, they look at each other just like about to grab the neck. I said, Oh, no no no, I cannot place the one from Linda Vista to work here, while the other one already works here I have to tell the mom, 'Okay you have to look another agency, for the community work.'

"But other than that if a Cambodian gang's in here and they see Lao kids come in and out, no problem. The same thing if a Lao gang's in here and they seeing Cambodian walk in an out, talking in Cambodian, they just do not bother each other."

Did this Lao-Cambodian rivalry exist in Asia?

"No, No. Just happened here. In 1980–82, they're still good friends. But somehow with the girls, coming in and treat the violence and afterwards retaliation come forth and back, forth and back. Even exploding to the level of drive-by shooting.

"Even now, the original first guy is already been away, but still the younger one have still continue the quarrel."

Car Tour
ROY MOODY

Roy Moody drives with his nice Smith and Wesson tucked into his belt, and his walkie-talkie by his side. Blocks of slab sided stucco boxes with little yards. "The Laos refer to it as the Market Street Area. It's in South Eastern Division. You can see it's not too far from where we came from, City Heights is just a couple of miles."

We rubber past a group of boys slouching home from school.

"Market Street gang members. They're Hispanics," Roy Moody says.

"Do they mess with Asian gangs?" I ask.

"Every once in awhile there's some conflict between the two. But it has more to do with machismo or saving for Hispanics, machismo for Asians is saving face. You know, words are exchanged.

"So the main gang in this area is Lao." He points to graffiti spray painted on a garage door. "'OKB,' 'Oriental Killer Boys,'" he reads off the doors as we pass. We are driving the streets of OKB turf, looking for gang kids hanging out and kicking back after school and the streets are bare.

"We might be out just a little bit early," Roy Moody says. "And it's a little bit cold.

"See the Neighborhood Watch signs? I'm very proud of it. In the Lao community we've got sixteen Lao Neighborhood Watch groups. And I was told that this would be impossible to do, given the history of setting up Neighborhood Watches in the community. It doesn't sound like a big deal. You gotta understand with the Southeast Asian countries, when their countries fell to Communism, they set up a series of neighborhood watches, but the purpose of those neighborhood watches was to report political indiscretions. So just the mere idea of that kind of system here, of course, they're going to be resistant to it.

"We meet, we try to set up two meetings a month. To try to get across the city. Then we have a Lao advisory board to the Storefront. We meet once a month to discuss neighborhood issues and problems with kids.

"We definitely stress that what the kids do, it will come back to haunt the parents. That's why it's so important to know what their kids are doing at all times.

"As a parent, you feel your kids are doing something wrong? You have a right to go into your kid's room. You have the right to go into the cars and look for illegal things. As a parent, not only do you have the right, you have the responsibility to do that. And we've gotten, in our Storefront, in a year, a year and half or so we've gotten about 28 firearms turned in. And they range from .22s to 9mm handguns to shotguns. We tell parents where to look. Look in the vents. Look in the fenders of the cars. Look under the engine. Look behind the heaters. Look under the beds. They find 'em. They call us and they turn 'em in.

"As a matter of fact, today, this morning we had a Cambodian father find…he found .22 hidden in the backyard, and he brought it in this morning."

We drive by a high school. Girls are on the field for cheerleading practice.

"There's been an increase in reporting and there's been in increase in the willingness to become involved with the police. It's very, very difficult. It took me over five years before I could get 'em started," Roy Moody says, searching for kids hanging out in baggy clothes.

"You know that's one of the things that is people come in, they say, Oh, we're going to do this, and we're going to do that. And then they disappear. And so, because I worked in this neighborhood for such a long time, I've got a little bit of credibility.

"And it's working. Crime only flourishes where it's tolerated. Somebody on the Neighborhood Watch reported Lao gang members were putting a stolen car into one of the garages, and so we went out there. I called for units, and units went out there. And the car was, in fact stolen. Nobody was around the car. But at least we have 'em watching. And so I think the community is getting the idea, that if they don't tolerate it, it won't happen.

"This area here is Gompers Park. At two o'clock this should start filling up. But it's cold right now, so it's going to be hard to find people hanging out.

He nods toward a row of garage doors and reads the graffiti. "See, 'OKB Jr.' 'LOK' means Little Oriental Killer Boys. 'Laos Pride.' And then the rest of this stuff is just tags.

"And then you have your Market Street gangs. They keep these alleys pretty clean. You know, they don't get a lot of city services back here. 'LOK,' 'Little Oriental Killer.' 'Gekko,' 'Rascal,' 'Bull.' Nicknames. Lao. Someone wrote 'OBS' and crossed it out. And '12 15 11' The 12th, 15th and 11th letters of the alphabet, L-O-K. They crossed them out. 'OKB Jr. L-O-K. Remember Little Oriental Killer Boy. OKB Jr. OKB. Laos Pride. Oakland CRIPS. Laos Pride. Fuck all them. OBS' crossed out. 'OKB. Laos Oriental Killer.'

"Now see you got 'TOC,' Tiny Oriental Crips, which is from the Linda Vista area. 'TOC #1.' A lot of 'TOC' and 'OKB,' they're relatives from Linda Vista and Chollas View Area. 'Penguin Jr. Lorrie. Blue. T-Fu Jr. T-Dog. LOK. OKB. TOC. OMC,' Oriental Mob Crip.

"LOC, technically they're just smaller OKB. 'OB' crossed out. 'Oriental Boys, crossed out, '187' in its place, the penal code for homicide.

"You had OBS come in here one night, back in 1990, and they

wrote OBS, which took a lot of guts for them to come down and do that in these alleys back here."

Interesting. War is waged on garage doors.

"Back in 1989, I had this beat. I was the only officer up here. Me and a partner. One patrol car."

STREET SCENE

It looks like a fight and doesn't look like a fight. People of all ages and roughly the same height watch on the sidewalk in front of their yards. Family groups watch the blur of bare arms and baggy pants from their doorways. Officer Moody stops the car. He talks to the fighters who've stopped fighting. I walk down the street and talk to a sixteen year-old Lao kid in baggy shirt and baggy pants.

"Whaddaya wanta know?" Drippy, asks with his hands in his pockets.

"You in a gang?" I ask.

"No," Drippy says. "I used to. I used to be in OKB for about like a year and a half. Get, like hang around for a long time. So, they just jump me in."

"So everyone gathered around and beat on you."

"Yeah," he says with a shy smile, like I've guessed the name of his girlfriend.

"Did you get to fight back?"

"Yeah. I get to fight back. But now, I just goin' to school. Stop all that stuff."

"Did you enjoy being in the gang? Was it fun?"

"Yeah, it was fun, a little while."

I turn to stout kid, a couple years younger and a few inches shorter than Drippy. "How about you, young man, are you in a gang?" I ask.

"Naw."

"Naw?"

"Naw."

"Sure?"

"Yeah."

"Wanta be?"

"Naw."

"Why not?"

"It's not cool."

"You dress like a gang kid."

"Yeah, but, I'm like...I jusssss. I used to play with them, but not no more. So I play with him." Nods to Drippy.

"You go to school?"

"Yeah, Gompers."

"How old are you?"

"I'm thirteen."

"What grade are you in.?"

"Seventh."

"How old are you, Drippy?"

"I'm sixteen. I'm in tenth grade."

"So, how do you get out of the gangs?"

"Stop playing with them. Stay home. Go to school. That's it. When you see them, we just talk to them and just go home."

Down the street, the Lao and Mexican crowd recognizes Roy Moody. He's taller than anyone here and is the only man I've seen in San Diego with hair this color of red. Short short hair, like a dry, well-mown lawn. The color and texture of his hair and his eyebrows make Roy Moody's face look like a furry, cuddly toy. He keeps himself on a short leash and works hard to consider everything he says, and communicate respect for his listeners when he says it. Everybody knows he has a nice Smith and Wesson 9mm tucked under his belt. But everybody on this block, at least, likes talking to the big guy being gentle and patient and polite.

"They don't beat you up before letting you leave the gang?" I ask Drippy, with an eye to the action around Moody.

"No they never do that," Drippy says.

"So is it hard to stay out of the gang?"

"It's not hard, just walk away."

"Then do they diss you when you walk away?"

"No, they don't diss me."

"You got brothers and sisters?"

"Yeah, I got three sisters."

"They hang out with gang kids?"

"No!"

"How old are your sisters?"

"Oh, one is juvie for being a gang. And one graduate already, preparing for college."

"How old is your sister in juvie?"

"Fourteen."

"And you're sixteen. Did you talk to her about being in a gang?"

"Yeah. I told her. I told her a lot of things. Why do you want to join a gang? Just going dying or going to jail."

"And what did she say?"

"She just go and play outside, you know. Hang around with the wrong crowd."

"So, how'd she get arrested?"

"I don't know. I didn't ask my parents that."

"Your parents work?"

"Yeah. My dad's a security, and my mom makes clothes."

"What do you want to do?"

"Go to school graduate. Be somebody."

Back in the car, Roy Moody says "Did you see the girl I was talking to out there? Now, see she's a pretty good student. She graduated, she's never been involved. You were talking to her brother who was involved. There's even a little sister who's been nothing but problems.

"Drippy said she was in juvie now."

"I think her sister said something about drugs. Fourteen years old. Run away numerous times. She's definitely got...but see the contrasts? You've got the oldest, who's not that old. What, she's eighteen, at the oldest right now. Her parents are good parents. Both parents work. The oldest has turned out great. The middle one is right on that borderline. He can go either way. And the youngest one is totally out of control. You know, that's not a dysfunctional family."

The Tiger and the Monk

Vitou finds the story of "The Tiger And The Monk Who Lives In The Forest" in the home made Xerox book. I ask him to tell it to me.

"The monk finds a tiger dead on top of the den of a big snake. The monk has the power to make somebody dead to be alive. The tiger wakes and gets angry at the monk and says, I was sleeping, and you woke me up and I don't get enough sleep. So I have to eat you because you woke me up. The monk tries to explain you were sleeping on a hole where a snake lives, and the tiger didn't believe him. The monk says that's not right. Ask any animal, the Tiger says. The monk ask the wolf if it's right for the tiger to eat the monk. The wolf thinks that ev-

214

eryday of his life he lives off the leftovers of the tiger's skill, so he doesn't want to make the tiger angry, so it's right for the tiger to eat the monk. So they asks the buffalo. The buffalo says people are no good. People make the buffalo work and then eat them, so it's okay for the tiger to eat the monk. So they go to the elephant, the people are bad, because they make the elephant work all day. So people are bad. Eat the monk. So they go to the rabbit and the rabbit says I cannot say anything. I have to see what happened where it happened. So they walk back to the hole and the tiger lays down over the hole and lays down as if to sleep and the snake comes out and bites the tiger and the tiger dies again, and the rabbit says, don't make him alive again."

Vitou laughs. With this book in his hand, he's a kid again. Some of his childhood had been on hold till now. He grins as he thumbs through the book of Xeroxed pages.

"I enjoy this. I read this a lot."

Same thing. Alligator lives in the lake. The lake dries up and the alligator's stuck. One day the farmer comes and frees the alligator and takes the alligator to water. Once in the water and feeling himself again, the alligator wants to eat the farmer. That's not right. The elephant says it's fair. The horse says it's only right. And the rabbit wants to return to where the alligator and the farmer met.

"In the Cambodian story, the rabbit is good, Vitou says, "The alligator and the wolf and the tiger are bad people."

Bulletproof Buddhists
ROY MOODY

"With the Lao and the Cambodian gangs, most of them are Buddhist. Theravada Buddhism. Your destiny's mapped out. And if something happens, it happened, it was mapped out, there's nothing you can do to change it. With Theravada Buddhism, what you do in this life, determines what you're going to be in your next life. And so even though they are gang members, they're very loyal to each other. And most of the older ones are very loyal to their families. And they're more than willing to share. I've seen them share money. I've heard about how like one gamer will get a lot of money and they'll more than gladly pass it out amongst the other gang members."

So the kids are good nonviolent practitioners of Theravada Buddhism? No, Roy Moody is not saying that.

"The only thing that...see these kids tend to believe...to take parts of what they want to believe."

He picks his words carefully, even as they flow. Sometimes a bit of a conversation with himself about the words he's picking flows out.

"I mean, we do have our drive-bys also, but we have so many that are willing to walk up because their Buddha will protect them."

Asian kids doing drive-bys. I make a note and listen on.

"One of the things that is definitely an important factor is the role of their religion. Buddhism. They definitely feel that Buddha will protect them. That's why we've had so many fatal homicides with Southeast Asians is that they will walk right up to their adversary.

"And in a group of other gang members, you know there might be ten or fifteen other ones there, but they will walk up, vastly outnumbered and shoot point blank range.

"See, they hear stories that their fathers and their uncles back in Laos, Cambodia, Vietnam, you know, 'Aw, I was shot, but nothing happened. The bullet bounced off of me. Or, The bullet went right in and right out, because Buddha protected me.'"

"We all know that different things happen in war. Maybe he was shot, maybe the bullet did pass through him and didn't hit any vital parts. But they hear enough of these stories that actually, especially with some of the original gang members in their late teens, early twenties actually do believe that their Buddha will protect. So you definitely have to look at the religion aspect of it."

Shades of the Boxers of the Boxer Rebellion

The Chinese insurrectionists known as "Boxers" of the "Boxer Rebellion" out to oust the whites from China said they were protected by Kwan Kung, the God of war and hero of the popular novel, Lo Kuanchong's, *The Romance of the Three Kingdoms*. Kwan Kung was such a powerful exemplar of personal integrity among the folk, the Buddhists made him the Buddha Who Defends the Realm, and the Taoists made him the guardian of borders. Heavy kung fu training and fanatical belief in Kwan Kung supposedly made the Boxers bulletproof. The only thing religion is good for, to an Asian, is making him bulletproof. Ironically, folklore has it, Kwan Kung as the god of war, destroys all magic. The 108 heroes of the *Outlaws of the Water Margin* are wrongfully outlawed in the corrupt Song dynasty, exiled, and condemned to wear the tattoo of the criminal. Ngawk Fay (Yue Fei), the great exemplar of loyalty, was trained in martial arts by the teacher of one of the heroes of the Water Margin. He's a legend because his mother proclaimed her son's loyalty by tattooing it on his back, and Ngawk Fay and his son became the Batman and Robin of the Song after the Water Margin. As the Song gave up chunks of China to the tribes who would become the Mongols and Manchus in the north, Ngawk Fay and his son fought to get them back.

Corrupt officials tricked him into approaching the Emperor in his private sanctum with sword in hand, and Ngawk Fay, even with his loving mother's tattoos on his back is condemned for attempting to assassinate the Son of Heaven. Legend has it corrupt officials bribed the family who supplied food to the jail to poison Ngawk Fay. At his tomb, destroyed during then restored after the Cultural Revolution in China, in Hangzhou City, next to West Lake, there are statues of a kneeling couple representing the man and wife who killed Ngawk Fay. People visiting Ngawk Fay's tomb spit on the statues.

Your Hand Is Your Friend
VITOU REAT

Vitou grins at a section on the meaning of dreams in Cambodian folklore.

If you dream you lose a tooth and it is clean, not bloody, it means someone close to you is dead

If you dream you lose a tooth and the tooth is bloody, it means a relative is dead.

If you dream you are fat, it is a bad omen.

He shows me a picture of a boy showing his hands, to a boy across the table, whose hands are on the table.

"One student lazy. One student not," Vitou says.

"This not a story, but just like a article to teach the children not to leave the food out or the flies can come. And flies not good cuz the legs carry disease. It's just like Chinese.

"This talk about you hands. It say your hand is your friend. Like you say, you hand help you to understand. I make my hand so you can better understand, and you do everything with your hands. He say that he gets smart because his hands help him. He write a lot with the hand. So this one," He points to the boy not using his hands, "doesn't know how to write. So it say, your hand is your friend, use it, don't keep it lazy. So you learn to read it, and the idea is good too.

"My teacher used to say that too. Use your eyes, you know, read! Don't be sorry for you eyes, use it all the time."

Gang Girls
RABBIT & BABOON

Rabbit is a twenty-one year-old baby with maybe a 9th grade education and two kids. She's small. She looks thirteen, maybe fifteen. She was born in Cambodia, came to the United States when she was seven, doesn't remember Cambodia. She speaks and reads three languages English, Lao, and Cambodian. In none of these languages does she have the words to say the father of her kids is doing life for murder. He killed a boy.

Bunny was a father and a murderer at nineteen. Rabbit didn't think much of it then. But now, Bunny, Jr. is about to start school. She tells him not to join a gang. And she tells him stories. The only stories of the only history she knows are stories of Bunny, Jr.'s father, a Cambodian gang banger since fourteen. The romance of the endless gangs are the myths and fairy tales, the tragedies she was never told. She doesn't want Bunny, Jr. to be jumped into a gang. But what else does the kid of the gang kids know but gang kids?

"Are you a gang kid?" I ask her.

"Well, I hang around with them," she says. "It's just that when I was young, I was fourteen, I ran away, and then I have no where to go, so I hang around with them cuz they stay up all night."

Wow, the ultimate in American free expression of self, the great rebellion of the spirit is to stay up all night. Her life changed forever at fourteen because she wanted to stay up all night.

"When I was a kid, I didn't even think my mother loved me. I mean, because I have a stepdad. And she pays more attention to her other kids than to me. They're on Welfare. My dad's on SSI.

"I ran away and I live with a friend. She was on welfare, but then she used to know me when I was real young, and she saw me and she took me in. She's on Welfare too."

"Hanging out means?"

"You kick back at the beach, drink, do whatever....Sometimes the girls have money. And sometimes it's the guys. I never have money though. But the guys have the money for us and they take us out."

There's no furniture. There's a mattress on the floor. An old motel couch she must have found dumped on the street.

"The last time I ran away we kick back at 4-7, the 47 OBS." She says "Four Seven," for 47th Street. "That's where I hang with them that time. They'll be smoking and everything. They ask me to, but then I don't want to get involved in it. They have a place for the guns. And if there's trouble, they bring it out. Last time, they were in some kind of trouble, right? With some other gang? And some other gang drive-by, and everybody was in each corner! They were hiding in back of the wall, there was some up a tree just ready to shoot 'em. And instead, it didn't happen. The cops came. And they took everybody. They got almost all the guns. Between ten and twenty. And the next day, the gang that they have a problem with came by and shot my cousin. And that's when they weren't ready. He was walking, and they came by and shot him. I mean, he was bleeding everywhere. Now my cousin's twenty-two. This happened about six years ago."

On the couch, under the long front window, a fifteen year-old girl nicknamed "Baboon" boasts of running away at eleven and belonging to a gang, the Asian Crips. The gray milky light of a cold afternoon, threatening rain, intrudes through the window. There's a triptych with an Asian theme in red on the wall. Something else junked from an old motel. That's it. The rest is a few battery-run electronic gadgets, a boom box. There's nothing in the next room. Nothing on the walls. Nothing over the windows. Nothing on the floor. Nothing. A nothing kitchen. A nothing bathroom. I plug my tape recorder into the wall. No electricity.

"How long have you been living here?" I ask.

"Five months now," says Rabbit. "At first when I got my place, I get to stay there for only a month, because the gangsters, they got me in trouble. They were making noise and everything. The neighbors complained, and then they would be cussing at my neighbors. And then my neighbors would tell my landlord, you know. There was nothing I could do."

"So you were kicked out of that place," I say.

"Yeah, and then I moved in at 49th," she says, "and I get to stay there for like three months. And they raided the place, I think for drugs and people they were looking for and everything. Well, they find some runaways you know. I tell them not to come, but still they come. Then, you know, they took 'em away, that's all. And some was on drugs, they took 'em in. And some that was on probation — took 'em in. I never got into *that* kind of trouble."

What kind of trouble is that? She's never been arrested.

"Well, they got me into a lot of trouble, and I have one kid at that time. And I have no where to go. I mean they won't accept me. The other place was at Auburn Drive, right there. And I get to stay there for like a year, because, the landlord knows my dad. For like a whole year nothing happened. But then after I'm about to move out, a SWAT team came over and everything. I don't know why! I was walking out of the house, and the SWAT team came, I mean they were carrying guns. A big one too! I got scared! I say, 'What is this?'

"I've seen gangs, like, jump people, you know. And I've been in a car when they drive by. Yeah. I don't know. A lot of things they do is bad. I see a lot. That time it doesn't scare me because it doesn't happen to me. Now, I know.

"But that time when I was with them? The people that they were hurting, I didn't feel sorry for them at all. Yeah, I know the people they were hurting. To me when I hang around with *them* it's not my business, you know. I just keep out. But then, you know, when I hang out with them, I can't disagree you know, because they won't like me.

"They wouldn't take me around any more. That's why I don't like to tell them anything they were doing was bad. They would diss me. They do gang rape, but they didn't do me.

"I don't go out with them now," she says. "Now, it's like they would just wave "Hi." Yeah, we're still friends, but now we don't get along that well, because I have my own family. I don't want to get involved in anything, because if I have them here, they're just like bringing problems to my family. And but, I'm still friends with them.

"My first boy friend that was in OBS was Bunny. Ever since then I haven't gone out with them, and I have his kid. It's like they give respect to Bunny. He even told them to keep an eye on us."

"What do you want to do in the next ten years?"

Baboon can't think ten minutes down the block. Ten years makes her show her tattoo. A Janus. The masks of Comedy and Tragedy. Under the masks, "Laugh now. Cry Later."

"I want to have a family," Rabbit says, "You know, someone who's going to care about me and my kids. I want to start working. I want to get my kids to go to school. I'm going to wait until they're five years old and both of them go to school, and then start to go to school."

"You ran away from home and are still friends with your mother?" I ask.

"Yeah, I used to think that she never loved me. But now I know if anything happens there's always my mom."

"Are you a good mom?" I ask.

"I don't think so."

"What can you do better?"

"Nothing, right now. I can take care of my kids, give them a bath everyday. Make sure they eat."

"Do you tell them stories?"

"No...Well, I tell them about their dad. He asked me about his dad. And I said, your daddy's in jail. And he goes, My daddy's in jail? Yeah. I ask him if he miss his daddy, he says, yeah. He says when is he coming out. I say, I don't know.

How Do You Survive?
Do You Walk the Streets? You Hook? What?

"How do you survive? Do you walk the streets? Hook? What?" I see I've struck a nerve.

"She just, you know," Rabbit says, instinctively rising to protect her friend, whoever she is. "No, she just come stay at, like either my house, or one of..."

"No, no, no, no!" Baboon says. "I don't hook or anything. I just sell dope and stuff. But I don't *hook!* "

"Would the boys like you to hook?" I ask.

"Umm mmmm!" Baboon shakes her head emphatically, pursed lips and all. "In our gangs, we don't sell like, you know...like that."

"Just drugs, not flesh."

"Yeah."

"Do you have a special boyfriend in the gang?"

"I used to go out with a few of 'em. But...." she tilts her head to the side to complete her thought.

"Hmmm" I say, as if I understand what she said.

"So what do *you* want?" I ask Baboon. "What's your future?"

Whoops! She's not ready for that question. "Or do you think about it?" There's a wordless whimper. Wrong question again. This is worse than asking if she hooks. "Is there anybody in the gangs you'd like to take with you? No? You obviously like the gangs. What do you like about them?"

"I don't! I don't like them," Rabbit says. "Now, I don't! Before I do. But now, when I think back, now that I have my own kids, I know how it feels like for a mother. Now, I know how it feels like for *my* mother, for me doing that to my mother."

"Do you feel the same way, Baboon?"

"She hasn't been through it yet," Rabbit says

"I'm not involved or anything, but my mom don't care about me," Baboon says proudly.

"Oh, she does," Rabbit says.

"She knows I go and sell out there to make money and stuff," Baboon says. "She didn't help me all through that time, she knows what I was going through. She didn't help. So, I don't care."

"I'm a boy. How would I get into a gang?" I ask.

"Okay," Rabbit says, "They jump you in."

"What? I gotta go out and get in a few fights?"

"No, there's not all the time in a gang you go out and look for trouble!" Baboon says defending some sense of gang ethics and moral proportion.

"If you want to get jumped," Rabbit says, taking over, covering for her friend. "If you want to be in a gang, right. The OBS right? All the OBS gonna jump on him."

"And beat him up," I say filling in her fade.

"Uh huh," she nods. "They don't know what they're going to do to him, but it's all of them. Fifty or something, they'll do it. And if they re-jump each other, like all of them just hit anybody! All of them hit anybody!"

"And if you want to get out of the set," Baboon says, "You gotta be jumped out."

"I gotta fight my way in. I gotta fight my way out," I say.

Rabbit nods, "Yeah," she says.

"And you've seen this," I say.'

"Um hmm!" Rabbit and Baboon both nod.

"And you say there are fifty?"

"Oh! Once they jumped each other down at the beach!" Rabbit gushes. "That one Cambodian beach? They were full of them! Full! in that place. And I was standing right there watching them jump each other in. But some you know, they can tell, you know, if he's down or not, because some would act like they're already hurt!" She laughs at the silliness of the crybabies.

"Some would act like they're really hurt already and they would stop. And then one would say, 'Oh, man! You need more! You need more!' And one would go, 'Aw, come on, man he got enough, come on! Attack!' But, they'll know! They'll know who's weak and everything."

"So weak means the guy who stops fighting first," I say. They nod.

Rabbit says, "I don't want my son to be in a gang. I'm not proud of it either. I'm not proud that my boyfriend's in a gang. A lot of things he do I'm not proud of."

"But you still love him."

"No, not anymore."

Officer Moody comes by to pick me up. He glances into the open doorway and asks if she has any food in the house. No. He fishes ten bucks out of his wallet and hands it to her. About an hour later we see her and her two kids and her fifteen year-old runaway friend, walking back from a restaurant. "I'm glad she really went out and got some food," Roy Moody says.

The next day Rabbit comes into the Storefront. It's a step. Roy Moody calls her caseworker and gives her leads on help finding Rabbit money for food, daycare for her kids, and three schools that might accept her. She may think it's too late, but five years from now, she'll wish she had started something five years ago, and five years after that she'll wish she had started school five years ago," Moody says.

"A lot of these older gang members have definitely said that they had wished that five years ago they had listened to what I said about staying in school, cuz they have no future, there's nothing for them. You know, they're not going to be picked up, like in the movies, by some Chinese…" And whoops, I knock over the Styrofoam cup of machine made coffee and the good officer Moody never finishes saying the Lao and Cambodian gang kids after watching too many subtitled Hong Kong videos dream of joining the Wah Ching, or a criminal triad, the Chinese M. M for Mafia.

The Wah Ching used to be what the police called Chinatown gangs of kids from Hong Kong, in the '70s. Now Wah Ching means organized crime from Hong Kong. The triads are centered in Taiwan. They're also known among the gang kids as the Chinese Mafia. America is their Swiss bank. America is their laundry. The triads send their dirty dollars to farms in Texas, to Chinese restaurants supplied by these farms, to Chinese games played at casinos on Indian reservations to be washed, fluff dried, and folded. Gang kids dream of taking the oath of a triad before Kwan Kung, the god of war, and sipping a tea of the blood of the brothers, and becoming a legend.

How deep and how common is this stuff among the Chinese?

A Concise History of the Tongs

Gangs used to be called "tongs" in the 19th and early 20th centuries. Some tongs were for legitimate businessmen. Some were for criminal business. When the tong wars between criminal tongs threatened to bring the National Guard in to end Chinese control of Chinatown, the good tongs banded together and formed the Choong Wah Wooey Goon to drive the criminal tongs out of Chinatown, like the 108 outlaw chiefs and their gangs banded together in their marshland stronghold to resist the corrupt Song court. The Choong Wah Wooey Goon and its member organizations are now the establishment in Chinatowns from Panama to Alaska. They own land. They own businesses on the land. They own banks. The recruit members. They attract members by appealing to a common culture and common values: folk lit.

The tong historian, writing in a recruiting pamphlet from the '50s, sounds like gangs sound today:

"From China, one of the oldest of civilizations beginning in 1848 there came to America an outpouring of Chinese who sought to better their personal fortunes, as men everywhere seek to do. Their first port of entry was San Francisco, which eventually became the capital City of Chinese America. The Gold Rush and then the building of the transcontinental railroad swelled the Chinese population. By 1851, with a Chinese population of 12,000 in the city, a need was felt for some type of social organization for mutual help and protection, and thus was born the formal Chinese association."

All Chinese organizations were modeled on the oath the three men from three different walks of life took to become blood brothers in the peach garden, told about in *Three Kingdoms*. The connection with childhood lit is not subtle or hidden:

"One of the most stirring periods of the Chinese people — a time of brave men, brutal warfare, and court intrigue — woven in the tapestry of Chinese history as the era of the Three Kingdoms is preserved for posterity by the Lung Kong Associations.

"Lung Kong is a confraternity of the members of the Four families of the surnames Lew, Quan, Chang, and Chew. Among the Chinese people this tale, told countless thousand upon thousands of times, gives the historic facts of four men whose spirit sense of sacrifice for the people and their bravery made them bigger than life, and therefore legendary.

"While serving the ritual and spiritual needs of the members of the Four Families, the Lung Kong temple in the United States functioned also as a fraternal organization. As did the others already created by other groups, Lung Kong fulfilled the social welfare needs of its people. From this period through W.W.II, the Chinese in America were subject to highly unreasonable legal restrictions, social pressures, an absence of civil rights, and unequal employment opportunities. In the oppressive atmosphere of those times they had to turn to themselves. They had to care for themselves. These conditions foster the social associations.

"These associations, like the Four Families, cared for their own sick, fed and housed their own unfortunate, buried their own dead.

"They banded to fight discriminatory legislation against the Chinese. They arbitrated in legal questions. All of these organizations, in spirit and practice, were akin to the pattern of the Four Families, blood brothers in helping each other and the Chinese people."

How does a gang become so organized and legit or criminal? It's happening now. Money. In the family association, or the district association, or the tong a brother says, "Brothers, I have $6,000 here I'm willing to loan out. What am I bid?" And Joe who wants to start a laundry, and Jake who wants to buy a car, and Jimmy who wants who knows what and any brother who wants the money, bids on it: "one percent," "three percent." Making the loan is an oath. Your word is your bond.

Bounhong Khommarath nods. "This still happen in Lao community," he says, "but very small scale among brother and sister among relative, uncle, but it's not on a large scale because of the issue of trust. If somebody got money and run away...but among brothers, uncles, aunts, and grandma close knit, relatives, yes. Especially want to help out a young couple to buy a car or something.

"We have like our regional association, like the people from this province get together, try to support each other. Especially when somebody dies. Everybody pitch in to help. Because we are now, after five ten years, we're still in survival stage. So we're not really that sophisticated.

"The loan money would only be in the family brother, sister, blood family."

Life Is War: The Stuff of Children's Stories

Why should people trying to stamp out the gangs or modulate the gangs into normal and still enjoyable childhoods know the childhood stuff of Asian culture? Why should full grown adults dip into the myth, lit, operas, and comic books of "Life is war. All behavior is tactics and strategy. All relationships are martial. Love is two warriors back to back fighting off the universe."

One might learn that there is a sense of honor and nobility in these kids that can be appealed to. One might devise a way to tell the kids the gangs are bad strategy. One might quote Sun Tzu and Br'er Rabbit, "The acme of military skill is in winning without taking a life or losing a life and taking the state intact." You want all the money in the bank. A strategy to get it without getting shot, getting arrested, getting wanted by the law might be better than sticking it up. And that might strike a chord. One might find a way of saying there are better, less lethal, less offensive, still very thrilling and macho ways for boys to show off for girls, make an intimidating presence, compete with the strong, get money, and still be a good soldier, be heroic, make history.

I can't remember when I've seen a cop want to respect the culture of the Asians he was policing. Or for that matter, a city. In New York, respecting the gang's culture meant social workers charged with turning the kids to the sunny side of the street went out shoplifting with the kids, to show they understood. They burnt out fast. Roy Moody is the first cop, and San Diego the first city to show enough respect for the Lao and Cambodian cultures to study them. Is he embarrassed when people tell him he's not like other white men, but a member of the family? The sad thing is there are, in too many cities, too many Asian American cops, no Asian immigrant, or refugee would treat like a member of the family.

"I went and I talked to the temple," Officer Roy says, "and I told 'em that one of the things we've learned is that the kids, that are teenagers, when they're more accepting of their own culture, they do better in school. They do better everywhere. And those kids that might not necessarily speak their own languages too well, or write, we're going to very much encourage them to do so."

It's just like the detective novels. The good cops have cultural mobility. Uptown to Harlem for some jazz. Down to Chinatown for some late night noodles. The locals at home or in the store let him in and call him by his first name.

Those Wedding Bells Are Breaking Up That Old Gang of Mine
ROY MOODY

"They don't really want to continue on with crime, but they have no options at all. The thing about it, with these gangs, a lot of gang members they want to get out. But a lot of their cousins are gang members, or their brothers might be gang members. The thing is they try to get out but they're sucked right back in. Especially when they can't find a job they get sucked right back into the gang. And they go through that gang cycle.

"One of the things that we've seen with a lot of Asian gang members is that they do tend to get married at an early age. And that seems to take them out. The sense of responsibility. A lot of things that we see with Asian gang members too, is that sense of family. Especially with the original Southeast Asian gang members. They seem to be more accepting of their cultures than the twelve and thirteen year-olds that we have today."

BOUNHONG KHOMMARATH

"And a few kid that been shot dead at age fifteen and sixteen. Yeah. And one is paralyzed, and that gives us a lot of leverage to deliver the message: Either you end like that one still in a wheelchair and blind. Or the other two that died.

"I been to both funeral. So then kids know the story, because San Diego is a large city, but not big enough to hide the secrets.

"Some of them who's overwhelmed with problems, their parents ship them out. We tell parents: Look, father if you do not do something, your son will end up in jail, or paralyzed, or been shot dead. So once we know that there is no other way to, we ask them to ship them out or move out. And then when he's coming back, he's already eighteen, he changes.

"They know that when they reach eighteen, the law is not treat them as easy as when they were fourteen years old. I see many kids that get out of the gangs get married and have two jobs. One full time and one part time job.

"So I seen it's very productive work that we outreach to the ones that wanna be gangs or acting out, somebody that work with them, give them guidance."

Youth Club

Roy Moody calls. He's upbeat, hopeful, enthusiastic. Parents have been turning in guns to the Storefront, no questions asked, since December.

"In exchange for guns — the first thirty-five didn't get anything, since they didn't have any incentive, but now, drop into the Storefront and turn in a gun, and get free medical services at Paradise Valley Hospital, or a US saving bond from San Diego First National Bank, or a month of free cable TV from Cox and free pay-per-view movies."

He's got a major project going. "We started a youth program." First meeting, 30 kids from South East to Mira Mesa. Junior high to high school. Mixed races. The Lao have their schools for the Lao. And the Cambodian their temple school for their kids. And the Vietnamese their schools. This is mixed races. All kinds of Asians. Even two Filipino kids have been coming to the meetings.

Second meeting, 63 kids. Third meeting tomorrow. He expects a hundred kids. Storefront one P.M. "I'll be there," I say.

Tomorrow comes and the air is full of the bullets of the Kurosawa rain from *Seven Samurai*. A million cars splash through the rain like hysterical villagers, and galloping bandits. The rain hits the streets of San Diego so hard, they seem to spark flames.

The girls arrive first, in pairs and small groups, dropped off by their parents. They shuck their coats for baggy T-shirts and baggy jeans or overalls of many colors. Then the boys in cars of their own. Baseball hats, jackets. Kids drift into the Storefront for about an hour. The girls take up most of the seats around the big conference table. The boys sit in groups against the window and the wall. A few boy-girl couples sit at the back, on unused desks and wave and do eye jazz to their friends. It's not the 100 kids Roy Moody had expected but 80 is a lot of kids. No teacher would want 80 kids from thirteen to nineteen years old for two hours in a classroom.

We Probably Would Have Had a Lot More If It Wasn't For the Heavy Rain

"We probably would have had a lot more if it wasn't for the heavy rain," Roy Moody says. He wants more kids.

"Part of the problem is parents said they were very afraid of letting their kids out of sight. But even the good kids need something to do. They just can't stay home, go to school, stay home, go to school. They need some sort of outlet.

"A lot of times those kids that are on the borderline could be pushed because their parents are so strict. But when we went out and talked to these parents, they said they would like some sort of Asian youth organization that was involved with the San Diego Police Department, because then the parents feel safer.

"I got this idea from the Oakland Police Department. I've traveled all over the United States, and everywhere I go I always look to see what their police departments are doing. The Oakland Police Department had what I thought was the most successful Asian youth program that I've ever seen.

"It's 100 percent supported by the Oakland Police Department. They only have one advisory committee, and the Asian Americans who sit on it are from the establishment, the elite. They conduct their meetings in English. In San Diego, the Lao and Cambodian and different Asian Advisory Committees conduct business in English and their own languages and members are from all walks of life. That makes our advisory committees unique," Roy Moody says.

Roy Moody's opposite number in Oakland "does a lot of fund raising." Moody likes the young Chinese Cambodian Oakland cop, but doesn't like the idea of cops "fund raising."

"I'm prohibited from going out and doing any fund raising on my own. That's why I have to rely on the Asian advisory committees. I can understand why we can't do it. Just the mere thought — I personally just would never walk into an Asian restaurant and ask for money. A policeman asking for money to support a good cause? People are going to give it to me whether they want to or not, just out of the fear alone. There's no way I could do that.

"What I really liked about this was that the kids, they pretty much do everything. They decide what activities they're going to do. They come up with their own budget. They run their meetings. They run their own committees. And, of course, it's just adult supervision over the top.

"The money's going to have to come from the kids. I've already told the kids we don't have any money. They're going to have to do their own fund raising. As you saw, there was an overwhelming response. They understand that. And in the meantime we'll look for what grants we can apply for. There are several people who've already expressed interest in donating money. There's a lot of different associations that have said this is a great idea, and they'd be willing to help out any way that they can. This is just getting off the ground, we'll find the money.

"And this was also a way of what I see of preventing some violence that's been occurring between different Southeast Asian groups, because, like I was saying before, a lot of Southeast Asian kids only interact in their own communities. And so you don't have Cambodian kids from Mira Mesa, interacting with Lao kids from Chollas View area, and the Vietnamese kids from City Heights. This is a way of bringing the kids together so that they can say, 'Hey! You know, these guys aren't any different than I am. They're maybe from a different culture. But they're the same."

The races of Asian kids are gathering at the Storefront, around Officer Roy Moody, San Diego Police, just as the 108 gangs of wrongfully outlawed men, from all parts of China gathered at the stronghold on Mount Liangshan around the humble clerk known as "the Timely Rain." It's a strange thing to say about a white man.

Two weeks later, on a sunny day, at the next meeting I see Roy Moody has taught the youth organization's officers enough Robert's

Rules of Order to run the meeting. The kids talk about raising $500 at a car wash in Mira Mesa, selling food from a booth at a Cambodian and Lao New Year's festival at Colina Park, and starting a basketball league. They decide on a design for their emblem, their logo, using elements from many of the designs offered by the kids. People from other agencies and community service organizations have shown up with their own kids to see if these kids can keep it together. Do they have the discipline? Can they keep their word?

I don't see Rabbit or Baboon here. Rabbit's too old, maybe too far gone. A kid who had to take a course on how to heat up bottle to feed her kid, it's too late for Rabbit to have a childhood. And Baboon is "Laugh now-Cry Later." Happy face. Sad face.

Two little boys, one just a bit younger and one just a bit older than my Sam. They fold paper gliders out of flyers announcing the gun exchange, and fly them in the little hallway between office in the back of the Storefront.

The nineteen year-old kid who teaches first grade at the Old Temple school gets stopped by the cops for looking thirteen behind the wheel of his car. He and the twelve year-old girl with him hear that I write for the mighty *San Diego Reader*.

When I speak to her, I find out the twelve year-old girl is twenty-one, and the San Diego Police have just hired her as a Cambodian Community Service Officer. She writes too, she says. She wants to be a writer. She's written several stories she'd like to publish.

"What kind of stories?" I ask.

"I write fairy tales," she says.

Sophea "Tommy" Ross gives me a copy of his magazine, *Cambodian Now*. I ask him if someone told him stories when he was a kid. Oh, yes. They both remember the fairy tales. I ask them if they've heard of the story of the parents who purposely take their little boy into the jungle and lose him, and when they want him back, are forced to leave the jungle alone and live in sadness for the rest of their lives.

Yes, they've heard that story. Do I like that story? Why do I like that story?

"I have come to San Diego with lots of money in my pocket. I will pay $1 million for each and every Cambodian and Lao and Hmong kid from newborn to eighteen years old," I say.

"My parents love me too much to sell me," they say.

"$3 million each. You've got five brothers and sisters. Plus you, that's $3 million times six. Your folks will have the good life. And if they won't sell, I'll raise my offer. And five years from now, I'm coming back with more money in my pockets to buy more Cambodian and Lao and Hmong and Vietnamese kids. And five years after that. And five years after that. What's going to happen to Cambodian and the Lao and the Hmong and the Vietnamese in San Diego?"

They look at me. Do they remember Pol Pot? Pol Pot in Cambodia, the Gang of Four in China, and gangs in San Diego rewrote the story. Here it's not, "Parents, please don't sell your children to monsters for the good life." Instead it's, "Kids, do not sell your parents for the life of laugh now, cry later." The result is the same. There will be no more. Not a soul, not a story, not a kid. I think they understand the story better than me.

Officer Roy is on the detective's list. He hopes to be assigned to Asian Gangs and be stationed at the Storefront. "But there are no guarantees." What happens in one's life may well all be written, but the good officer has not read it yet.

He's also on the sergeant's list. The engines of gang prevention and control he's built, the Neighborhood Watch groups, the advisory councils, the gun exchange, and now the Asian Youth Organization are not self-maintaining, though he says they are. Everything in the Southeast Asian communities works by personal example. If Roy Moody is promoted out of the Storefront and away from the Southeast Asian communities, what he built over the last six years might sputter out. It's a delicate time. Summer's coming. But right now, it's spring. It's Saturday morning. The sun is out. The Marines fly pairs of pretty twin tailed F-18s out over the road, loop around over the blue water and sleek back the way they came. People drive their Miatas topless. The 16 Neighborhood Watch groups are working. Gang leaders are off the street, and gang activity down. Sophea's teaching first grade at the Old Temple, this morning, then writing for the special New Year's issue of his magazine. Twenty kids actually show up ready to wash cars at $3 a pop. Officer Roy tells the girl holding the money to button her pocket and towels off a wet Jeep. They make a little more than their $500 goal. About $3 more. I have my car washed and drive into downtown San Diego to show it off.

Author Biographical Notes

Nash Candelaria

Candelaria is a descendant from an old New Mexico family. His novels have been described as landmarks of Hispanic literature, and his most recent work is a novel, Leonor Park. His "Rafa trilogy" of novels includes Memories of the Alhambra (1977), Not by the Sword (Bilingual Press, 1982), a 1983 American Book Award winner, and Inheritance of Strangers (1985). His short stories have appeared in a number of literary magazines and anthologies, and a collection has been published, The Day the Cisco Kid Shot John Wayne. He and his wife live in Santa Fe, New Mexico.

Frank Chin

Chin is a Seattle writer unavoidably detained in LA. His books include *Gunga Din Highway* (Coffee House Press, 1996), *Donald Duk* (Coffee House Press), and *Chinaman Pacific & Frisco R.R. Co.* (Coffee House), which received the American Book Award. In 1972 his *Chickencoop Chinaman* was the first Asian American play on the New York stage. Chin was coeditor of the first anthology of Chinese and Japanese American literature, *Aiiieeeee* (1974), and a second volume, *The Big Aiiieeeee* (1991). He was a recipient of a Lannan Foundation Literary Fellowship.

Victor Hernández Cruz

Cruz's books include *Paper Dance: 55 Latino Poets* (Persea Books, 1994), *Red Beans: Poems* (Coffeehouse Press, 1991), and *Rhythm, Content and Flavor: New and Selected Poems* (Arte Publico Press, 1988). He has also authored *By Lingual Wholes* (1982), *Tropicalization* (1976), *Mainland* (1973), *Snaps* (1969), and *Papo Got His Gun* (1966). He was the winner of the World Heavyweight Poetry Championships at Bumbershoot, the Seattle Arts Festival, and the winner of the World Heavyweight Poetry Bout at the Taos Poetry Circus. He read at the Dodge Poetry Festival in New Jersey where the poets were taped and interviewed by Bill Moyers and featured in the series "The Language of Life" for PBS. Cruz has been living in Puerto Rico for the last seven years where he writes in both

Spanish and English and keeps a keen eye on falling avocados. A new collection of his poetry and prose will be released in 1997 from Coffee House Press.

Lawrence DiStasi

A Lecturer of Comparative Literature, UC Berkeley Extension, DiStasi is the author of *Mal Occhio: The Underside of Vision* (North Point Press, 1981) and *Dream Streets: The Big Book of Italian American Culture* (Harper Row, 1989). He is Project Director of *Una Storia Segreta: When Italian Americans Were "Enemy Aliens,"* a traveling exhibit about the little-known restrictions, evacuations, and internments imposed on Italian Americans during World War II. He lives in Berkeley, California.

Chitra Banerjee Divakaruni

Divakaruni was born in India and spent the first nineteen years of her life there. She lives in the San Francisco area with her husband and two children, and teaches creative writing at Foothill College. Her books include three books of poetry: *Dark Like the River, The Reason for Nasturtiums,* and *Black Candle* (Calyx, 1991). Her latest book is a collection of short stories, *Arranged Marriage* (Doubleday, 1995), and she has been anthologized in over 30 collections. Divakaruni is the editor of *Multitude: An Anthology of Cross-cultural Readings* (McGraw Hill, 1993). She is the recipient of an Allen Ginsberg poetry prize, a Pushcart Prize, and two PEN Syndicated Fiction Project Awards.

Joseph Geha

Born in Zahle, Lebanon, in 1944, Geha came to the United States in 1946 and was raised in Toledo, Ohio. Before coming to Iowa State University, where he is a Professor of English, he taught at The University of Toledo, Bowling Green State University, and Southwest Missouri State College. Geha authored *Through and Through: Toledo Stories* (Graywolf Press, 1990); his short stories, essays, poems and reviews have appeared in many publications, and his plays have been produced in regional theaters. His fiction has been anthologized in *The Pushcart Prize XV, Best of the Small Presses,* and selected for inclusion in the Permanent Collection, the Arab American Archive, of the Smithsonian Institution. In 1988 Geha was awarded a fellowship from the National Endowment for the Arts. He lives in Ames, Iowa, with his wife, novelist Fern Kupfer, and two daughters.

Robin Hemley

Currently Professor of English at Western Washington University, Hemley was born in New York and grew up in the Midwest. His books include: *The Big Ear: Stories* (John F. Blair Publishing, 1995), *Turning Life Into Fiction* (Writer's Digest Books, 1994), *The Last Studebaker* (Graywolf Press, 1992), and *All You Can Eat: Stories* (Atlantic Monthly Press, 1988). Hemley's stories have been widely anthologized, nationally and internationally, in such collections as *20 Under 30* (Scribners), twice with other winners of the Pushcart Prize (*XV* and *XIX*), and *The Best American Humor of 1994* (Touchstone). His essay in *Homeground* is from a memoir-in-progress.

Lawson Fusao Inada

A Professor of English at Southern Oregon State College, Inada's *Legends From Camp* (Coffee House Press, 1995) was a winner of the American Book Award and a finalist for the Los Angeles Times Book Award. *Before the War: Poems As They Happened* (William Morrow, 1971) was the first volume of poetry by an Asian American to be published by a major publishing company. Additionally, Inada has been published in many anthologies, including *Edge Walking on the Pacific Rim* (Sasquatch). He is the coeditor of two anthologies of Asian American writing, including *The Big Aiiieeee!*.

Pico Iyer

Iyer was born in 1957 in Oxford, England, and was educated at Eton, Oxford, and Harvard. He is a longtime essayist for *Time* magazine, and his pieces appear frequently in magazines such as *Condé Nast Traveler*, *Harper's*, and *Tricycle: the Buddhist Review*. He is the author of three nonfiction books: *Video Night in Katmandu*, *The Lady and the Monk*, and *Falling Off the Map*, plus a novel, *Cuba and the Night*. He lives in Santa Barbara, California, and in Japan.

Laura Kalpakian

Kalpakian is the author of five novels and two collections of short stories. Her mother was born in Constantinople, and her father is from a large Mormon family in Idaho. These two very different cultures have enriched and broadened her work, allowing her a range of possibilities from the European settings of *Cosette: The Sequel to Les Misérables* (Harper Collins, 1995) and in *Fair Augusto and Other Stories* (Graywolf Press, 1986); to the desert town of St. Elmo, California, portrayed in

These Latter Days (Times Books, 1985), *Graced Land* (Grove Press, 1992), and *Dark Continent and Other Stories* (Viking, 1989). *Graced Land* aired in 1993 as a TV movie titled *The Woman Who Loved Elvis*, starring Tom and Roseanne Arnold and scripted by Rita Mae Brown. Kalpakian was a winner of a National Endowment for the Arts Fellowship in 1990. She has also been a book critic for the *Los Angeles Times*. Kalpakian is a native Californian and now lives in Washington State with her two sons.

Thomas King

King was born in 1943 and raised in Roseville in the central valley of California by his Cherokee father and his Greek mother. He holds a Ph.D. in English/American Studies from the University of Utah, and has worked in Native Studies programs in Utah, California, Minnesota, and Alberta, Canada. He is the author *Green Grass, Running Water* (Houghton Mifflin, 1993), which won the Canadian Authors Award for fiction, *Medicine River* (Viking/Penguin, 1990), which won the Josephine Miles Award/Oakland PEN award, and *A Coyote Columbus Story*, a children's book, (Groundwood Books, 1992). *Truth and Bright Water* (rights sold in 1995 to Knopf, Canada) is a novel. King is currently working on two children's books, a radio comedy show, and a collection of short stories. He resides in Guelph, Ontario, with his partner Helen Hoy and two of their three children.

Russell Leong

Leong was born in San Francisco's Chinatown in 1950. A poet and editor, he has worked as a window washer, receiving clerk, tour guide, and academic book editor. He is currently editor of *Amerasia Journal*, published by the UCLA Asian American Studies Center, and editor of *Asian American Sexualities: Dimensions of the Gay and Lesbian Experience* (Routledge Books, 1996). He is the author of a volume of poetry, *The Country of Dreams and Dust* (West End Press, 1993), which received a PEN Oakland Josephine Miles Literature award. An earlier version of his piece in *Homeground* was published in *Tricycle: the Buddhist Review*.

Shirley Geok-Lin Lim

Lim was born in the historic town of Malacca before Malaysian independence in 1957. She attended the University of Malaya in Kuala Lumpur and Brandeis University. She now lives with her husband and son in Santa Barbara, California, and teaches English and Women's Studies at the University of California. Her works include *Among the*

White Moon Faces (Feminist Press 1996), *Life's Mysteries: The Best of Shirley Lim* (Times Books International, 1995), *Monsoon History: Selected Poems* (Skoob Pacifica, 1994), and she coedited *The Forbidden Stitch, An Asian American Women's Anthology* (Calyx Books, 1989), which was a 1990 American Book Award winner. Lim has poems, short stories, and articles in over 40 anthologies. Works in progress include two novels and a book of poems.

Colleen McElroy

McElroy is Director of Creative Writing at the University of Washington where she teaches Creative Writing, Third World Literature, and Women's Literature. Her educational background is language-centered: from speech pathology and language acquisition to linguistics and the oral tradition. She is the author of six poetry collections, including the most recent, *What Madness Brought Me Here: New and Selected Poems, 1968–88* (Wesleyan University Press, 1988). She has published two short fiction collections, *Driving Under the Cardboard Pines* (1990) and *Jesus and Fat Tuesday* (1987), and a textbook, *Speech and Language of the Preschool Child.* With the help of a Fulbright Research Fellowship to study folktales/oral traditions of Madagascar, she has written *Over the Lip of the World: Among the Storytellers of Madagascar* (forthcoming from University of Washington Press). Another forthcoming book is *No Stops Until Darwin* (memoirs). Her work has appeared in numerous literary journals and anthologies, as well as in translation in Russia, Italy, and Malaysia.

Naomi Shihab Nye

Nye, born in 1952 of a Palestinian father and American mother, grew up in St. Louis, Jerusalem, and San Antonio, Texas. She is the author of four full-length collections of poems: *Hugging the Jukebox*, a national Poetry Series winner, *Different Ways to Pray, Yellow Glove.* and *Red Suitcase* (BOA Editions Ltd., 1994). *Words Under the Words, Selected Poems* (Eighth Mountain Press/Far Corner books) was published in 1995. Forthcoming from Simon & Schuster are *Lullaby Raft* (a picture book), *I feel a Little Jumpy Around You*, a collection of paired poems for teenagers coedited with Paul Janeczko, and *Habibi*, a novel for young readers. Nye was one of the featured poets on the Bill Moyers poetry series "The Language of Life" on PBS. She has worked as a visiting writer in schools for 21 years, and currently is poetry editor for the *Texas Observer.* She is married to the photographer Michael Nye and they have one son, Madison.

Ishmael Reed

Reed is the author of more than twenty books, including novels, essays, plays, and poetry. His most recent novel is *Japanese By Spring*, and his most recent nonfiction is *Airing Dirty Laundry* (Addison-Wesley, 1993). His *Writin' is Fightin'* (Atheneum), from which the selection for *Homeground* came, was published in 1988. A Professor of English at the University of California, Berkeley, he has been a Harvard Signet Fellow and a Yale Calhoun Fellow. Reed has been a finalist for the Pulitzer Prize and was twice nominated for the National Book Award.

Sandra Scofield

Scofield is the author of six novels, most recently *A Chance to See Egypt* (Harper Collins, 1996). Her second novel, *Beyond Deserving*, was a finalist for the National Book Award and won an American Book Award. Two of her books have been cited by the *New York Times Book Review* as "Notable Books of the Year." She is the recipient of other honors, including nominations for the Oregon Book Award (*More Than Allies*) and for a First Fiction Award from the American Institute of Letters (*Gringa*). Scofield grew up in West Texas, the child of a working class family, and though she has lived in other parts of the country, the last 20 years in Oregon, she continues to draw on her childhood in much of her writing. She is committed to fiction, primarily, as the way a writer can open up the consciousness of readers to lives they have not lived.